ADOPTION
GLOBAL PERSPECTIVE AND ETHICAL ISSUES

About the Editor

Jagannath Pati, holding Master degree in Social Work, LLB and Ph.D. in Social Sciences, is presently Deputy Director in Central Adoption Resource Agency (CARA), Ministry of Women & Child Development, Government of India. He was granted Sr. Fulbright Fellowship for the year 2005-06. Dr. Pati was attached with Department of Social Work, California State University of Long Beach, California, USA as an honorary faculty and completed his post-doctoral work on "Best Practice: Placement Protocol and Service Models for Children without Families in USA—A Comparative Study".

ADOPTION
Global Perspective and Ethical Issues

Edited by

Jagannath Pati

CONCEPT PUBLISHING COMPANY, NEW DELHI-110059

Cataloging in Publication Data—DK
Courtesy: D.K. Agencies (P) Ltd. <docinfo@dkagencies.com>

Adoption : global perspective and ethical issues /edited by Jagannath Pati.
p. cm.
Contributed articles.
Includes bibliographical references.
Includes index.
ISBN 8180694429

1. Adoption. 2. Adoption—Moral and ethical aspects. 3. Children's rights. I. Pati, Jagannath,1963-

DDC 362.734 22

ISBN 81-8069-442-9

First Published 2007

Published and Printed by
Ashok Kumar Mittal
Concept Publishing Company
A/15-16, Commercial Block, Mohan Garden
New Delhi-110059 (INDIA)

Phones : 25351460, 25351794
Fax : 091-11-25357103
Email : publishing@conceptpub.com

Dedication

The book is dedicated to the memory of millions of children around the world who have been subject to neglect and abuse. These children are often exploited, as they do not have family to care for; those separated from their families and treated as orphan and abandoned.

Preface

We come across countless information on abuse of child domestic workers in Morocco, the plight of internally displaced persons in Bogotá and Cartagena, multiple placements in foster care in the United States, police beatings, rape, and torture of children in Papua New Guinea, stigma and discrimination against HIV-Positive mothers and their children in India and Russia, abuse and exploitation of child domestic workers in Indonesia, hidden abuses against detained youths in Rio de Janeiro, child soldiers and the Tamil Tigers in Sri Lanka, hazardous child labour in El Salvador's sugarcane cultivation, child combatants in Colombia, renewed war in northern Uganda, child soldiers in the west Asian crisis, discrimination against Palestinian Arab Children in Israel's schools, children and violence in Colombia, large number of neglected children and problem of child labour in India, children in confinement in Louisiana, HIV/AIDS children's languishing in Kenya and other African countries, cruelty and neglect in orphanages in different parts of the globe and many other news of such kind, affecting our children population of the globe.

Over the past 20 years, our understanding of the complex problems of child abuse and neglect has increased dramatically. This increased knowledge has improved our ability to intervene effectively in the lives of troubled families. Likewise, we have a better grasp of what we can do to prevent child abuse and neglect from occurring. Children in need of care and protection include several categories of children, i.e. street children (including missing and abandoned children), child labour (including child domestic labour), children who have been abused (sexually, physically and emotionally), child victims of the flesh trade, special needs children, child addicts, children in conflict with law, children in institutions, mentally ill children, children affected by HIV/AIDS and similar situations all over the globe.

We have international instruments, national laws and innumerable rules/guidelines in each country to implement various policy issues, action plans, strategies and measures and the contradiction is that countries lack resource centres which could contribute to agenda building and best practice in the area of children and young people and supplement the efforts of policy-makers, researchers, civil society and other interested groups, by providing access to key research, debates and announcements. There is dearth of information on services and measures available for children in developing countries. The information on all children services rendered by Government, NGOs and other institutions should be readily available to public.

The UN General Assembly 2002 Special Session on Children and the Millennium Development Goals recently announced at the UN; recent outcomes of the discussion on 16th September, 2005 on "Children without Parental Care" at the office of the High Commissioner for Human Rights; General Comments on Implementing Child Rights in early Childhood (1st November, 2005) prepared for Forty-first Session, Geneva, 9-27 January, 2006; discussions held during 17-23 September, 2005 by the Special Commission on the Practical Operation of the 1993 Hague Inter-country Adoption Convention and the Rights of the Child in Internal and Inter-country Adoption—"Ethics and Principles: Guidelines for Practice" developed by International Resource Center for the Protection of Children in Adoption (International Social Service), Geneva discuss about ethical issues, practices and rights of vulnerable children in general and children without family in particular.

Prevention of abandonment and encouraging other appropriate means of non-institutional care, curtailing delays at all level beginning from the identification stage to children's reintegration in the family and final rehabilitation, additional protection for older and special needs children (fast-tracking such children while deciding rehabilitation issues), promoting transparency at all stages are some of the important priorities now.

Our efforts to prevent homelessness and neglect must continue to grow and improve. Even though geography is an important divide, each country must borrow from the other its best practice and ethical standards that are in vague for most disadvantaged children. While there is lot of ignorance and knowledge gap amongst most of the service providers, professionals and child care staff involved in rehabilitation of orphan and abandoned children, it's meaningful to come out with such kind of volume.

The research on ethics in dealing with homeless children is rife with conflict of interest. As far as inter-country adoption is concerned, sending countries are usually developing countries and receiving countries are economically developed countries. In recent times, there has been lot of anti-publicity on inter-country adoption and it has been termed as selling of children to foreign countries. Research also shows that various stakeholders related to adoption process have been unable to translate ethical principles into behaviour. This has been due to the fact that there has been no transparency across adoption process in most of the developing countries. There is need to develop uniform ethical standards in adoption to enable prospective adoptive parents to take informed decision.

I personally do not consider institutional care or long-term foster care as an alternative to a permanent family and adoption should be the most preferred way of rehabilitation if joining their family of birth is not an option for them. This will entail much more work on the part of the social work community and the officials; however, the words "unknown" or "abandoned" should not be acceptable as the end of the story. Recently there has been lot of negative publicity in international adoptions and mostly this is due to lack of transparency across adoption process. On the whole, the children suffer most. Often social workers and adoption agencies have confusion about best interest of child while deciding its placement. People also talk about alternate facilities such as group foster care/specialized institutional care in the place of inter-country adoption mostly for older and special needs children as in such placements; they are detached of their culture, race, food habits and communities. In addition, there are attachment issues, disruptions, other matters like post-adoption issues and search of roots. But the fact remains that even older child or special needs child has a right to be with a family and he/she should be placed preferably in domestic adoption or if not possible in international adoption as there are large number of loving families waiting for such children. Possibly, we need no more institution except for those children who need special protection and care; we need a set up promoting family foster care from the day one the baby is detached from her biological mother. A vision of every child living in a safe, stable, permanent home, nurtured by healthy families and strong communities is what we all desire to make a reality.

The book reflects that childhood is the most important stage of life which has to be preserved and children should be provided with the resources they need to grow into healthy, contributing members of society and hence the best interest of the child becomes the priority in all decisions affecting them.

The edition which has been contributed by many subject experts, has dealt issues related to childhood, ethical issues in adoption procedure, transparency across adoption process and procedure related to adoption. Family renders physical, emotional, and material security necessary for the overall development of the child and provides opportunity to realize his/her dreams and aspirations. In today's world, adoption protects abandoned, destitute and neglected children from abuse, exploitation and social maladjustment. The intention is that every child should have a safe, stable, permanent life nurtured by healthy families and strong communities.

Acknowledgements

Many people have helped to bring this volume to publication, fianlly. I must thank all the paper contributors. An edited book depends on the hard work of many individuals and teamwork. I am grateful to the Fulbright granting authority for enabling me to contact so many authors of repute to contribute to the book while working in California State University of Long Beach during 2005-06. This project was completed during 8 months' stay in Long Beach, California. This was in addition to my research project which was based on a comparative study on child welfare systems in India and the United States. Thanks to my parents, who have always inspired me to put hard work in life and my wife, Varsha and children (Aaruni and Kasturi) who have cooperated me a lot during the period.

I am indebted to Prof. John Oliver, Director, Department of Social Work, California State University of Long Beach, USA and Prof. Eiteen Mayers Pasztors of the Department for their guidance and support during the period.

Jagannath Pati

Contents

PART III
ETHICAL ISSUES

List of the Contributors

Chivonne Hagan received her Masters in Social Work from California State University, Long Beach and is currently working at Kinship Center, a licensed non-profit adoption agency located in Santa Ana, California. Her perspective on adoption stems from personal family experiences (having four adopted siblings from Eastern Europe), research, and current work experiences. Chivonne is passionate about educating prospective adoptive parents on adoption related issues.

Ms. Chivonne Hagan
1901 N, Heliotrope Dr. Santa Ana, CA 9270, USA
E-mail: chivonneh@hotmail.com

Christine Futia, a Market Research Director is an adoptive mother living near Chicago, USA. She is an adoptive parent of three children from India and she promotes Indian children to visit their homeland. She also runs such a camp known as "SPICE Indian Heritage Camp".

Ms. Christine Futia
5501 Keeney St., Morton Grove, IL 60053, USA
E-mail: cfutia@aol.com

Jagannath Pati (Editor) is attached with Central Adoption Resource Agency (CARA), Ministry of Women & Child Development, Govt. of India and is a Senior Fulbright (2005-06) who was placed to work in Department of Social Work, California State University of Long Beach, USA, as an honorary faculty. Dr. Pati is working as Deputy Director in CARA, a central authority in the matter of adoptions in India.

Dr. Jagannath Pati, Dy. Director
Central Adoption Resource Agency
Wing No. 2, IInd Floor, West Block-8, Sector-1,
R.K. Puram, New Delh-110066
E-mail: jpati@rediffmail.com

Josephine A. Ruggiero, Professor of Sociology at Providence College, is an applied sociologist, international adoption researcher, and the mother of three teenage siblings whom she and her husband adopted as non-infants from Russia in 1994. Prior to adopting, Dr. Ruggiero and her husband were foster parents and were trained and approved to adopt domestically. Her years as a graduate student at Fordham University, where she received both her M.A. and Ph.D. degrees in sociology, shaped Dr. Ruggiero's interest in minority groups and social change. Her long-standing interest has been on women and family issues. Professor Ruggiero has published numerous pieces, including journal articles on a variety of subjects, critical essays, a teaching-activities manual, book chapters, and book reviews. She has also conducted empirical research, presented papers at a variety of pro-fessional conferences, and written and spoke extensively on the subjects of older-child domestic and international adoption. Her book, *Eastern European Adoption: Policies, Practice and Strategies for Change*, published by Transaction Publishers, is forthcoming in the Spring/Summer, 2007.

Prof. Josephine A. Ruggiero
Professor of Sociology and
International Adoption Researcher, Providence College
Providence, Rhode Island 02918-0001
E-mail: jruggier@providence.edu

Louise Anita Williams is Founder, Managing Trustee of Love Humanity International now functioning from Mumbai, India (www.lovehumanity.org). Louise's successful business career was in the field of sales, marketing and advertising, advising multi-national organizations like Walt Disney Productions, Mitsubishi Electric, American Isuzu Motors International, etc. Always being active in the community, she was appointed and served as a Commissioner for the Status of Women in Orange County, California and served on President Ronald Reagan's Presidential Task Force. Louise was born in Portland, Oregon in the USA and was raised in southern California. She has one daughter and she now resides in India.

Ms. Louise Anita Williams, Managing Trustee
Love Humanity International
B-4, Sea Breeze Plaza, Nargol- 396135
Gujarat, India
E-mail: louise@lovehumanity.org

Valji Bagha is a grassroots level social worker involved with Love Humanity International.

Valjibhai Bagda, Executive Director
Love Humanity International
B-4, Sea Breeze Plaza, Nargol- 396135
Gujarat, India

Dr. Nilima Mehta has been in the field of child rights, child protection, juvenile justice, adoption, foster care, family counselling and other community outreach programmes for over twenty five years. Dr. Mehta has been an Honorary Consultant with several organisations like UNICEF, CRY, CHILDLINE, ICSW, ICCW, IAPA, FSC, as well as the Central and State Government for research policy development and review of legislations. She is the author of "Ours By Choice – Parenting through Adoption" published with UNICEF support. She is a visiting faculty member at the College of Social Work, Bombay University, and the Department of Social Work at the S.N.D.T. University. Dr. Mehta is currently the President of the Bombay Association of Trained Social Workers (BATSW), Vice President of IAPA (Indian Association of Promotion of Adoption), Chairperson of FSC (Family Services Counselling), and the Chairperson of the Government appointed Child Welfare Committee, Mumbai.

Dr. Nilima Mehta
Chairperson, Child Welfare Committee, Mumbai,
5 Normandie, 25 Carmichael Road
Mumbai 400026, India
E.mail: nilimamehta@gmail.com

Pal Ahluwalia is the Professor of Ethnic Studies at the University of California, San Diego and the Research-South Asia Chair and Professor of Post-colonial Studies at the University of South Australia. His recent books include *Politics and Post-colonial Theory* and *Edward Said*, both published by Routledge. He is currently working on a book titled *Out of Africa: Post-structuralism's Colonial Roots* to be published by Routledge. His work has been translated into Arabic, Korean, Japanese and Spanish. He is the editor of three Routledge journals, *Social Identities, African Identities* and *Sikh Formations*.

Prof. Pal Ahluwalia
Professor of Ethnic Studies, University of California
San Diego and Research SA Chair and
Professor of Post-colonial Studies,
University of South Australia
E-mail: pal.ahluwalia@adelaide.edu.au

Paul Sachdev, Professor Emeritus, School of Social Work Memorial University of Newfoundland, CANADA earned his Ph.D. in Social Welfare at the University of Wisconsin-Madison in 1975. He has taught and extensively published in the areas of child welfare and reproductive health care. Among his previous books are: Adoption: Current Issues and Trends (1984); Unlocking the Adoption Files (1990); International Handbook on Abortion (1988); Perspectives on Abortion (1985); Abortion: Readings and Research (1981) and *Sex,* Abortion and Unmarried Women (1994). Paul Sachdev received Memorial University President's Award for Outstanding Research. He is the founding editor of "Advances in Social Work", and an international editor of the Journal "Medicine and Law." He is also on the editorial board of Adoption Quarterly.

Prof. Paul Sachdev, Ph.D.
Professor Emeritus, School of Social Work
Memorial University of Newfoundland
St. John's, NL, A1C 5S7, Canada
E-mail: psachdev@mun.ca

Peter Selman is Reader in Social Policy and Visiting Fellow in the School of Geography, Politics and Sociology at the University of Newcastle upon Tyne, where he teaches courses in Comparative Social Policy and Adoption; a worldwide perspective. His main areas of research interest are child adoption, teenage pregnancy and demographic change and public policy. He is currently Chair of the Network for Intercountry Adoption and a member of the Board of Trustees of the British Agencies for Adoption and Fostering. During the past six years he has also been co-director of two major research projects on the Education of Young Mothers for the Department for Education and Skills (Selman *et al.* 2001) and the Teenage Pregnancy Unit (Dawson & Hosie, 2005).

Prof. Peter Selman, Reader in Social Policy,
School of Geography, Politics & Sociology,
University of Newcastle, Claremont Bridge level 5
Newcastle upon Tyne NE1 7RU, England.
E-mail: p.f.selman@ncl.ac.uk or pfselman@yahoo.co.uk

Reesa Sorin is Coordinator of Early Childhood Education and Arts Education at James Cook University, Cairns. She has researched in the areas of children's fears, emotional literacy, conceptualizations of childhood, student mobility and adult learning. In 2005 she helped to develop the Sorin and Galloway "Ten Constructs of Childhood". She is currently applying the typology to childcare policies and to interviews with children, parents and caregivers in Australia and Canada.

Dr. Reesa Sorin
School of Education,
James Cook University,
P.O. Box 6811,
Cairns, QLD 4870, Australia
E-mail: Reesa.Sorin@jcu.edu.au

Greta Galloway is working as Sr. Lecturer in School of Social Work & Community Welfare, James Cook University, Australia.

Dr. Greta Galloway, Sr. Lecturer
School of Social Work & Community Welfare,
James Cook University, P.O. Box 6811,
Cairns, QLD 4870, Australia

René A.C. Hoksbergen (1940) studied psychology at Amsterdam University. Dutch adoption specialist, has done research on education and adoption since 1975. Written a large number of books and articles in several languages. Since 1998, he has been involved in research project on situation of adoptive children born in Romania and he consults adoptive parents and grown-up adoptees.

Prof. René A.C. Hoksbergen, Ph.D.
Adoption Department, Utrecht University

Jan ter Laak (1944) Ph.D., is a developmental psychologist at the University of Utrecht, the Netherlands. His are a interest is the assessment of such children. He was the chairman and member of the test committee of the Dutch Psychological Association. During last years, he has been cooperating on several research projects with Rene Hoksbergen in the Netherlands and abroad. Both are working at Utrecht University, Heidelberglaan 2, 3584 CS Utrecht, Netherlands.

Jan J.F. ter Laak, Ph.D.
Department of Developmental Psychology,
University Utrecht, Faculty of Social Sciences,
P.O. Box 80.140, 3508 TC Utrecht, The Netherlands
Corresponding author: R.A.C.Hoksbergen@fss.uu.nl

Prof. Victor Groza is a Professor of Social Work at Case Western Reserve University (CWRU), Mandel School of Applied Social Sciences. He received the Ph.D. from the University of Oklahoma and joined the faculty of CWRU in 1993. He serves as a consultant to public and private child welfare agencies and has conducted research, training or technical assistance in other countries including Romania, India, Belize and the Ukraine. His primary research interests focus on: (1) an examination of the institutional care of children, ways to improve the care of children who must reside in institutions, and the negative impact on child development from early trauma due to institutionalization; and (2) family, children and service system issues in domestic, older-child adoption and international adoption.

Prof. Victor Groza, Ph.D.
Mandel School of Applied Social Sciences
Case Western Reserve University, Cleveland, OH 44106
E-mail: vkg2@case.edu

Curtis Proctor received his Master of Social Work from the University of Iowa. He has completed his doctorate in social work from the Mandel School of Applied Social Sciences at Case Western Reserve in Cleveland. He has published research on international adoption and gay and lesbian youth. His current research interest is the Indian Child Welfare Act. He is also a vocal and stage performer.

Prof. Curtis Proctor, Ph.D., Assistant Professor,
School of Social Work, Wichita State University,
Wichita, KS 67260

Introduction

"In the green years of childhood, the young begin their irreversible march into the future with the resolution and sweet calmness of innocence. The march of childhood goes on as long as the human race endures an affirmation of new hope and the freshness of life that comes with every generation. The message proclaims another chance for mankind". (UNICEF)

The unit of civilisation is the family, which offers the healthiest physical environment. The most susceptible member in the family to all external conditions is the infant. In most of the developing countries, as a result of poverty and less access to resources, a number of families are not in a position to take care of their infants and young children, which is something painful. The innocent child suffers from mother's womb and in many times, a child is never planned. In India, unwed mothers and biological parents on the ground of poverty have surrendered their children to adoption agencies as a result of social stigma. In most of the cases, the baby is deserted either near a residential home or in an abandoned place or in the hospital/nursing home. Countless of such children are having similar fate in India and in other developing countries, as well.

Even though family patterns have changed, it is still a fact that the close and warm relationships and the care given within a familial frame is of vital importance for the well-being of children. But broadly, we find institution based childcare system in developing countries and in Europe and in United States, family foster care is the most prevalent rehabilitation practice when children and young people cannot live with their natural parents.

Broadly children in need of care and protection can be divided into the following categories:

(i) Children who are homeless (abandoned or relinquished or become homeless for other reasons, i.e. war, natural calamity or separated from parents);
(ii) Children who need special protection, i.e. having special needs, HIV and handicapped children;
(iii) Children who are neglected and abused.

Children who experience child abuse, neglect, or family violence are at risk for poor development not only during their childhood but also throughout their lives. The hidden consequences of child abuse and neglect can result in long-term health and cognitive effects and developmental delays. The wellbeing of children is crucial to any society that include their physical health and safety; educational achievement and cognitive attainment; and social and emotional development. Childhood is the important phase of life and has got to be made meaningful for all such children who are without any home or who are in need of care and protection.

It is widely acknowledged that the effective resolution of child abuse and neglect must include prevention, treatment, and follow-up services under a highly coordinated, comprehensive service delivery system where all players and providers work in concert. The multi-disciplinary team approach for child protection has the potential to provide a highly coordinated, comprehensive service delivery system (Mills & Untalan, 1992).

Experiences of institutional care all over the world show that the risk of neglect and exploitation is high. Children are helpless, and assaults both by staff and by other children at the institution have proved to take place. Studies show, for example, that the children with disabilities are more vulerable to the risk of being subjected to assault of various kinds. There are traumatic childhood experiences of institutional care, which often constitute physical and emotional abuse. The situation in developing countries has not been investigated in the same way as in the west, but it is probably the same. The relative isolation that institutional life involves and the often inadequate supervision in the form of official inspection and control are factors contributing to the risks of assault against the children.

The UN Convention on the Rights of the Child, 1989 recognizes family as the fundamental group of the society and the natural environment for growth and wellbeing of all its members and particularly children. However, in reality, millions of children become homeless without a nurturing family environment which is a fact not only in developing countries but also all over the globe.

The CRC and other human rights instruments also emphasize the role of the parents. Parents or, when applicable, the extended family or legal guardians have the primary responsibility to take care of, support and guide the child in a way that is in the child's best interest. The state shall render appropriate assistance to parents and legal guardians (Articles 3, 5, 8 and 27). If the child is deprived of his or her family environment, the state shall provide special protection and assistance (Article 20), but it is the right of children placed by the state for reasons of care, protection or treatment to have all aspects of that placement evaluated regularly (Article 25).

New perspectives on childhood contribute to a different understanding of the interaction between adults and children.

The social ethics of childhood is concerned less with moral or spiritual development than with the child-related assumptions, beliefs, and responsibilities of adults and societies. In a similar way to issues of women, minorities, and the natural environment, attention to the distinctive experiences of childhood should reshape contemporary ethical understanding itself in fundamentally new ways. Children are, uniquely, full human beings who, nevertheless, cannot speak up or act in the public realm fully for themselves (John Wall, 2005).

In most countries in a situation where children have to be placed in out-of-home care, foster care is the first choice. A basic assumption in our perception of children and adolescents is that they should be part of a family. On a general level in many countries, the image of 'family'—what it is and what it does—is a powerful ideal that structures societal institutions oriented to children and young people (Makrinioti, 1994). The good family is a potent figure of thought in society at large and even more so in out-of-home care. In foster care this idea is fundamental (Gillis, 1997; Colton & Williams, 1997).

"Children are human beings with human rights. However, people around the globe tend to think otherwise. Most birth parents tend to think, 'I have given birth to these human beings and they are my property to bring up as I wish.' Some sell their children. Some abuse their children. Some use their children as labourers. Some offer their children as domestic servants. Some train their children to be beggars. The list goes on and on. When and how should ethics enter the picture for parents? It doesn't! Parents do not think of ethics when raising their children. Most feel they are in-charge and that the children must do as they say, even if wrong", says Louse Williams, a Philanthropologist. In her opinion, each and every child comes into this world as a pure individual. Their views and attitudes are acquired from their caregivers and environment. Therefore to create positive change, one must empower children to grow into self-sufficient citizens of tomorrow so that they may give back to their community, country and the world.

Children are entitled to standards of care and protection that guarantee their rights. Many states are failing to monitor the quality of care for children placed in institutions or in alternative families. It is the primary responsibility of states to establish policies, laws and services for the protection and care of children, in accordance with the CRC. These should address standards of childcare and regulate practice and agencies providing the services. States should also monitor and take action regarding all agencies and other groups within their borders that support the provision of childcare in foreign countries that is contrary to the spirit and intention of the CRC. The issues facing children in need of care and protection are not going to be resolved unless the CRC is implemented holistically and indivisibly. It is important that our knowledge of child development and different forms of childcare in their cultural contexts is improved. While some research has indicated that community-based care is less costly than institutionalized care, more rigorous empirical cost-effectiveness analysis must provide convincing evidence that community-based care represents the optimal use of resources without compromising the quality of childcare (http://www.savethechildren.net/alliance/resources/last_res.pdf).

Henry Dwight Chapin, a pioneering paediatrician, concluded in 1908 that, "The collecting of many little children under one roof is not good for them; no matter how well managed the institution." The next year in 1909, at the first White House Conference on children, and then during the next eight decades, physicians and child welfare specialists concurred that: (1) publicly funded programs (including income maintenance) to support family life is preferable to removing children from their relatives except in cases of serious maltreatment. And (2) when removal from relatives is unavoidable because of abandonment, profound neglect, or maltreatment, infants and young children should be provided with long-term family substitutes through prompt adoption or, at a minimum, care in stable foster families.

The study of children and childhood is now an accepted part of social science. The academic growth of childhood studies began in the 1980s, with three trajectories, parallel and sometimes overlapping but nonetheless distinct. The first of these established that childhood is a social phenomenon rather than a biological fact, the second developed new methods of research with this population, which presents both practical and ethical challenges to researchers, and the third, based in but not exclusive to academic research, focused on investigating the lives and conditions of especially vulnerable children. (down loaded from http://www.knowing-children.org/upload/nus/concept_paper_May2006.doc)

One of the new departures in the late twentieth century has been the growing attention to children and the discovery of both 'children' and 'childhood' as a research area. Feeding on a range of local, national and international policy concerns, children have become visible in ways than they were not before. The concerns relate to the inclusion of children in the development process, the abuse and deprivation of children and the contextualisation of the rights associated with 'childhood'. In the mainstream construction of childhood, children have henceforth been seen as individuals with an autonomy that should be safeguarded and fostered (G. K. Lieten, July 2005).

In the recent past, as a result of ratification of Hague Convention, both receiving and sending countries through their central authorities are obliged to ensure procedural safeguards for internationally adopted children. Various socio-psychological compulsions have resulted in inter-country adoptions defying national boundaries, which is of course a blessing in disguise for the children who are not able to find adoptive parents in their own country. The guiding principle of best interest of the children has always been emphasized in various international conventions, and meets.

The circumstances of adoption changed dramatically after Second World War. The involvement of Americans in wars outside the United States, in Europe, Japan, Korea and later in Vietnam, coupled with a decline in infants available for adoption in the United States, gave rise to the practice of international adoption. Trans-racial adoptions also referred to as inter-racial, inter-ethnic, or trans-ethnic adoptions; involve the adoption of a child by parents of a different race or ethnicity. In practice, trans-racial adoptions refer to mostly to the adoption of children of colour by white families (Hollingsworth, 1998). Many of the children adopted were European and Japanese war orphans. Additional adoptions followed after the civil war in Greece (1946-49), the Korean War (1950-53) and the war in Vietnam (1954-1975). But war and its aftermath are not the only factors leading countries to allow their children to be adopted abroad. Desperate poverty and social upheaval have been critical factors in the adoption of children from Latin America, the former Soviet Union and Eastern Europe over the last twenty years. In China, government population control policies contributed to abandonment of infant girls and overcrowded orphanages, factors in the government's decision to facilitate international adoptions (Gailey & others).

The western society particularly United States is a place where adoption of unrelated children is a way of life and large number of children (neglected and/or abused) find their alternate families within the society. There are large numbers of overseas adoptions too and in most of the cases, children do well and the country has created large number of resources to benefit such children.

Thousands of couples or individuals from receiving countries regard inter-country adoption as the solution left at the end of a long, painful road that has typically included unsuccessful fertility treatment, applications for domestic adoption turned down or placement on a long waiting list. In the last two decades, inter-country adoption has progressively changed. From its initial purpose of providing a family environment for children, it has now become more demand driven. Increasingly in industrial countries, inter-country adoption is viewed as a way for childless couples to satisfy their desire for a child (Chantal Saclier, 2000).

During the adoption process, violations of the most basic rights of the child can occur. These violations are often perpetrated under the cover of the supposedly humanitarian aim of the act and "justified" by the simplistic view that a child will somehow be "better off" in a materially rich country. Therefore, it is important to understand the meaning of childhood and ethical issues involved in the rehabilitation process of such children who are deprived of family care. Children without families are most vulnerable in society. Investing in them and their healthy development has benefits for society, for parents and families as a whole. A field like the rehabilitation of abandoned, orphaned and destitute children calls for total dedication to the highest standards of professionalism, competence, integrity and social vision.

Chapter Outline

As it has been widely agreed, the issues such as lack of transparency across adoption process and procedural delays at each level need to be addressed in each country involved in international adoption. The volume has been divided into three parts. Part I deals with issues related to construction of childhood, basic nature of a child, effects of institutional living on attachment and the rights of children (in UK), Part II deals with some global issues, i.e. open adoption, adoptions in and to the United States and global perspective and trans-national adoptions. Ethical issues and safeguards in adoption placement have mostly been covered in Part III. Various Annexure included in the volume are very much relevant to the issues discussed.

PART I

1. Dr. Reesa Sorin and Dr. Greta Galloway

Rights-based approaches are increasingly used as a framework for developing and providing protection mechanisms and welfare services for children around the world. Understanding construction of childhood is important while serving child in need of care and protection. In a number of situations professional social workers confront major dilemma while dealing with children and thus it is significant to understand each construction of childhood behaviour.

Researchers at James Cook University have discovered 10 different child "typologies" that group children's behaviour and adults' perceptions of them into distinct archetypes. Reesa Sorin and Greta Galloway researched popular fiction and history books looking for recurring themes in the way children were perceived and presented. Dr. Reesa Sorin and Dr. Greta Galloway discuss ten important construction of childhood i.e. the child as innocent—the adult as protector, the child as evil—the adult as good/moral, the snowballing child—the differing adult, the out of control child—the powerless adult, the noble/savior child—the dependent adult, the miniature adult and the adult in training, the commoditized child—the self-interested adult, the child victim—the absent adult, the agentic child—adult as co-constructor of being. It's important to understand appropriate transactions with children as any construction of childhood necessarily and simultaneously engages us in the process of constructing adulthood. Beginning from childcare worker to the people working at the policy level, all need to have orientation about appropriate construction of childhood to better understand childhood reality. Knowing these typologies can help parents and those who care for children.

2. Louise Anita Williams and Valji Bagda

We all perhaps cherish a dream that children everywhere should be treated with dignity, respect, understanding, and compassion. In such a world, every child can grow into adulthood with a generous capacity for love and trust. The UN Convention on the Rights of the Child, 1989 recognizes family as the fundamental group of the society and the natural environment for growth and wellbeing of all its members and particularly children. However, in reality, millions of children are found destitute and abandoned without a nurturing family environment not just in developing countries but also all over the globe.

"When coming into this world, there is no such thing as a bad child. Each and every child comes into this world a pure individual. Children are not born orphans; that is unless it was a mistake and the father is not known. Children's views and attitudes are acquired from their caregivers and environments. Therefore to create positive change one must empower children to grow into self-sufficient citizens of tomorrow so they may give back to their community, country and the world", says Louise Anita Williams, a philanthropist who is promoting effective parenting and responsible childcare in India.

In India, we require right attitude from all stakeholders who are directly or indirectly connected with children's wellbeing. With increasing diversity of family forms, and the changing roles and pressures within families, understanding how family factors interact with the child's own characteristics and those of the family's wider social context, in determining children's adjustment is a complex task. In most of the cases, the adults are responsible for the fate of the children and once we realize the fact and have commitment to work for their best interest, the goal that we cherish for children become achievable.

3. Chivonne Hagan

In many countries, thousands of children spend their childhood in large institutions without love and attachment or individual attention from adults. Early institutionalisation increases the risk of attachment difficulties. It can slow the child's emotional, social, and physical development as well as affect the child's ability to make smooth transitions from one developmental stage to another. In most of the countries which are having institutionalized based child welfare system, children are usually subjected to administrative procedures and routines and fewer efforts are made for providing personal care. All such children need help with developing secure attachments and emotional expressiveness, and that interventions focusing on these needs can help minimize deficits in social development. Chivonne Hagan, is a trained social worker working in the area of adoption and foster care in the state of California, USA and she has referred a number of studies that lay emphasis on promoting personal connection or attachment at early childhood.

4. Peter Selman

Prof. Peter Selman, a specialist on adoption matters, has covered a number of issues on children in need of care and protection and children in conflict with law in United Kingdom. The UN Convention on the Rights of the Child (UNCRC) was ratified by the UK Government in December 1991. The Convention provides a set of minimum standards relating to children's civil, political, economic, social and cultural rights and as such represents a comprehensive framework by which to examine the impact of all legislation, policy and practice relating to children's rights. He discusses about commitment to children's rights in the UK, role of Ombudsman, United Nations Convention on Rights of Child (UNCRC), UK's experience and status on the rights of children, child poverty and the incidence of children in public care, issue of corporal punishment, juvenile justice, child participation, and children's rights in inter-country adoption. His comparative analysis with different countries such as Korea is interesting.

PART II

5. Paul Sachdev

Open Adoption is one of the many options available to birth and adoptive families who are looking to adopt a child. In western societies, open adoption of unrelated children is some thing very common unlike developing countries. This type of adoption is a unique relationship that a Birth Parent and Adoptive Family form when a child is placed in adoption. Adoptive parents sometimes welcome the birth parents into their lives almost as extended family members. Research of open adoption information has shown that children raised in open adoptions have better overall adjustment and higher self-esteem than those raised in closed adoptions. In USA, open adoption is catching on particularly fast in the Midwest and western parts of the country. It is less common in much of the East Coast and parts of the South. In certain societies, family adoptions are much prevalent but not open adoption. Dr. Paul Sachdev, Professor Emeritus discusses some of the implications of open adoptions. The author is of the strong opinion that although some data are available about how birth and adoptive parents experience openness, but much more rigorous research is needed to understand the effects of openness on children's social and emotional outcomes and family relationships.

6. Josephine A. Ruggiero

U.S. inter-country adoptions nearly trebled from more than 8,000 to more than 22,000 between fiscal years 1994 and 2004. Adopting a child from a foreign country is a complex process with a variety of domestic and foreign government requirements that prospective parents must meet. Despite the existence of such U.S. and foreign government regulations, a number of factors in foreign countries, such as corruption, may lead to abuses in inter-country adoption procedures. In recent years, some of the countries have suspended their inter-country adoption programs in response to concerns over abuses in inter-country adoptions, as well as to review their inter-country adoption processes and improve safeguards. The 1993 Hague Convention on Protection of Children and Co-operation in Respect of Inter-country Adoption (Convention) provides additional safeguards by establishing uniform standards for inter-country adoptions.

Prof. J.A. Ruggiero talks about the trend of international adoptions of children to the United States and how inter-country adoption has been a part of United States social life. United States citizens started adopting children from other countries in substantial numbers after Second World War (1939-1945). More and more US citizens are expanding their families through adoption for various reasons. The author has raised gender specific issues and has come out with lot of facts that may be helpful for researchers to conduct studies on international adoptions. In fact, people in the developing countries have a genuine desire to come and settle in United States, a place with lot of diversities that offer more opportunities for growth. The country encourages all multi-cultural activities and freedom for all to grow and remain active. But for quite some time things are changing as we see a return migration from USA to the country of origin for several reasons. It is presumed that less and less children may be available for inter-country adoption in United States in the days to come for several reasons, i.e. efforts made by developing countries to attain Millennium Development Goals (MDG), more domestic adoptions resulting in the country of origin and moratorium in some of the sending countries for international adoptions due to notice of unethical practices.

7. Pal Ahluwalia

Trans-racial adoption refers to the adoption of a child of one race by parents of another and trans-national adoption means international adoption. It is perhaps the most controversial form of adoption today. While trans-national adoption is very much prominent in case of children placed in international adoptions in USA and Europe, there are also trans-racial adoptions within USA/ UK itself of African American children by white parents because of the large numbers of African American children in foster care, and because of the large numbers of white families wishing to adopt.

It is a fact that children adopted from a different race suffer from racial discrimination and in some cases disruptions are likely to occur. But many children who are internationally adopted are very resilient and thrive in their new homes once they are loved and provided stimulation. There are various ways and means now in the receiving countries to tackle such problem and meet challenges of cross-cultural and trans-racial adoption issues. While studies of adoption disruption do not find race to be a discriminating variable, there are numerous anecdotal stories of very serious difficulties in establishing racial identity among trans-racially adopted children. Whether or not the best interests of children are served by trans-racial adoption is currently open to debate. Prof. Pal Ahluwalia has got very critical opinion about trans-racial adoption and believes that one of the most significant consequences of inter-racial or trans-national adoption is that it makes adoptive parents aware of the shocking racism that their children have to endure.

The question is whether several options are left before considering inter-racial adoptions and in case of inter-country adoptions, whether the country of origin has got adequate resources to deal with such children through family foster care and sponsorship etc. Again the question is whether the home-country alternatives will find answer to all children's needs and the system could be foolproof from delays and unethical practices as noticed from time to time? My understanding about the issue is that it is always desired that children are placed in adoption within the same race and colour.

PART III

8. René A.C. Hoksbergen and Jan J.F. ter Laak

In today's world a couple has the opportunity to have a child with the assistance of reproductive technology, surrogacy and ovum donation. In traditional surrogacy, the surrogate mother is artificially inseminated with the sperm of the intended father or sperm donor. In gestational surrogacy, the surrogate mother is not genetically related to the child. Eggs are extracted from the intended mother or egg donor and mixed with sperm from the intended father or sperm donor in vitro. The embryos are then transferred into the surrogate's uterus. The entire procedure includes various stakeholders like professionals in the fields of reproductive medicine, psychology, legal representation and investigation etc. An article on the RESOLVE website reports on qualitative comments of 150 donor insemination (DI) parents surveyed in a San Francisco study, indicating that most that undergo DI do not plan to tell their offspring. "Secrecy: The Unresolved Dilemma of Donor Insemination," by Robert Nachtigall and Gay Becker, summarizes parental views ranging from those who plan to disclose to their children (most of whom cite their children's right to know as the reason) to parents who want total secrecy, often to avoid social stigma, explanations and judgments. Some wives said they choose non-disclosure out of deference to their husbands' wishes. René A.C. Hoksbergen and Jan J. F. ter Laak discuss the controversial topic of the application of modern reproductive technology, its ethical consequences and rights of such children.

9. Dr. Nilima Mehta

Although ethics in adoption is a hot topic, adoption specialists and professionals are unsure about how to serve the best interests of children who need to be adopted and how birth parents, adoptive parents, and adult adoptees ought to be served. This failure to identify and prioritize ethical standards in adoption has resulted in a lack of ethical decision-making and inadequate—and sometimes fraudulent—treatment of those seeking adoption—related services. One of the most critical ethical issues in adoption is the way that adoption impacts real people: birth families, adoptees as children and as adults, prospective adoptive parents and adoptive families.

Adoption has a lifelong impact and the issues are complex. Key ethical challenge is ethical counselling for members of the triad and counselling by a professional/trained social worker is the most important intervention in the process, i.e. at the time of surrender of children or separation of children, for the prospective adoptive parents who desire to adopt a child, for the adoptive parents encountering problem with the child and for adopted children when they are grown up and search for their biological parents. Dr. Nilima Mehta, who has long been dealing with children issues in India, is of the opinion that the dilemmas that crops up in the process of adoption are because of a certain kind of conflict between the rightness or wrongness of the actions and the goodness or badness of the consequences.

10. Victor Groza and Curtis Proctor

Escorting children placed in international adoption from the country of origin is an area, which has attracted less attention so far. Adoptive parents, representatives of foreign adoption agencies or adoption agencies of the country of origin usually escort children to their place of destination. In fact, this is additional safeguard for the child to be escorted by his adoptive parent/s. When prospective adoptive parents come to escort their child or children, they get a chance to mingle with the baby even if for few days before making final departure, they get to know more information about the baby's food habits, preferences from the child care staff of the adoption agency and more importantly, they have the last chance to take the informed decision about the proposed adoption. While sending countries do not have a uniform escort policy as far as escorting of internationally adopted children is concerned, most of the countries stipulate adoptive parent/s to escort the children as they would have more understanding about the culture and heritage of the country of origin and also later they are in a position to handle issues like "search of roots". In case of India, as per 2006 Inter-country Adoption Guidelines, the adoptive parent/parents will have to come to India and accompany the child back to their country. But in exceptional cases, where there is a problem of escorting by adoptive parents, there can be relaxation to such provision keeping in mind the best interest of the child/children as provided in Para 10.3 of the Guidelines. This can be on case-to-case basis. As per guidelines of Euro-Adopt, an escort ought not to travel with more than 2 children. The organization should avoid making arrangements for escorting large groups of children at the same time. Prof. Victor Groza and Prof. Curtis Proctor have to say that it is usually in the child's best interest for the parent/s to travel to the birth country and take them home.

11. Christine Futia

A large number of children from developing countries find their homes in the United States. Recently, Heritage tours have become very popular in reconnecting children to their roots, learning about their birth culture and gaining first-hand experience with their country of origin. In some cases optional "Talk Times" are offered to the adopted children struggling with their identity search by trained adoption social workers or adoption professionals during the tours. The ultimate objective of the tours is to give children— a sense of belonging as they experience their birth country with other adoptive children. It is exciting to note that children adopted from many different countries here in USA gain a lot from a heritage tour to their country of origin. Typically, they make the trip accompanied by one or more of their adoptive parents as well as friends they may have made through heritage camps and other Indian cultural activities for adoptees in America. Mrs. Christina Futia, who herself is an adoptive parent, is very positive about the long-term benefits of heritage camps and heritage tours. In reality, in most of the cases, it is nearly impossible to find more information about biological parents, which means that such programs are immensely helpful in addressing identity, self-esteem or attachment issues.

Older adoptees in USA have access to lot of internet sources about connecting with each other particularly to those belonging to their country of origin and there are also large numbers of agencies working on this area. Heritage tour is certainly a good practice for connecting older adoptees to their country of origin.

12. Jagannath Pati

Child adoption in India has been a prevalent social practice from ancient times but with a different perspective. Earlier the practice was to adopt a child from one's own family or near and dear ones. The adoption of an unrelated child into the family had its beginnings in the sixties. Professional intervention of child welfare agencies in the process of adoption began only in the early seventies. This led to systematisation of the procedures so that the best interest of the child, adoptive parents and the birth parents could be protected. The adoption program saw significant changes in the eighties at the legal, social and practice levels. Adoption of an unrelated child into the family gained acceptance and more Indian couples came forward to adopt. The national adoption program received an impetus because of the lock of promotional efforts by the Government and various social and child welfare organisations.

In India, there are large numbers of orphan and abandoned children who are not in the database. Their journey of pain and pleasure begins from the mother's womb and it is a continuous journey. All such children have right to their childhood and all basic civic amenities of life including a loving family to grow. There have been some recent developments in India; a couple of progressive legislations for their rights and safeguards and fresh guidelines on adoption matter. The problems in India's child welfare system are largely due to a lack of accurate database and not having a support system to achieve targets. Fundamental ignorance of facts becomes the basis for policy decisions that impact the lives of many children. In India, at any time there are not more than 10,000 children for adoption in all adoption agencies listed by Central Adoption Resource Agency. There is need of a paradigm shift in interventions to the rehabilitation of children in need of care and protection from needs to a rights approach and from residential care to a family based. In case of inter-country adoption, safeguards and ethical practices as stipulated under Hague Convention on Inter-country Adoption-1993 must be adhered to both in letter and spirit by adoption agencies and authorities. Reorganizing adoption system in India has become almost inevitable to curtail procedural delays and have more such children in the database. For such endeavour, placement related decision should remain with the government while other services may be rendered by adoption agencies which are usually non-government organisations.

References

All Africa Global Media/The Monitor, Kampala.

Downloaded from http://www.savethechildren.net/alliance/resources/last_res.pdf

Chantal Saclier (2000), *Inter-country Adoption: Development, trends and perspectives*—Edited Publisher: British Agencies for Adoption and Fostering.

G.K. Lieten (July 2005), *Tradition, Globalisation and Childhood.* Amsterdam: IREWOC, downloaded from www.childlabour.net

Gailey, Christine Ward, Race (2000), Class and Gender in Inter-country Adoption in the USA, at 298-303, Intercountry Adoption: Developments, Trends and Perspectives, Peter Selman, ed. (2000).

Gillis, J.R. (1997), *A world of their own making: a history of myth and ritual in family* life. Oxford: Oxford University Press.

Hollingsworth L.D. (1998), promoting same race adoption for Children of color, social work 43/2.

John, Wall (2005), *A New Social Ethics of Childhood in a Globalizing World Childhoods—2005,* Conference, Oslo.

M. Colton and M. Williams (Ass. Prof. Univ. Calgary) (ed.) (1997), *The World of Foster Care: An International Sourcebook of Foster Care Systems,* Aldershot, Arena.

Makrinioti, D. (1994), Conceptualisation of Childhood in a Welfare State: A Critical Reappraisal. I Qvortrup, J.M. fl. (red.) *Childhood Matters: Social Theory, Practice and Politics,* Aldershot: Avebury.

Mills & Untalan (1992), *Inter-disciplinary Perspectives in Child Abuse and Neglect,* Praeger Publishers.

Robert C. Fellmeth (2002), *Child Rights & Remedies.* Contributors, Clarity Press, Atlanta Publication.

The Growing Concern about Children in Residential care© International Save the Children Alliance contributed by, Andrew Dunn, Elizabeth Jareg and Douglas.

UNCRC materials and a number of materials browsed from http://www.crin.org/hrbap/index.asp and http://www.uncdf.org etc.

W. Schramm (1964), *Mass Media and National Development.* Stanford, Calif: Stanford University Press.

World Bank (1999), *World Development Report: Knowledge for Development.* New York: Oxford University Press.

(downloaded http://www.knowingchildren.org/upload/nus/concept_paper_May2006.doc).

http://www.resolve.org/site/PageServer?pagename=pubs_pubs_sec http://www.humanscape.org/Humanscape/2004/Nov.

Part I

CHILDHOOD, ATTACHMENT ISSUES AND CHILD RIGHTS

1

Constructions of Childhood

Constructions of Self

REESA SORIN and GRETA GALLOWAY

Introduction

Throughout history, notions of what constitutes a child and defines childhood have been strongly contested. Childhood is now largely recognized as a constructed notion developed, perpetuated and contested by powerful adults who act and speak on behalf of politically and economically disenfranchised children. Wrigley (2003) argues that these adult constructions of children "necessarily involve profound questions of moral judgement that rest on implicit ideas of children's place in the social order" (p. 693). Shifts within the economic and political state itself force us to re-evaluate and re-conceptualize childhood to meet changing circumstances (Mason & Steadman, 1997). Myriad examples exist within literature to demonstrate this ongoing project of defining childhood (see for example Aries, 1962; Branscombe, Castle, Dorsey, Surbeck and Taylor, 2000; Corsaro, 1997; Hutchinson and Charlesworth, 2000; Mead and Wolfenstein, 1955). While this literature focuses on defining children and childhood, it is less overt in recognizing that through processes of defining the "other", adults are necessarily and simultaneously defining themselves. It is through this process that adults, either consciously or unconsciously, locate themselves in relation to children rather than as a mutually exclusive entity. In this paper, we present nine different constructions of childhood through which we elucidate the demands, these constructions place on children and adults in their relationships with each other. A focus on relationship, rather than a discrete focus on either the characteristics or responsibilities of children or adults, provides an additional site for psycho-social and political engagement of children with adults. This is not possible, however, if we remain unconscious of the basic underpinning constructs of this engagement.

Those of us working with children recognize that it is at the interface between these constructions of childhood that we confront major dilemmas in our relationship with them. Each construction jostles with the other for pre-eminence. In this sense, these categories are not mutually exclusive. That is, we may work with children, even the same children, from multiple definitional perspectives. Hutchison and Charlesworth (2000) articulate this in their example of the 1989 United Nations Convention on the Rights of the Child, wherein there is an explicit call to extend human rights to children (with the expectation that the child is agentic and can act on these rights) whilst simultaneously recognising childhood as a time of immaturity and vulnerability when children are in need of care and protection (the child as innocent). Similarly, children who are focused on under policy directives of "child protection" are engaged through a paradigm of "child as innocent". At the point at which the child acts out their abuse on others, though they are more likely to be engaged through a paradigm of "child as evil". This recognised, however, a focus on the intersection between constructions of childhood is outside the scope of this paper. The task of this paper is to present a typology of childhood which explicates both the power of the child and the power of the adult as a first step in developing a political consciousness of our engagement with children. Like many typologies this is presented outside of notions of culture, class, gender, ability, age (etc.). It is hoped that the typology presented provides a tool for people working either directly, or indirectly, with children, to interrupt their taken-for-granted notions of children and childhood to expand that which is possible in the relationship between us. This will force us away from expectations of linear or singular change, from either the adult or the child, to a recognition that change within either definition will provoke change in both.

Ten Constructions of Childhood: Ten Constructions of Self

Literature analysis suggests that there are ten ways in which childhood is conceptualised. These are, the child as innocent; the child as evil; the snowballing child; the out of control child; the child as noble/Saviour; the child as miniature adult; the child as adult in training; the child as commodity; the child as victim; and the agentic child. Each of these constructions is presented in terms of its defining characteristics, images or examples of this type; power and a critique of each construction.

The Child as Innocent: The Adult as Protector

This construction has been presented since the late Middle ages, from depictions of the child saint, and with the belief that adults should care for the young and innocent (Branscombe *et al.*, 2000). Childhood is located as distinct from adulthood—a time of pure innocence which will never be recaptured and a time and carefree space which should be the best of our lives (Branscombe *et al.*, 2000; Hutchison and Charlesworth, 2000; Wood, 2003). Froebel's notion of kindergarten depicts this through imagery of literally, a garden of children in a state of "primitive kindness" or natural goodness (Aries, 1962). The innocence of the child simultaneously makes them incompetent, vulnerable and dependent, a blank slate ready to be moulded by adults. Under this construction, children should be, and deserve to be, loved and guided by caring teachers in order for these innate qualities to manifest (Branscombe *et al.*, 2000).

The innocent child is present in works of fiction, as well as non-fiction, including works of Dickens, where children are portrayed as weak and suffering, in need of our (adult) pity and protection (Wolfenstein in Mead and Wolfenstein, 1955). It is found in Alcott's "Little Women", where a central character, Jo, dreads growing up and her mother states that children should be children for as long as possible (Wood, 2003). Hoffman (2000) positions this as a primary force within Japanese education, stating "Traditional Japanese views of children stressed not their supposed development in terms of movement toward a superior state of adulthood but the innate moral and spiritual superiority of childhood over adulthood" (p. 194).

This construction of childhood is evident in codes of ethics and codes of conduct towards children, most importantly the United Nations Convention on the Rights of the Child, which states that in all actions towards children, "the best interests of the child shall be a primary consideration" (United Nations High Commissioner for Human Rights, 1989). Similarly, this construction underpins child centred education practices as demonstrated through Early Childhood Australia's Code of Ethics (Early Childhood Australia, 2005a) and Australian Child Protection policies and practices (Mason & Steadman, 1997). While the "best interests of the child" are fore grounded in these and other policies, these are for the large part defined outside of the child's own agency. Their innocence is conflated with their simultaneous ignorance or naivety. James *et al.* (1998) state it thus: "If childhood innocence is to be nurtured at all costs, then we must attain publicly recognisable standards in the treatment of children…children can no longer be routinely mistreated, but neither can they be left to their own devices" (p.14).

Walkerdine (1999) argues that this is a predominant paradigm at the beginning of the 21st century as we seek to protect our (innocent) children from those who would harm them. She cites several examples of events which act upon the fears of adults and entrench "protection". These examples include, the Dunblane tragedy where teachers and children were killed by a gunman; adult fear of children's relationships with others in cyberspace, as is evidenced by computer programs such as Net Nanny. Faced with these fears of adults, children become subjects of protection, surveillance and control.

Within the discourse of the child as innocent, children are granted little power; they are perceived of as incapable of making decisions and positioned as needing adult protection. They are therefore at the mercy of adults (Corsaro, 1997). Adults are perceived as having power and responsibility over and for the children with whom they interact. They are christened as nurturers and moulders (sculptors) of the child. If the child does not respond in ways which society deems appropriate, then it is because they have not been loved, cared for, taught, moulded appropriately. Parents, teachers, therapists and welfare workers have not done their jobs properly (Gibson, 1998; Wintersberger, 1994 in Hutchison and Charlesworth, 2000). The adult's power comes from their (assumed) capacity to guide and protect children. They are expected to control (or limit) the child's environment and type of stimulus to which they are exposed, such as the amount of time children can watch TV as well as what they can watch (Buckingham, 1994).

This construction of childhood is criticised in terms of its assumption that adults always act in goodwill towards children. Further, it denies the child a voice in their own lives and decisions, allowing adults to speak and give consent on their behalf (Dockett, 2002; Fasoli, 2001; Wood, 2003). Hutchison and Charlesworth (2000) argue that childhood becomes sentimentalised in this construction. Dockett (2002) concurs that this is a nostalgic view but more seriously, it is one that stops us taking children seriously— they are cute and cuddly.

There is also an over concentration on outcomes of socialisation to explain the phenomena of childhood rather than other variables, such as development, genetics and/or free will (Corsaro, 1997), whilst remaining devoid of a wider socio-political and material understanding of the lives of children. Therefore, this framework of child as innocent is over-reliant on standardised, psychological "universal" knowledge of an homogenous entity, "children" (Dockett, 2002). The outcomes of this framework are that school and other curricula and the world are sanitised in their presentation of and to children (Dockett, 2002). We control what children are able to see, do and participate in, because this state of innocence is to be preserved, not only for the child's good but as a societal end in itself (i.e. this state of innocence is good for all of us). Silin (1995 in Woodrow, 1999) urges us to recognise that when we construct safe, nurturing and sanitised environments for children we separate them from their own knowledges and disconnect them from their own experiences of life.

The Child as Evil: The Adult as Good/Moral

Notions of the evil child come from prehistoric and early Christian times when it was perceived that children were evidence of their parents' (evil/sexual) intimacy. This construct allowed for practices of infanticide and incest to persist (in Greece, Rome, Africa and China). Children who were considered less than perfect were drowned, exposed to the elements or starved (De Mause, 1982, in Branscombe *et al.*, 2000). Hobbes felt that children left to their own devices would display their intrinsic evil. The evil child arises from the concept of original sin, that is, all children born are essentially demonic, although this is not intentional (i.e. they are driven rather than in control of this "evil"; James *et al.*, 1998).

This view prevails through literature like Golding's (1954) "Lord of the Flies". The child as evil is an underlying construct of the regulation of children in educational settings, where children are regulated in terms of dress and behavioural codes. Regulation can also occur through imposing drug regime upon the child. This construction of childhood forms the basis of research that positions children as objects to be studied in the search for better methods of establishing conformity and ease of teaching practice (Woodrow, 1999). While the adult who views the child as innocent restricts the curriculum and alternative world views available to children, adults with constructions of the child as evil seek to restrict the child him/herself (Sorin, 2003). The child is positioned as "an untamed threat" (Corsaro, 1997, p. 9) who must be controlled and trained to "fit in". This construction of childhood is maintained not only through Christian beliefs, but through mass communication about child killers (e.g. the James Bulger case, where a toddler was murdered by two young boys in England); destructive energies of young people (e.g. as depicted in "Schoolies Week" imagery (in Australia, this celebration occurs at the end of High School and is displayed in newspapers as involving drugs, alcohol, sex and irresponsible behaviour around property) and imagery of deviant and violent youth (Guppy, 2005). These events are often followed by some call to control and "tame" young people through detention, curfews or "boot camps".

Walkerdine (1999) notes that adults may simultaneously position some children as innocent and "other" children (usually the children of those who have themselves been "othered", for example, Indigenous, migrant, intellectually or mentally disabled, and poor) as evil. These children are a threat to the social order and its reproduction. This allows for the control of some children more than others within the state.

In this construction of childhood, children are seen as intrinsically driven by their own needs, desires, nature and pleasure. They do not have real power therefore, since they are not choosing to act this way, but are driven by the "demon within" (e.g. Freud's theory of people being driven by sex and aggression). Parents, teachers and others who work with children are expected to control this innate evil. When they cannot or will not do this, they are seen as weak and blamed for not controlling the "evil" child. Evil is innate but is manifest in children because adults lack control of their children or abdicate their control over them. Current discussion in Australia about fining parents for the misbehaviour of their child/ren, for example, operates from this typology.

The power of adults within this construction of childhood comes from the intrinsic goodness/morality of adults who have passed from this naturally evil state to a more mature state. Our society becomes sustainable through adult transmission of this goodness or morality. This picture of the evil child simultaneously depicts adults as "good". Beatings and harsh discipline from adults may be seen as good for the child. Corporal punishment is often viewed through this lens, where the adult claims "It did me good (or at least no harm), so it will do you good."

As in the construction of the child as innocent, there is an over concentration on outcomes of socialisation, within this paradigm of the child as evil. This paradigm does not consider the issue of real material social conditions, such as poverty and unemployment, conditions under which some children live. Children are seen as driven through psychological processes rather than as actors in their world.

The Snowballing Child: The Deferring Adult

This child, while not out of control, seems to be in charge of adults and situations around them. Snowballing children make inflexible demands of adults. If things don't go the child's way, the child either withdraws or goes on the attack, either verbally or physically. Within this construction, it can feel like the child has more influence on their parents/adults than the parents/adults have on them. Images of the "spoiled brat" who has all the toys and accessories he/she wants, but remains unsatisfied and continues to demand, perhaps best fits this construction. Advertising to children supports this image, where children are offered a plethora of goods and services to be acquired through manipulation of their parents. Online shopping and wish lists are examples of this. Children who choose what and where to eat and refuse to eat meals prepared by adults have assumed this construction.

The child sees power as a birthright, based on the parent giving them authority. They get a little power, and it snowballs. Adults are too busy or distracted, so give them more and more of their own power. This power is used by the child to further their own desires, needs or interests (unlike the Noble or Saviour child who uses this in the interests of others). This child has illegitimate power—that is, their power does not derive from themselves but from an abrogating adult. This child is neither at the mercy of adults, as is the innocent child, nor driven through intrinsic forces, as is the evil child, but gains power through the lack of adult influence. The power they gain may or may not be useful in their own long-term interests, but it is the short-term gratification that conditions this behaviour.

The adult may feel guilty about something to do with their relationship with the child. They may wish to "shut the child up", or they simply don't think about the long-term nature of their relationship with the child, so they hand (their) power over to the child. This could start off in small ways, but then snowballs. The adult doesn't take control or say no. For example, the child may go to bed whenever they decide regardless of the impact this has on themself or those around them either in the short or long-term, or parents/adults feel like they "talk 'til you're blue in the face", then give up and let children experience consequences for themselves. The adult could take the power back, but often doesn't know how to, or the snowball is so big now that it seems impossible.

In this image, the adult is very much seen as responsible, or rather irresponsible. Any power the child has is power that has been taken from the adult, rather than power in the child's right. The opportunity to negotiate power and autonomy is denied, as the adult defaults power to the child. This denies both the adult and the child agency in their relationship.

The Out-of-Control Child: The Powerless Adult

Challenging adult authority is part of childhood (Corsaro, 1997), but the out-of-control child uses power in negative ways, such as violence, to get people to do what they want them to do. They may internalise power and control in ways that ultimately incapacitate them, for example by getting sick (*anorexia nervosa*). These children may also use protective policies against adults (for example, the small number of children who allege physical or sexual abuse by significant adults when this has not occurred). They can be found in the pages of newspapers having committed violent crimes without being sanctioned for this behaviour (Robson, 2005). This stands in contrast to the evil child, who will be sanctioned. The out-of-control child, while seemingly powerful in the short-term, is ultimately not protected by the state or other authority, as continuation of such behaviour will lead to sanctions upon the child reaching adulthood.

These children, however, can be found in the works of narrative therapists, Epston (1989) and White (1988/89; 1991) who engage out-of-control children in ways that allow for the child to increasingly come under their own control. Temper tantrums, for example, are understood in narrative therapy as events through which the child loses control of themselves and come more directly under the control of the temper tantrums (this is the process of externalising the problem). In the event of ongoing temper tantrums, the child becomes labelled as somehow dysfunctional. Their parents may also label themselves, or be labelled by others, at least as ineffective. In this process, narratives begin to build about both the child and their parents, which privilege the version of themselves as under the control of the temper tantrum. This story, it is believed, camouflages the story about children and their parents as agents in their own lives and authors of their own narratives. Through narrative processes, Epston and White help children and adults rediscover these liberating narratives that help them regain control over the problems or issues (in this case temper tantrums) in their lives. In these ways, Epston and White provide alternatives to the evil/innocent narrative and pave the way for working with children and adults as agentic (see below).

While the out-of-control child initially assumes power in their relationships with adults, this is transitory, as they (eventually) feel out of control and believe that no-one is there to help them regain control—of themselves, their lives. Significant adults of the out-of-control child feel powerless and even defeated in regaining influence with the child.

Within this image, the power of anarchy as a force for societal change is negated. A prevalent view of children within this image as described above is that they should come under their own control, with adults helping them in this process. In this image, the notion of a co-constructed relationship between the child and the adult is negated, as the child is focused upon as an isolated entity.

The Noble/Saviour Child: The Dependant Adult

Like the innocent child (above) the noble child is beautiful and beloved, but in addition has the power to save not only other children, but adults, families, communities and even the world. This image of the child saint, or saviour, emerged in early Christian times with the recognition of Jesus' wisdom as a child and the Christian tenet that "a little child will lead" (Branscombe *et al.*, 2000). An example of the noble child cited by Wolfenstein (in Mead and Wolfenstein, 1955) is the hero in the Italian film, The White Line: "The boy hero of this film embodies the essentials of the Christ—legend. He forgives his enemies, he bears the cross, he dies for the sins of others; by his example he teaches his follow-men that they should love instead of hate one another" (p. 279). In the 1980s the Milan family therapists depicted a number of child "problems" as attempts by the child to solve much broader family problems which they perceived, even at a subconscious level, as a threat to the integrity of the family. They provided myriad examples of this; a child getting major headaches or developing other health problems enables a "dysfunctional" couple to remain together as they worry about the child rather than focusing on their own marital problems. Similarly, a child consistently sleeping with their parents could be seen as providing a solution to parents who have some sexual difficulties (Boscolo, Cecchin, Hoffman, and Penn, 1987).

Noble/Saviour children are presented in literature like J.K. Rowling's (1997) Harry Potter (and indeed his friends, Hermione and Ron). Despite his own loss (his parents' deaths) and suffering he is positioned through his birthright to place himself on the line in order that others might be protected. Children who look after their parents may be viewed this way, but this seems to depend on the "worthiness" of their parents. If the parents are disabled, for example, then the child is given noble/saviour status (Pengelley & Anderson, 2005). If a child is looking after parents who are abusing drugs or alcohol, other adults are more likely to be viewed as child abuse, since this behaviour is assumed to result in a loss of the child's innocence.

In the noble/saviour construction of childhood, children assume power; to save, reconcile, take over adult responsibilities. This may be because the parent/s absolve/s themselves of responsibility or literally cannot undertake that which is expected. The power of the child is assumed through circumstances, rather than choice, and rightfully should belong with the adult. The child is neither agentic (has real choice, is able to make informed decisions) nor innocent; the responsibility is placed upon them (through acts of commission or omission) rather than it being their free choice.

The noble/saviour framework of childhood is created by powerful adults (e.g. therapist, grandparents, society) rather than children themselves, and assumes that we can understand the subconscious of children. This image may be a reframe of another image (such as the miniature adult or the child-in-training—see below). Like other constructions of childhood, this framework may be seen as deterministic, since it relies on an understanding of a system (whether this be family or any other system) as homeostatic (Bateson, 1972), that is, a system which during crisis will revert to "how things should be", thus propelling even young children into activities which make their system (family, home) seem "normal". The child then carries out activities normally the reserve of adults/parents, which "allows" the adults to revert to some form of dependency.

The miniature adult and the adult-in-training: children and adults as the same and the adult as teacher.

Literature describes two different, yet similar types of child categorisation, the miniature adult and the adult in training, with some understanding that the former prescription of children predates the latter.

Miniature Adult

This construction of childhood is one in which children are depicted as the same as adults. Childhood is not perceived as a separate phase of development (as it is in the child as innocent typology). For example, in Ancient Greece and Ancient Rome, children of slaves had to perform adult work alongside adult workers (Branscombe *et al.*, 2000). During the middle ages, children were depicted in art as having adult behaviours, proportions and facial features (Osborn, 1991 in Branscombe *et al.*, 2000). Relatively recently, during the Industrial revolution, children were made to work long hours in mines and factories in harsh conditions (Branscombe *et al.*, 2000). In the majority world, children (often poor and black) are frequently treated as miniature adults, performing factory work, used as soldiers and as sexual prey of adults. This is often over looked by most in the minority world, who benefit from this labour (in the availability of cheap shells from the Philippines, soccer balls from South America, carpets from India). This suggests that some children around the globe are constructed differently than "other" children. Even in the majority world, however, Postman (1983) points out the increasing representation of children as the same as adults in television sitcoms from Gary Coleman, in "Different Strokes" to the present "Franklin" (Noah Gray-Cabey) in "My Wife and Kids". Children who commit crimes are often presented as miniature adults with some sections of society calling for children to be tried alongside adults for particular crimes (Postman, 1983).

Adult-in-Training

This construction positions children as working through various motor, psychological and social tasks, or stages, to reach adulthood. Advertising campaigns that tout children as our future promote this image. Developmental psychologists like Piaget, Erikson and Freud popularised this view of children as "human becomings" rather than "human beings" (Hutchison and Charlesworth, 2000). Children are thus perceived of as a "defective form of adult, social only in their future potential, but not in their present being" (Corsaro, 1997, p. 6). School curricula that push children to achieve outcomes and to compete and achieve on standardised tests, operate from this construction of childhood (Woodrow, 1999).

Neil Postman (1983), in his now classic *The Disappearance of Childhood*, provides compelling evidence of the miniature adult/adult in training as a strong contemporary construction of childhood. Postman (1983) argues that society has shifted from notions of the child as innocent, due largely to forms of media that are universally available to children and adults in their adult-centric form. He argues that we no longer protect children from the world when news is broadcast into our living room without censorship (one can think of the recent media coverage of the Iraq war and the events of 9/11). He presents other indicators of this construction in terms of clothing, which is now styled similarly for children and adults; children who engage in paid work or who work for their parents. In the recent movie, "Shall we Dance", a young Jennifer Lopez is put to work in her parents' laundry. Similarly, children are driven to "appointments" with friends, music teachers, soccer coaches (etc.).

The power of the child as adult-in-training or miniature adult lies in their capacity to learn and participate in a world constructed for them by adults. The power of the adult within these categories lies in their capacity to harness the abilities of the child to suit adult imperatives. The adult can be tyrannical or a loving guide or facilitator (see Woodrow, 1999 on the latter). Adults have power to socialise children from the basis of their own knowledge, resources and networks. The adult in this construction is knowledgeable or otherwise powerful, while the child is simultaneously positioned as less knowing—an apprentice to the adult, and less powerful (bio-psycho-socially and politically) (Sorin, 2003).

Woodrow (1999) argues that this is a socio-politically deterministic model of childhood. She contends that within this construction, neither the adult nor the child is intrinsically, personally powerful rather the relationship between adults and children is simply the means through which the social order is reproduced. Similarly, Hoffman (2000) notes the impoverished emotional connection between children and adults who are positioned within this construction. She believes the adult-in-training is a particularly western approach to childhood based as it is upon individualism and meritocracy (Hoffman, 2000). Developmental approaches to children focus on deficiency in the child—"developmental milestones", "developmental delay", and "readiness" are key terms signifying this approach (Hoffman, 2000). Critics of this approach argue that children in this adult-in-training typology are positioned without authority until they attain adulthood (Corsaro, 1997; Hutchison and Charlesworth, 2000).

The Commodified Child: The Self-Interested Adult

In juxtaposition to the Victorian image of the innocent child, the late twentieth century and the early twenty-first century commodified child is one who "has become an object to be consumed by an adult audience obsessed with childhood and youth" (Wood, 2003, p. 8). Wood notes the use of children as marketing tools for clothing, toys, greeting cards and other franchise. However, dual images are presented of the innocent, Victorianesque child (including pictures of doe eyed, passive black children), along with that of the child as pseudo adult, the "Lolita" images of child pop stars (e.g. Britney Spears), models, and beauty queens (e.g. Jon-Benet Ramsey), which sexualise childhood in much the same way as Carroll's 19th century photographic images (Wood, 2003). Similarly the waif model of the 1990s (e.g. Kate Moss) represents the child-woman. "Her large, mascaraed eyes connote the face of a child, while her engorged red lips suggest readiness for penetration. Her boyish body heightens the illusion of the fuckable child" (Goldstein, 1997, in Wood, 2003).

It is not only those of pornographic persuasion, however, who compete for the money derived directly from their interaction with children. Ethicists and caring parents make a case for the reproduction of children for bone marrow matches, while still other adults engage in the buying and selling of children for body parts (Woodrow, 1999). Those of us within welfare, health and education sectors are forced to compete with each other to increase our market share of income for the services we provide to children. Government sectors and non-government sectors in health, education and welfare fields represent their work with children in ways that they hope will help them obtain this "market share". Intercultural and country adoptions are increasingly expensive at both the private market and regulated market level. As of many other adults, we could as aptly ask of welfare, health and education directors, "where is the voice of children in programs and services submitted for their benefit, and upon which so many professionals rely for their income?"

Within this construction of childhood, children are largely powerless. While some of these commodified children no doubt have an illusion of power (e.g. child movie stars, models and beauty queens), since they derive material benefit from use of their image and/or labour, and may even feel a sense of "power over" some adults (i.e. those who have come to rely upon them for their income) it is, nonetheless, powerful adults who broker these images and (re)construct the child as a saleable item. The adult holds the majority of power within this construction since they are able to manipulate the economy through the use of children.

A critique of the child as commodity largely revolves around the amount of agency the child has to consent to how their image and/or body is being used as a means for making money (or other goods/needs) for adults. As Woodrow (1997) states of Anne Geddes' work, "what capacity...does a premature baby have to resist being placed in a strange man's hands in its first day out of the humidicrib, or a six-week-old child to be draped naked over a large pumpkin for the camera's eye?" (p. 17). Lewis Carroll's photographic images border on pornography, looking at the innocence of childhood through a voyeuristic lens and thus sexualising childhood. According to Wood (2003), "the presence of [Carroll's] camera acts as an unwanted intrusion (or penetration) into their world and this fantasy of a 'pre-fall' innocence" (p. 4).

Similarly, this construction of childhood unsettles those of us forced to operate within an economic system that consistently demonstrates its indifference to the most vulnerable population groupings, whilst pedagogically adhering to a different construction of childhood (child as innocent; evil; noble; adult-in training; agentic etc.). Unlike the construction of the child as innocent, where the child receives the protection of "good" adults, the commodification of childhood and particular groups of children, makes us aware of the self-interest of adults, and confronts us with the idea that adults may not always act in the child's best interests (Woodrow, 1999).

The Child Victim: The Absent Adult

Sadly, this child goes largely unrecognized. The victim of social and political forces, this is the child who lives through war or terror, famine or poverty. While this child is voiceless, so too are the adults in the immediate environment, as they are either suffering alongside the children or absent altogether.

We usually notice these children only when they have become commodified by the media, who use their images (without their knowledge or permission) to demonstrate world strife and to appeal to the charity of those more fortunate (Sorin, 2005) or through reports, such as UNICEF's State of the World's Children. These may be the faceless, nameless oppressors who run the economic and polictical world agendas. They are often NOT presented—that is, we are made to think that the economy is rational and drives itself. These children are the casualities of "rational" market and political forces. Their plight is not recognised as resulting from the actions of very powerful economic and political leaders (Rees, Rodley and Stilwell, 1993).

While they usually seem worlds away, victim children are a silenced, disenfranchised group in schools and communities in every country. They are the children who live in poverty or neglect, whose presence is often ignored as teachers and society in general get on with their everyday functioning. They may miss out on textbooks, excursions, toys and family holidays, but as they aren't attention-seekers, other typologies often override their presence (Sorin, 2005). Neither the child victim, nor the adults in that child's life hold even an illusion of power. Voiceless, their existence only becomes apparent when teachers, social workers or philanthropists attempt to give them means of expression (Silin, 2005 in Yelland, 2005) and more often determine "best" ways of educating, protecting and socialising them. In some ways, this resembles the innocent child, whose voice is denied and overridden by well-meaning adults, in this case outside of the child's immediate circle.

The Agentic Child: The Adult as Co-constructor of Being

The agentic child is positioned as a capable and competent agent who appropriates and reproduces aspects of their culture through interaction with others (Corsaro, 1997). Rather than focusing on aspects of interaction that limit opportunities for children to participate in the real world (James & Prout, 1990 in Corsaro, 1997), this is an optimistic construction. James *et al.* (1998) argue, for example, that childhood has social status in its own right, with its own agenda. Rather than "becoming" (as in the miniature adult or the adult-in-training), the child is talked about as "being". "The child is conceived of as a person, a status, a course of action, a set of needs, rights or differences—in sum as a social actor" (James *et al.*, 1998, p. 207). Childhood is a time of meaning making and active participation in the world. The agentic child is competent and capable. Adults are co-learners who negotiate, challenge and guide through reflection on their own experiences. They negotiate and share power with children (Woodrow, 1999).

Within this image, children and adults alike construct childhood. In this co-constructivist framework, the child is an "active and eager learner" (Corsaro, 1997, p. 9), internalising experience while participating in and reproducing society (Corsaro, 1997). Hoffman (2000) argues that "concepts of the self are powerful molders (*sic*) of the adult the child will become". One can explore early education, then, as "pedagogy of the self" (p. 194). The ideas we have about ourself are fundamental to what we learn and how we participate.

Children constitute a private world created and sustained by them. In describing the "tribal child", therefore, James *et al.* (1998) seek in scholarship "a commitment to childhood's social worlds as real places and provinces of meaning in their own right and not as fantasies, games, poor imitations or inadequate precursors of the adults state of being" (p. 28). While affected by the adult world, childhood is an independent place. "Children are not pathological or incomplete; they form a group, a body of social actors, and as citizens they have needs and rights" (p. 32).

Research or any other relationship between adults and children is with children rather than about them. Their voices are given serious consideration (Sorin, 2003). Cannella (2000) envisions a new field of childhood studies that celebrates diversity and values the multiple voices of children. She suggests denaturalising childhood and positioning children as equal partners in life and in educational decision-making. Similarly, Zelizer (1985) discusses research of the 1980s that clearly positioned children's voices in the quest for increased public and private space.

There is evidence of this construction of childhood in Reggio Emilia classrooms, where the child is seen as an active, curious and self-motivated learner curriculum is negotiated and emergent—actively designed with and by students focusing on their strengths and abilities. This paradigm views children as "possessed of individual agency, as competent social actors and interpreters of the world" (James and Prout, 1995, cited by Mason and Steadman, 1997, p. 35; Hoffman, 2000). This view is also evident in the Systematic Training for Effective Parenting (STEP) program (Dinkmeyer and McKay, 1976), which teaches parents how to actively listen to and negotiate with their child/ren. Current school curricula, such as the Media strand of the Queensland Arts Syllabus, similarly teach children to interact with various media, including language, to negotiate their experiences (Queensland School Curriculum Council, 2001). Many policies and practices are being reviewed and rewritten with this newer image of childhood in mind, such as Early Childhood Australia's Code of Ethics (Early Childhood Australia, 2005b), the new Queensland Early Years Curriculum (Queensland Study Authority, 2004) and the National Association for the Education of Young Children's Standards and Accreditation Performance Criteria (National Association for the Education of Young Children, 2005).

Within this construction of the agentic child, children and adults both have power, which is negotiated as a critically conscious component of their relationship. The child is empowered through their relationship with the adult, who lends their power, strength, resources to the child, rather than imposing this upon, or doing for the child.

The adult has power that is shared with the child. The adult is also empowered and made knowledgeable, wise and influenced through their relationship with the child. Postman (1983) points out, for example, the influence children have on adults in terms of language use, with adults adopting terminology used by children.

The agentic construction of children rejects the view of the child as passive and innocent (Fasoli, 2001; Woodrow, 1999). It is somewhat at odds with both the deterministic model of childhood and the pure constructivist model that focuses on the child's actions as if these are separate or dislocated from the actions of others (Corsaro, 1997). Nonetheless, co-constructivists recognise that the agency of both children and adults is "constrained by a number of limited choices" (James *et al.*, 1998, p. 25) available to them in their interactions with each other. Thus Cannella notes the "illusion" of choice in American classrooms when these choices themselves are already predetermined (in Hoffman, 2000). In its ideal form, this image is congruent with what many teachers profess as a basic tenet of their philosophical framework.

Conclusion

In this paper we have provided a typology for understanding the ways in which we as adults construct childhood. We have argued that any construction of childhood necessarily and simultaneously engages us in processes of constructing adulthood. Of the adult and child types presented in this paper, it is only through the construction of the agentic child that the power between adults and children becomes balanced as adults and children work together to build relationships of mutual respect and growth. It is hoped that the typology presented in this paper provides a means for adults and children to critically reflect on the relationship they either consciously or unconsciously invoke, each in relation to the other.

References

Aries, P. (1973), *Centuries of Childhood*. Suffolk, U.K.: The Chaucer Press.

Bateson, G. (1972), *Steps to an ecology of mind*. New York: Ballantine Books.

Boscolo, L., Cecchin, G., Hoffman, L., & Penny, P. (1987), *Milan Systemic Family Therapy*. New York: Basic Books.

Branscombe, N.A., Castle, K., Dorsey, A.G., Surbeck, E., and Taylor, J.B. (2000), *Early Childhood Education—A Constructivist Approach*. Boston: Houghton Mifflin Company.

Buckingham, D. (1994), Television and the definition of childhood in Mayall, B. (ed). *Children's Childhoods: observed and experienced*. London: The Falmer Press.

Cannella, G.S. (2000), Critical and feminist reconstructions of Early Childhood Education: continuing the conversations. *Contemporary Issues in Early Childhood*. Vol. 1, No. 2, 215-221.

Cleverley, J. and Phillips, D. (1988), *Visions of Childhood—Influential Models from Locke to Spock*. Sydney: Allen and Unwin.

Corsaro, W. (1997), *The Sociology of Childhood*. USA: Pine Forge Press.

Dinkmeyer, D., & McKay, G. (1976), *Systematic Training for Effective Parenting: Parent's Handbook*. Circle Pines, Minn: American Guidance Service.

Dockett, (1998), Why are they putting flowers on the fence? Child initiated curriculum and images of children. Seventh Australia and New Zealand Conference on the First Years of School—New approaches to old puzzles—Reconceptualising the early years of school presentation. Australian National University (13-16 January).

Early Childhood Australia, (2005a), *Code of Ethics*. Accessed online: http://www.earlychildhoodaustralia.org.au/abtus_resources_cofe.htm

Early Childhood Australia, (2005b), *Early Childhood Australia's Code of Ethics Agenda*. Accessed online: http://www.earlychildhood-australia.org.au/news_archives_jan2005.htm#Agenda

Elliott, A. (2000), "Visions of Children and Childhood" in *Every Child*. Vol. 6, No. 3, 6-7. Canberra: Australian Early Childhood Association.

Epston, D. (1989), *Collected Papers*. Adelaide: Dulwich Centre Publications.

Fasoli, L. (2001), Research with children: ethical mind-fields. *Australian Journal of Early Childhood*. Vol. 26, No. 4, 7-11.

Gibson, L. (1998), Teaching as an encounter with the self: unravelling the mix of personal beliefs, education ideologies, and pedagogical practices. *Anthropology and Education Quarterly*. Vol. 29, No. 3, 360-371.

Golding, W. (1954), *Lord of the Flies*. London: Faber.

Guppy, D. (2005), Kid Crim—Child, 12, faces court again on 18 charges from theft to drugs. *The Cairns Post*, 23/24 April.

Hoffman, D. M. (2000), Pedagogies of self in American and Japanese Early Childhood Education: A critical conceptual analysis. *The Elementary School Journal*. 101(2), 193.

Hutchison, E.D. and Charlesworth, L.W. (2000), Securing the welfare of children: Policies past, present and future. Families in Society: *The Journal of Contemporary Human Services*. V. 81, I 6, 576-595.

James, A. Jenks, C. and Prout, A. (1998), *Theorizing Childhood*. Oxford, U.K.: Blackwell.

Mason and Steadman (1997), "Conceptualisation of Childhood and its Implications for Child Protection Policy". *Family Matters*, 46, Autumn 1997.

Mead, M. and Wolfenstein, M. (eds). (1955), *Childhood in Contemporary Cultures*. Chicago: The University of Chicago Press.

National Association for the Education of Young Children (2005), NAEYC. Early Childhood Program Standards and Accreditation Performance Criteria. www.naeyc.org

Pengelley, J., & Anderson, L. (2004), Our silent carers, *The Cairns Post*, Wednesday October 6, p. 7.

Postman, N. (1983), *The Disappearance of Childhood*. London: W.H. Allen.

Queensland School Curriculum Council (2001), *The Arts Syllabus*. Available online at http://www.qsa.qld.edu.au/kla/arts/syllabus.

Queensland Study Authority (2004), *Early Years Curriculum Guidelines*. Available online: http://www.qsa.qld.edu.au/preschool/prep/index.html

Rees, S., Rodley, G. & Stilwell, F. (1993), (eds.) *Beyond the Market: Alternatives to economic rationalism*. Sydney: Pluto Press.

Robson, L. (2005), Child's Play. *The Sunday Mail*, May 1, p. 9.

Rowling, J.K. (1997), *Harry Potter and the Philosopher's Stone*. London: Bloomsbury Publishing.

Sorin, R. (2005), Images of childhood: Perception and Practice in Early Childhood Education. Canadian Children—*Journal of the Canadian Association for Young Children*. 30, 2, 4-8.

Sorin, R. (2003), Research with young children—a rich glimpse into the world of childhood. *Australian Journal of Early Childhood*, 28(1), 31-35.

United Nations High Commissioner for Human Rights (1989), Conventions on the Rights of the Child. Accessed online: http://www.unhchr.ch/html/menu3/b/k2crc.htm

UNICEF (2005), *State of the World's Children*. Available online www.overpopulation.com/archives/years/2005/000004.html

Walkerdine, V. (1999), Violent boys and precocious girls: regulating childhood at the end of the millennium. *Contemporary Issues in Early Childhood*, 1(1), 3-23.

White, M. (1988/1989), The externalising of the problem and the reauthoring of lives and relationships. In *Dulwich Centre Newsletter*, pp. 3-21.

White, M. (1991), Deconstruction and therapy. In *Dulwich Centre Newsletter*, 3, pp. 21- 40.

Wood, A. (2003), Constructions of childhood in art and media: Sexualised innocence. AgorA: Online *Graduate Humanities Journal*. 2.2 Available at: http://collection.nic~bnc.ca/100/201/300/agora/2003/v2n02/157.htm

Woodrow, C. (1999), Revisiting images of the child in early childhood education: Reflections and considerations. *Australian Journal of Early Childhood*. Vol. 24, No. 4, 7-12.

Woodrow, C. (1997), Questioning representations of children and childhood. *Every Child*. Vol. 3, No. 2, 17.

Wrigley, J. (2003), Symbolic Childhood review. *Contemporary Sociology*. V. 32, I. 6, p. 693.

Yelland, N. (ed) (2005), *Critical Issues in Early Childhood Education*. Berkshire, England: Open University Press.

Zelizer, V.A. (1985), *Pricing the Priceless Child—the changing social value of children*. New York: Basic Books.

2

Strengthening Family Efforts for Helpless Children

LOUISE ANITA WILLIAMS and VALJI BAGDA

Children are human beings with human rights. However, people around the globe tend to think otherwise. Most birth parents tend to think, 'I have given birth to these human beings and they are my property to bring up as I wish.' Some sell their children. Some abuse their children. Some use their children as labourers. Some offer their children as domestic servants. Some train their children to be beggars. The list goes on and on. When and how should ethics enter the picture for parents? It doesn't! Parents do not think of ethics when raising their children. Most feel they are in-charge and that the children must do as they say, even if wrong.

Children and ethics is such a huge topic and as such, where does one begin? What ethics or standards do agencies that work with children follow? What do teachers or other childcare providers follow? For that matter, what type of ethics do parents follow?

The word ethics itself contains great values. Let's look at each letter:

- Empathy
- Transparency
- Honesty
- Integrity
- Commitment
- Sincerity

If we measure institutions working with children with these

standards, how many of them would be up to the mark? In India, the figure may be negligible, and for this, institutions only cannot be held responsible as it is a hard reality in India, and the conditions that prevail here are such, that it is very easy to do or practice something wrong rather than right. All over the globe, there is recognition of the fact that most of the problems in children are due to lack of connection or attachment with their family.

Children in India are traditionally an essential part of the family unit. The child rearing process during infancy has by and large been *laissez faire* with flexible rules and restrictions. Kindness to the young ones is an essential element of child-care. Within the folds of the large joint families, children grow under the charge of multiple caretakers. But because of certain reasons, large number of children are deprive of family care and such children need loving and caring family to be looked after.

All over the world, there is realisation that strengthening family efforts that will bring positive changes in growing children. We need to teach young men and women that certain types of behaviour are not acceptable in dating relationships. We need to teach parents that certain types of behaviour are not acceptable toward children. We need to encourage parents to be more responsible when they bring children into the world. We need to instill in parents (and future parents) the qualities that make parents responsible, loving and caring parents.

The Preamble to the Hague Convention Provides

"Recognizing that the child, for the full and harmonious development of his or her personality, should grow up in a family environment, an atmosphere of happiness, love and understanding, ... Recognizing that inter-country adoption may offer the advantage of a permanent family to a child for whom a suitable family cannot be found in his or her state of origin" to which *the UN Convention on the Rights of the Child* adds:

> "The States Parties to the Present Convention...
>
> Convinced that the family, as the fundamental group of society and the natural environment for the growth and well being of all its members and particularly children, should be afforded the

necessary protection and assistance so that it can fully assume its responsibilities within the community,

Recognizing that the child, for the full and harmonious development of his or her personality, should grow up in a family environment, in an atmosphere of happiness, love and understanding ...

Have agreed as follows ...

Article 21

(a) States Parties that recognize and/or permit the system of adoption shall ensure that the best interests of the child shall be the paramount consideration and they shall ...

(b) Recognize that inter-country adoption may be considered as an alternative means of child's care, if the child cannot be placed in a foster or an adoptive family or cannot in any suitable manner be cared for in the child's country of origin;"

By signing and ratifying the United Nations Convention on the Rights of the Child, India has committed to ensure the following rights of children under 'Protection' (Doris Rao, 2004, downloaded from http://www.humanscape.org/Humanscape/2004/Nov in Feb 2006)

- The State shall facilitate reunification of families by permitting travel into, or out of, their territories.
- Parents have the primary responsibility for a child's upbringing, but the State shall provide them with appropriate assistance and develop child care institutions.
- The State shall protect children from physical or mental harm and neglect, including sexual abuse or exploitation.
- The State shall provide parentless children with suitable alternative care. The adoption process shall be carefully regulated and international agreements should be sought to provide safeguards and assure legal validity if and when adoptive parents intend to move a child from his or her country of birth.
- Disabled children shall have the right to special treatment, education and care.

- The State shall protect children from economic exploitation and from work that may interfere with their education or be harmful to their health or well being.
- The State shall protect children from the illegal use of drugs and involvement in drug production or trafficking.
- All efforts shall be made to eliminate the abduction and trafficking of children.
- Capital punishment or life imprisonment shall not be imposed for crimes committed before the age of 18.
- Children in detention shall be separated from adults; they must not be tortured or suffer cruel or degrading treatment.
- Children involved in infringements of the penal law shall be treated in a way that promotes their sense of dignity and worth and aims at reintegrating them into society.
- No child under 15 shall take any part in hostilities; children exposed to armed conflict shall receive special protection.
- Children of minority and indigenous populations shall freely enjoy their own culture, religion and language.

Children are most vulnerable, as well as helpless in society, especially those without families. Investing in them and their healthy development provides benefits to society, caregivers, parents, and families as a whole. A field like the rehabilitation of abandoned, orphaned and destitute children calls for total dedication to the highest standards of professionalism, competence, commitment, integrity and social vision.

Numerous agencies around the globe dealing with children appear to think and act in the same manner. They begin to look at children as a commodity instead of looking at their welfare. The people heading children institutions are ignorant of ethical practices that could be followed for working with children.

Another agency in Mumbai operates homes for orphans where a husband and wife are employed full-time to care for at least 25 children in a three-bedroom house without any furniture except mats for sleeping. When doing a site visit it was shown that the agency had four homes in one society. Cooking for all of the homes was done in one kitchen. Would a normal family live like this? Are the children better off than living on the street? Most likely, yes. But does this prepare them for the society at-large? What are the chances of a family having 25 children? Also, in a normal family of the past, the father would work and the mother would be the main caregiver. However, this is quickly changing to where both parents work and the charge of raising the children is passed on to domestic workers or, if the parents live in joint family, the grandparents.

We come across disturbing news in the press in India about adoption agencies stealing babies or little children just for the monetary advantages of placing them up for adoption. In addition, each adoption agency is in competition with each other instead of working hand-in-hand to serve the rights of the children. How do we stop this? Children may be little people, but they are human beings with human rights. The children must have advocates. They need people who truly care about their well being and their futures. How do we get people to work collectively for the good of children?

The results of agencies that have misused the legal systems for their personal benefit have made it very difficult for those with a pure heart to do good for children. There are huge problems in India and it is very difficult to do good things for the hapless children. Those who use the government system incorrectly for personal gain or illegal reasons ruin it for those with a pure heart.

There was a Western man who had a shelter in Mumbai for young boys living on the streets. It was discovered that he was sodomizing the boys and giving them out for sexual pleasure. After the shelter was closed by the authorities and while talking with a resident of Mumbai about the situation, it was amazing to hear his response...the individual thought it was bad that the shelter had been closed down as the boys, even though used for sexual pleasure, were better off than living on the street. With this mindset of the people, what may be done to create brighter futures for children in India, let alone think of ethics?

In the year 2001 or 2002 it was discovered in the state of Andhra Pradesh that numerous agencies were trafficking children into child labour or the sex trade and all agencies had to be closed down.

Abuse of girl children, rape and trafficking of young girls from one place to another are very much common in India. While in most of the cases, the victims do not register cases due to fear of social stigma, the perpetrators are not punished due to lack of sufficient evidence.

In May 2006 an 11-year old girl was raped by a man in a village in Uttar Pradesh and the village Panchayat (governing body of the village) acquitted the rapist with a fine of just Rs. 10,000 (approximately US$ 200)!

In India, a country where both the *Ramanaya* and *Mahabharat* are the ideal epics and Holy books to guide the life of the people in which a war between two kings, Lord Ram and King Ravana, was fought to establish the self-respect and dignity of Sita, wife of Lord Ram, who had been abducted by King Ravana, and another woman, Draupadi, whose *sari* was pulled off, a rapist is set free in this manner. Does this make sense?

In Maharashtra as per the latest figures available, out of the total cases of rapes, 65.03 per cent were committed on minor girls, out of which 49.12 per cent of the girls were between 14 and 18 years of age and 9.79 per cent were below 10 years of age. In the year 2001, 1300 cases of rape were registered in the state. Whereas in 2005, the figure was higher at 1,539 out of which 44.51 per cent of the rape cases were of minor girls.

These figures don't depict the real picture of this grave condition as there are more rape cases, as much or more, which police complaints are not registered. There are many reasons for not registering a police complaint on minor girls. One of them is that rape is considered as a social stigma and the life of the raped girl is ruined and she has to live out her whole life with this stigma. Another reason is the horrible way in which the police handle rape cases where girl or boy children have to pass through enormous mental torture, which is not less than mental rape. If the rape is committed by a family member, then complaints are not usually lodged just to save the family's honour.

As we all know, children come in contact with relatives, neighbours, teachers, servants, tutors, etc. These are all people they know...thus the possibility of sexual abuse is very high, as most cases of known sexual abuse are committed by someone known by the children. Children on the street are usually first prey to sexual abuse and they have no one to turn to.

Cases of sexual abuse of children are registered as normal rape cases under Indian Penal Code and there are no special laws for sexual abuse of children. Laws protecting the children must be passed providing stringent punishment for child abuse and rape. In addition, parents and childcare providers need to learn how to teach sex education to children in a way that is not alarming. The children must be acquainted with this issue and should be taught how to behave in various embarrassing situations. In USA, sex education is imparted in the school when the children are very young say 10-11 years. The children get to know about their rights to their body and are taught as to how they have to react to situations, no individual should touch their private parts and if they are touched, what to do about it etc.

An organisation in San Diego, California in the USA, Chadwick Children's Center, has developed a non-threatening, child-friendly environment where children who have been physically or sexually abused may be examined safely and where the necessary evidence for the police is collected without threatening or scaring the child. By following their methodology, the children need to be examined one time only. A video taped interview by a trained professional is taken as early as possible. Then when the case goes to trial, the children appear in the court room by video tape only, thus saving undo pressure on the children's psyche.

Another problem of ethics and children is within the police department. One such case that comes to mind is when a young boy of about 9 years of age in Rajasthan was missing. When his parents went to the police, the police refused to file a complaint. After approximately one week the boy was found by his mother in front of a mosque begging. He appeared to be under some type of drug and did not recognize his mother.

Then there is the problem of children being used for begging. One day while travelling in New Delhi there was a horrible scene on the side of the road, the capital of India. A woman was beating a very little girl. She was beating her in such a cruel way, which was worse than the way people beat animals. When asking the taxi driver to stop, he sped rapidly from the scene stating that if he would have stopped, it would cause great trouble. That little girl was used as a beggar and she was beaten by a gang member.

Children are used as beggars throughout India in both small and large cities, which is operated by a nationwide network of gangsters for whom begging is a big business. Children are abducted for this purpose and some are even deformed intentionally so they will make better beggars. This must be stopped. These children need protection.

In 1989, while visiting an orphanage in Andhra Pradesh, it was found that the head was living lavishly in a huge two-story bungalow on a beautiful piece of land full of coconut trees. He had approximately 50 orphans living in the back of the property in a shed with beds stacked four high. The orphans had cavities in their teeth, wore rags as clothes, attended the village school and ate plain rice and *dhal* for food, while the head of the orphanage sent his natural children to English Medium schools, fed them the kings' food and dressed his children in the finest clothes. The orphans were treated as slaves and had to clean the property and do all the chores in the house. And all of this was happening while living on donated money raised in the USA. When confronted about the discrepancies, the head did not see any problem.

In India, discrimination prevails against girl children as unwanted. In Rajasthan, it was customary to drown newly born girl babies in milk and kill them. Now, due to laws being passed and awareness created by the government and NGOs, this practice has stopped, but it has taken on a new form of killing the girl fetuses in the womb itself after discovering the sex of the child. The Government of India has banned Sonar tests, even though girls are killed before or at the time of delivery. Due to this very unethical practice in India, the ratio of boys to girls is 1000:900 and even in some states it has fallen to a ratio of 1000:826.

There is one horrible incident that happened in May 2006 in Rajasthan. A newly born girl child was cruelly killed by feeding her steel screws, safety pins and a poly bag through her feeding pipe.

Another type of discrimination is due to the Caste System. Children belonging to the scheduled castes have to suffer insults and various atrocities throughout their childhood and even into adulthood.

Here's a different type of example. While talking with a gentleman from a very well-respected affluent family, and who leads a well-known multi-national company in India, he shared a story about his son. When his son was 4, they chose the best private school for him to attend. On the first day, when he came home, both parents noticed welts on his back from being hit with a ruler. When questioning the boy, he told them that the teacher beat him with a ruler because he was slow in getting his book out of his knapsack. I asked the father what he did. He told me he sent the boy back to school. A week later he talked with the head priest and the incident was denied. He then talked with the teacher and got almost the same reply. Throughout the boy's education he would come home monthly with some type of evidence of being hit with a ruler and the same thing was happening to the other children as well. When asked why he kept the boy at that school he replied that it is known as the best school in his area and he had no other choice. Where and when do the child's rights enter the picture? Where does ethics?

In India, recent research (UNICEF, 2005) showed that there are large number of orphan children between the age of birth and 14 years. From this number of orphans various research studies estimate that from 13 to 17 million are living on the streets, most of them are complete orphans without mother or father. To survive they resort to begging, crime, prostitution, etc. Something must be done for these innocent human beings. These children need permanent loving family-like homes where they are raised with well-trained loving individuals providing the role of parents.

Other research shows that 49.5 per cent of children in India between birth and 14 years of age suffer from severe psychological abuse; 42.1 per cent suffer from severe physical abuse, not including being hit with the hand (Hunter, Jain, Sadowski and Sanhueza 2002); 63 per cent of girls living in Delhi have been sexually abused by a family member (Sakshi, 1997). In a study of a 1000 girls from 5 different states in India, (Rahi, 1997), 50 per cent of the girls said that they had been abused when under 12 years of age, 35 per cent had been abused between the ages of 12-16 years of age.

What are we to do? Agencies must join together and change their focus. Most agencies today are developed to focus on stopping something. Therefore that 'something' must continually be in existence for the agency to be in business. Instead, it is recommended that everyone focus on the positive. If one wants peace, don't focus on stopping war. Focus on being peace. If one wants good health one must not focus on stopping a disease, but to focus on good health. In one wants children to be raised without violence, then it is important to focus on teaching individuals alternative ways in which to raise children in a teaching, loving, abuse-free manner. The only way this can happen is through childcare education for parents, teachers, childcare providers, clergy, etc.

Let's look for a moment at the root cause of violence in the youth of today. According to Dr. James Prescott, a neuro-psychologist, human violence is fast becoming a global epidemic. He states in one of his numerous research papers that unless the causes of violence are isolated and treated, we will live in a world of fear and apprehension. Unfortunately, violence is often offered as a solution to violence. Imprisoning people will not solve the problem, because the causes of violence lie in our basic values and the way in which we bring up our children and youth. He is convinced that the deprivation of physical sensory pleasure is the principal root cause of violence. On the other hand the biology of love is in the giving of physical sensory pleasure, the affectional bonding in the maternal-infant relationship, and the paternal-child relationship.

After conducting years of research at the National Institute of Child Health and Human Development in the United States, Dr. Prescott feels that the single most important cause of violent behaviour, the developmental depression that precedes it, and the later drug/alcohol abuse that is used to treat the emotional pain that underlies the rage of uncontrolled violence is the failure of physical affectional bonding in the maternal-infant relationship; the paternal-child relationship and the failure of adolescent sexual affectional bonding.

When young children are not touched, held or surrounded with affection, the neural systems required to experience pleasure are not developed, which leads to an individual and a culture that is self-centered, violent and authoritarian.

Rene Spitz, an Austrian born psychoanalyst known for his studies of the effects on infants of hospitalisation with extended separation from mother, noticed that most institutionalized infants, who had the best medical and physical care, but no 'mother love'—no one touched, held or hugged them—had depressive and autistic-like behaviours. With deprivation of physical affection and body contact, which is the biology of love, these infants and children withdrew into their own world and in extreme cases, they gave up and died.

Experimental studies of isolation-reared infant monkeys documented that maternal-infant separation constitutes a specific form of affectional deprivation that involves the touch and movement sensory systems and results in a variety of abnormalities of brain development that includes structural, neurochemical and neuroelectrical abnormalities. These deprived animals engage in mutilations of their own bodies. Animals deprived of touching early in life develop impaired pain perception and an aversion to being touched by others. Physical violence and physical pain become therapies of choice for those deprived of physical pleasure.

In short, it is the failure of physical love in human relationships that begins with the failure of that physical love when the infant is not permitted to bond with the body of its mother, which then begins the infant's journey of depression, rage, hatred and violence for not being loved. Thus begins the peril of infant and child daycare centers, which impedes, if not prevents, the affectional bonding between mother and her infant/child and, thus, all later affectional bonds.

In 2005, when visiting an orphanage in Mumbai, I saw a small very thin infant crying. I asked if I might pick up the baby and hold it. The head mistress refused. She stated that there are not enough people in the orphanage to hold babies so it is best that it does not get used to being held.

When coming into this world, there is no such thing as a bad child. Each and every child comes into this world a pure individual. Children are not born orphans; that is unless it was a mistake and the father is not known. Children's views and attitudes are acquired from their caregivers and environments. Therefore, to create positive change one must empower children to grow into self-sufficient citizens of tomorrow so they may give back to their community, country and the world.

And to empower children one must work with both children and adults. After all, adults are the ones who provide love and guidance for each child growing up. But with adults believing that children are their personal property, how do we change their mindset?

In 1917, a Catholic priest, Father Flanagan, living in Omaha, Nebraska, USA, believed that there was no such thing as a bad child. To prove his theory he borrowed money, bought a large home in the city, and began taking in delinquent boys. A few years later his theory was proven correct. He again borrowed money to buy a farm so he could care for more boys. The farm later became known as Boys Town. Today, it is known as Girls and Boys Town. It is a full fledge city for the sole purpose of rehabilitating children who society rejects. Years later, in 1996, a course entitled Common Sense Parenting (CSP) was developed following the principals laid down at Girls and Boys Town.

Here in India, it is most important to empower children to grow into self-sufficient citizens of tomorrow who may one day effect positive change in the future for their community, country and possibly the world. With this mission, we need to emphasize parental education to most than any other priorities for children.

Responsible child care program may include the following modules:

1. Common Sense Parenting (CSP)
2. Preventive Healthcare with emphasis on HIV/AIDS prevention
3. Family Planning

Worldwide research of programs using CSP shows positive outcomes:

- 90 per cent decrease in out-of-home placements or runaways
- 40 per cent decrease in reported child behaviour problems in the age group of from 3 to 16 years
- 19 per cent decrease in potential of parent/childcare provider physical abuse

These positive outcomes occur in all types of families...single or two-parent families, in joint families, non-traditional families and across socio-economic, ethnic and racial lines.

Government ought to patronize strengthening family efforts which are most required in India in view of the fact that there are large numbers of children who do not have childhood of their own. The best of the institutional care cannot replace the warmth of family care where there is scope of attachment to other family members. These children are on the streets, in the orphanages and also are working as child labour. We need lot of resources for training for training trainers/teachers so they are able to reach as many parents, childcare providers, teachers, NGOs, Government organisations, etc. as possible to offer new alternatives in raising children in a loving, teaching manner.

Maharashtra is a progressive state and it has implemented almost all the schemes of Government of India. The situation in others states may be worse. Physical punishment in schools is an accepted fact and parents usually do not protest.

Another way to empower children addresses the issue of orphans in India. LHI intends to provide, manage and monitor loving family-like homes for orphaned, neglected and/or abused children where they are raised and nurtured in supportive family-like environments with married couples provide the role of parents/caregivers.

Each individual home for one family will comprise a well-trained married caregiver/parent couple and up to six (6) children. The husband will be employed in his line of work or profession within the city where the home will be located and the mother will be a stay-at-home full-time mom.

Children of both sexes, at the time of acceptance into a home, range from birth to 10 years of age. Every effort is made to assure that siblings are kept together. The children in each home will grow up together as brothers and sisters in a loving, abusive free, family atmosphere.

All basic and emotional needs will be met, which include:

- Love—it is a known fact that love heals all things
- Physical and emotional security
- Protective, safe and abuse free homes
- Nutritious meals
- Clothing
- Healthcare
- Education through university
- Vocational training if lacking the aptitude to go to university
- Spiritual and family values

In the normal everyday world, every family has relatives. The role of grandparents or other relatives such as aunts, uncles, cousins, etc., will be filled by individuals who have been screened and who have passed the Responsible Childcare Training Course.

Each aspect of the program is to be monitored, reviewed and fine-tuned on a continuing basis. Policy and procedures are to be followed and modified as needed to care for the children in safe, teaching, loving environments. The methods used by Girls and Boys Town, the developers of Common Sense Parenting that is used in our Responsible Childcare training, will be used as our benchmark, taking into consideration the Indian culture. In Indian context where large number of orphan older children are considered ineligible for domestic adoption, group foster care and guardianship by responsible families can be considered as suitable alternative while inter-country adoption still remains an important option.

3

The Effects of Institutional Living on Attachment

CHIVONNE HAGAN

Attachment Theory

The process of attachment is commonly referred to as the dance by those who study it (Perry, 2001). The dance consists of the reciprocal relationship between the primary caregiver and infant; in which bonding takes place, with the ultimate goal of healthy secure attachment. John Bowlby was the first to write about attachment theory and the importance of the emotional bond that an infant shares with the one who cares for him (Bowlby, 1969). This initial emotional bond leads to attachment, which provides infants with a framework for healthy future relationships throughout childhood and into adulthood (Perry).

Healthy attachment is a response to constant care giving. When an infant cries and the caregiver responds, by meeting the infant's needs, trust is formed. Once the caregiver responds the infants usually stops crying, and engages in eye contact with the caregiver. Once an infant receives sensitive, attuned care it often begins smiling and cooing, which makes the care reciprocally enjoyable for the caregiver. The crying allows the infant to acquire proximity to the caregiver, and the response of the infant ensures that proximity is maintained (Bowlby, 1969). When a caregiver offers an attentive and sensitive response to an infant's needs, demonstrating an ability to read an infant's cues accurately, the infant in turn will feel safe and secure. Responding to an infant's needs promptly and accurately is the key to forming an initial attachment. Additionally, infants respond to those who bring them pleasure. Due to this fact infant attachment is promoted by caregivers who interact with them socially, and engage them in playful acts (Rycus & Hughes, 1998).

An infant's ability to form attachments begins at birth; therefore a child who is adopted in early infancy has the same ability to attach to adoptive parents as a child who remains with their birth parents, considering that both environments supply the infant with nurturance and stability (Leon, 2002). Difficulties in attachment arise when an infant is in a neglectful or abusive environment in which attachment building responses, provided through sensitive care, are not provided by the same caregiver on a consistent basis. Attachment serves the purpose of allowing a child to internalize the love that is shown to them, and promotes feelings of safety. Without secure attachment the child may be easily overwhelmed and anxious. The response to these feelings may either be outward anger or disassociation from feelings altogether.

Ainsworth made a great contribution to attachment theory with her study of the 'strange situation'. A synopsis of her study is that she took infants and exposed them to a variety of stressful situations, which included separating them from their mothers followed by reunification. The procedure took place over a time span of 25 minutes. During this separation infants are exposed to an unfamiliar setting, unfamiliar people and being along. When the mother and infant reunited, infant responses were evaluated and categorized based on the evaluated behaviours, and what those behaviours inferred about the infant's level of attachment (Ainsworth, Blehar, Waters & Wall, 1978). Secure attachment is what is seen in infants who experience a healthy reciprocal relationship with their primary caregiver. A securely attached infant uses the caregiver as a secure base in which he can venture away from as time goes on knowing that he can always return to the caregiver when uncertain of the world around him.

Insecure attachment takes on different forms. Avoidant insecurity is when infants are able to leave the caregiver with comfort to explore the world around them, yet show little care or emotion upon return. Resistant insecurity is when infants do not want to separate from their caregiver and show little to no interest in exploring the world around them (Ainsworth *et al.*, 1978; Marvin et al, 2002). The problem with this categorisation is that not all infants fit into one of these categories, and that some infants perform in the strange situation like that of a well attached child, yet due to neglect show abnormalities in their attachment behaviour on a day to day basis (Rutter, 1995). Due to this finding the category of ambivalent or disorganized attachment is often used to describe such behaviours.

Bowlby (1969; 1970), and Ainsworth (1969), both found that attachment can occur even in an abused child. When a child is given attention of any sort, that child typically becomes attached to the caregiver (Ainsworth; Bowlby). Not all attachment is healthy. Unhealthy attachments are often found in children who have suffered abuse at the hand of their caregivers. Situations of neglect, such as those found in institutional care, are examples of circumstances in which attachment fails to take place altogether.

Patterns of Attachment

The primary caregiver-infant relationship is vital in forming attachment in an infant during his first year of life. Parents who find high amounts of pleasure in caring and interacting with their infants are shown to have infants that are more securely attached. Parental feelings toward their child contribute to the level of attachment that a child will demonstrate (Bowlby, 1969; Condon & Corkindale, 1998; Feldstein, Hane, Morrison & Huang, 2004; Perry, 2001). How a caretaker responds to an infant's cues often directly relate to how that individual related to their own caregivers at infancy. This may be an insecure pattern, caused by previous neglectful care giving. In this case the caregiver would have to take notice of his own emotions when responding to the infant, in order to ensure that the reciprocal relationship provided by the caregiver is conducive to infant attachment (Marvin *et al.*, 2002). In a random intervention study of 130 adoptive families with 6-month old adopted children, findings suggested a weak, yet apparent connection between parental sensitivity and disorganized attachment (Juffer, Bakermans-Kranenburg & van IJsendoorn, 2005). Helping parents identify their attachment patterns, and assisting them in increasing the sensitivity of their responses to their infant's attachment patterns are useful in facilitating attachment. A good fit between the parents' attachment style and the infants' attachment style is beneficial in increasing positive attachment behaviours (Marvin *et al.*). The reciprocal nature of attachment should be considered when applying this concept to infants cared for in an institutional setting. In an institutional environment the caregivers are employees of the institution, rather than parents of the infants, and are caring for large numbers of children for a low salary.

In extreme cases, patterns of insecure attachment can result in a diagnosis of Reactive Attachment Disorder. Reactive Attachment Disorder is one of the few diagnoses that can be given to a child under the age of 3. For diagnostic purposes, attachment disorder is viewed in two subtypes, inhibited type and dis-inhibited type (American Psychiatric Association, 2000). A child with behaviours that are categorized as inhibited subtype present as socially awkward, and will not respond to social interactions in an age appropriate way. This child may appear withdrawn and will fail to initiate and respond to social interactions. A child with behaviours that are categorized as dis-inhibited subtype present with indiscriminate sociability, and may seek proximity to adults without showing selectivity for those familiar to him or her (American Psychiatric Association; Zeanah & Boris, 1999). Inhibited and disinhibited types of attachment disorder often take place in post-institutionalized infants and children with an increased risk due to extreme neglect (Zeanah, Boris & Scheeringa, 1997). Reactive Attachment Disorder is uncommon in prevalence (American Psychiatric Association). It is important not to assume that a child has Reactive Attachment Disorder due to the appearance of poor attachment behaviours. Insecure attachment behaviours often exist outside of the disorder (Zeanah & Fox, 2004). For the purpose of this curriculum the focus will be on attachment behaviours rather than Reactive Attachment Disorder.

Attachment and the Infant Brain

Forming attachments is genetically determined in human beings, yet infants need constant interaction with a primary caregiver in order to reach their genetic capability. In the first two years of an infant's life the right hemisphere of the brain undergoes a large growth spurt. The limbic system, which is where the developmental changes that result in attachment and the regulation of emotions take place, is located in the right hemisphere of the brain. Trauma in the first two years of life can be responsible for possibly altering the limbic system and therefore permanently impairing the brains ability to control emotions and develop attachments (Schore, 2001). Since neuropsychological growth occurs rapidly in infancy, these early years are of utmost importance for allowing an individual to achieve their maximum potential in life (Juffer *et al.*, 2003). This rapid brain development causes the infant brain to be vulnerable to early neglect or abuse (Schore). By the time an infant turns three his brain will be 90 per cent developed, and templates have been developed that will affect all future interactions and relationships (Perry, 2001). Without proper bonding experiences in infancy, attachment is at risk for failure, and infants are at risk of potentially losing the ability to self soothe and regulate their emotions.

When an infant suffers deprivation of any kind the result is a loss of homeostatic balance, which results in emotional distress. Until the distressed state ends and balance is returned the infant must focus all of their regulatory resources on reorganisation instead of being able to take in new experiences and learn from them (Schore, 2001). Therefore, early impairment in neurological development creates potentially irreversible effects in the structure of the infant's brain (Perry, 2001). Just as positive early experiences enhance brain development, negative early experiences hinder brain development in infants (Schore). Brain scans of individuals who suffered severe early deprivation showed that trauma actually alters the human brain (Gray, 2002). Fortunately, neuroscience research shows that the human brain has astonishing plasticity, a fact that provides hope to post-institutionalized children and adoptive parents alike (Gunnar, Bruce & Grotevant, 2000).

Characteristics of Poor Attachment

When an infant does not meaningfully and significantly attach to their caregiver there are a variety of ways that this can manifest in the infant's life. In extreme cases, which are rare, severely neglected infants can lose the ability to form significant and meaningful relationships in the future. Typically, infant neglect results in a myriad of ways, ranging from mild social discomfort to social and emotional problems that may deeply affect their lives and the lives of their loved ones (Perry, 2001). Often a child with poor attachment may present with typical behaviours for the most part, yet such a child may lack the fundamental understanding of reciprocal love and dependency. Children that are raised in an institutional environment learn what to say and do to please adults, yet do not typically learn any emotions behind such behaviours (Hughes, 1999). Infants who have experienced neglect often learn to self soothe when sensitive care is not received. Rocking, head banging or other ways of injuring oneself are examples of self soothing that may be found in infants who have experienced severe neglect (Perry).

With severe attachment problems a myriad of behaviours may exist. Deprivation, when severe and prolonged can lead to deficits cognitively, socially and physically (Judge, 1999). Physical, cognitive and emotional development is affected by an infant's initial ability to attach to a caregiver (Hopkins-Best, 1997). Some typical behaviours that may result from poor attachment include: lack of eye contact, indiscriminate affection, lying, and increased manipulative behaviours that are effective in splitting caregivers to create turmoil. Typically cause and effect thinking will be poorly developed for these children and they may have trouble moving past concrete thoughts. A child who has not attached in infancy may have a poorly developed conscience, a lack of empathy, a lack of impulse control and an interest in morbidity (Adoption UK, 2002; Gunnar *et al.*, 2000; Perry, 2001). Outward signs in a poorly attached child may demonstrate as speech or developmental delays. A poorly attached child may also struggle with bed wetting or soiling, abnormal eating patterns and may have poorly developed social skills causing them to have trouble forming peer relationships (Adoption UK; Hughes, 1999).

In a quantitative study conducted by Repacholi and Trapolini, using 48 children, the findings suggested that children with insecure attachments also suffer with deficits in social understanding (Repacholi & Trapolini, 2004). With decreased social understanding common situations such as peer relations at school may be challenging to a poorly attached child. It is typical for children with poor attachment to lack appropriate boundaries both physically and socially (Stein, Faber, Berger, Kiliman & Albers, 2004). These children often misread facial cuing which leads to misunderstanding in social situations. Often a child with poor attachment will fail to understand that it is possible for an adult to have their best interest in mind, and want to have a relationship with them (Hughes, 1999). Without this basic understanding it is difficult for a child to trust an adult, and instead adults are seen as people to manipulate in order to get needs and wants met.

A common misconception is that clinging to the caregiver is a sign that the child is securely attached. Clinginess is not an indicator of attachment, and in actuality is typically an indicator that the child is experiencing anxiety. Anxiety is often result of an insecure initial attachment (Ainsworth, 1969). Furthermore, it is important to realize that the very behaviours that are thought of as attachment behaviours are not necessarily what is observed in securely attached children. A child with dependent behaviour is not more securely attached then a child with independent behaviour (Ainsworth; Bowlby, 1969). From an infant's interaction with a sensitive caregiver and through developing quality attachments, the infant learns that he or she is valued and significant. When a caregiver remains physically close to an infant it prevents the infant from forming anxiety regarding whether or not their needs will be met. In this way a child's initial attachment is the beginning of a child having a sense of themselves and positive self-confidence (Olson & Kholmogorova, 2003). When a child receives proper care and nurturance as an infant they in turn learn that the world is a safe and loving place. When these experiences are lacking the child fails to learn how to regulate their emotions. Without learning how to self-regulate the world is often a frightening and over-whelming place (Stein *et al.*, 2004).

Attachment is the key to teaching children autonomy. When a child is well attached they feel comfortable exploring the world around them. The ability to learn independence creates self-confidence in a child (Rycus & Hughes, 1998). A securely attached child has the building blocks necessary to maintain typical child development emotionally and mentally.

Child Development and Attachment

When learning about child development it is important to take into consideration that most theories assume that the child has received basic nurturance, care, socialisation and has formed solid initial attachments. With these assumptions children typically develop in stages that can be recognized and categorized accordingly. Without a child having the opportunity to form an initial attachment to a caretaker, their development may be delayed (Karen, 1998). Attachment is developed throughout infancy and individuals continue to form attachments throughout life. During the first year of life, infants thrive due to interactions with their primary caregiver in which their sensory system is stimulated. These interactions stimulate the infants' brain leading to feelings of enjoyment, interest, and happiness in an infant (Hughes, 1999).

A study of 163 internationally adopted children suggests that attachment disorder behaviours can be identified in an infant of merely 3 months (O'Conner, Bredenkamp & Rutter, 1999). At approximately 7 to 9 months a securely attached infant will begin to be wary of strangers and show preference for their caregiver. The initial sign of secure attachment occurs when an infant exhibits stranger wariness and begins to protest separation from the familiar caregiver (Zeanah & Fox, 2004). Although the first signs of attachment do not occur until 7 months, the building blocks to attachment begin at birth. Newborns recognize their mothers by scent, and at approximately 2 months distressed infants respond faster to their preferred caregiver. Attachment is not as clear at this point due to the fact that infants can also be calmed by strangers during 2 to 7 months. However, the calming may not be as immediate, and depending upon the infants' temperament the primary caregiver can often calm the infant almost instantly (Zeanah & Fox).

According to Eric Erikson (1959; 1963), developing basic trust is crucial in the first year of an infant's life. This initial trust is the basis of attachment, and a child's attachment in the first year of life sets the tone for their future attachments throughout the life (Bowlby, 1970; Erikson; Perry, 2001). This is not to say that without this initial attachment future attachments can not occur. However, for some children without this initial attachment future attachments may be a struggle, and may require work on the part of the child and their family (Rutter, 1995). A study of 217 children adopted from Romanian and United Kingdom orphanages showed that attachment disturbances occurred in children that were institutionalized for the first six months of life. These findings illuminate the importance of the caretaker—infant relationship and the detrimental effects of this relationship failing to occur in the highly developmental period of the first year (O'Connor & Rutter, 2000).

Typical development following the first year of life for an infant is based on the assumption that attachment to a primary caregiver was successful for the infant. Before a toddler can begin to seek independence, a solid year of dependency should be obtained in which the caregiver provides love and stability (Hopkins-Best, 1997). In the second year, the toddler is taught to identify with extended family members, and socialisation outside of the immediate family is increased. At this point the primary caregiver provides a secure base for the child to venture away from and return to when overwhelmed or scared (Boris & Zeanah, 1999). A secure base is the foundation for a toddler's independence. Typical development into the third year for a toddler consists of learning to feel empathy, control behaviours, and control ones own emotions. When a child does not experience initial attachment there is limited basis for further healthy development (Hughes, 1999).

International Adoption

International adoption is becoming common practice among American families. In fact, one out of every six families that chooses to adopt outside of their family adopts internationally (Steltzner, 2003). Children born in Eastern Europe are the main source of adoptees from overseas (Judge, 1999). China is the greatest single country source of internationally adopted children, with Russia following closely behind. Between the years of 1998 to 2002, more than 60 per cent of all internationally adopted children in America were born in either China or Russia (Meese, 2005).

Economics appears to be the main reason for the surge of adoptable children in Russia (Isupova 2004; Steltzner 2003). After the fall of Communism, the structure of living in Russia changed dramatically. Unemployment rates were high and families without work could no longer care for their children (Steltzner). Poverty, insufficient social ties, alcoholism, and social stigma are a few reasons that mothers are choosing to relinquish their children to orphanages (Isupova). Social norms in the former Soviet Union dictate that women should have children in their twenties and thirties within the parameters of marriage. Women who become pregnant that are considered too young, too old, or unwed can be stigmatized by their society. Families who have children with disabilities are also stigmatized (Isupova). This stigma often leads parents to relinquish their children to orphanages. During the time these children wait to be adopted they reside in baby houses, hospitals and orphanages, all of which are government run institutions.

Shared emotional, cognitive and social developmental impairments are commonly found among children who resided in institutions (Olson & Kholmogorova, 2003). There are approximately 155 institutions for children under the age of 18 in Russia. Warehouse style institutions are the least costly method, and therefore are common practice in Eastern Europe. Children with learning disabilities account for up to half of those in institutions (Parfitt, 2003). Due to the lack of staffing, children are left with minimal supervision. There may be up to ten infants per caregiver, and for children over the age of three there may be up to twenty children per caregiver (Judge, 1999). Children often are indiscriminately friendly towards all people, which is a result of not forming proper attachments (Judge). Lack of stimulation, poor nutrition, and minimal human interaction may result in delays that affect physical, emotional and social development in children (Judge). Due to the instability and lack of care in an orphanage children view caregivers as rejecting and learn that their needs cannot be met by others. Avoidance, manipulation, and denial of all feelings are survival mechanisms employed by institutionalized children (Chapman, 2002). When attachment ceases to take place, many parts of the child's psychological development suffer. Attachment affects a child's ability to develop relationships, regulate emotions, control behaviour, and develop a sense of self (Hughes, 1998).

Life in an Institution

Despite adverse institutional circumstances that children adopted internationally experience, for the most part children are extremely resilient and tend to make excellent progress once they adjust to a stable family environment (Gunnar *et al.*, 2000). This adjustment takes time due to the possible neglect and abuse that children may have endured while living in an institutional setting. Children living in institutional settings are susceptible to deprivation on a number of levels. There are base level needs for food, clothing, shelter, and medical attention. Often children face deprivation that begins at this basic level, and often caregivers are so overwhelmed at meeting these basic needs for children that secondary needs such as stimulation to improve their cognition and social development fail to occur. Tragically, achieving stable attachment based relationships is often overlooked, due to staff changes throughout the day, and staffing shortages on the weekends. Children are also grouped by age, and may be in a hospital initially, then placed in a baby house throughout infancy, and later moved to an orphanage when approaching childhood. This constant change in environment and caregivers make it virtually impossible for children to develop stable relationships (Gunnar *et al.*).

Children in orphanages often learn to seek love wherever it is available (Gray, 2002). Children in this environment often tend to be indiscriminate and seek attention from inappropriate sources. Indiscriminate attention seeking is an example of a behaviour that children rely on to help them survive in the orphanage, yet can create problems once the child is in a home environment. Poor discrimination among caregivers in the orphanage allows a child to move from caregiver to caregiver in order to get his needs met, yet in a home environment it is crucial that the child attaches to their parents and learns to turn to them for all of their needs (Hughes, 1998).

Institutionalized infants and children alike are exposed to a variety of circumstances that put them at risk for poor physical and emotional health. Lack of food, clothing, medication, neglect, abuse and exposure to infectious disease are all possibilities when living in an institutional environment internationally (Jenista, 2000). Institutionalized children are often deprived of human touch due to the small number of caregivers assigned to a large number of children. Bottles may be propped up in a crib as a solution for not having enough caregivers to feed all of the infants (Steltzner, 2003). Research suggests that the longer a child is in an institution the more prone they become to present with poor attachment behaviours, yet this does not mean that all children that are institutionalized for long periods of time will struggle with attachment (Judge, 2004; O'Connor *et al.*, 1999).

Post-institutionalised Behaviour

The transition from an institution to a family home is often challenging for both the child and the parents. Post-institutionalized behaviours are often frustrating and overwhelming for parents who are adopting children that have spent time in an institutional facility such as an orphanage of baby house internationally. In order for infants and children alike to function in an environment of extreme deprivation and neglect certain survival skills are learned. Trust, which leads to attachment must be achieved between a parent and a child before these survival behaviours can be relearned. These children often view adults as unsafe and unpredictable. They see caregivers as neglectful and possibly cruel. They have learned to be silent, to disconnect, to avoid and to manipulate in order to survive. It is crucial to remember that the very behaviours that cause a child's struggles in an American family may have been the reason they have survived in an institutional setting (Hughes, 1997).

A study of 163 internationally adopted children adopted before the age of two found that children with poor attachment behaviours concurrently had trouble forming peer relationships. Additionally, a large number of children presenting with poor attachment behaviours at the time of adoption no longer exhibited these behaviours by the age of four (O'Connor, Brenenkamp, & Rutter, 1999). This study addressed the socially awkward nature that often accompanies poor attachment, and provides insight into the resiliency of children when placed in loving and nurturing environments.

A study of 117 children adopted from Romania found that a longer period of institutional living typically resulted in more severe attachment related behaviours (O'Connor & Rutter, 2000). It is crucial to remember that not all children who have lived in institutional settings have the same experience and that poor attachment is something to research and become familiar with, but is not inevitable for all children (Nickman *et al.*, 2005). A quantative study of 124 children adopted from Eastern European orphanages suggested that it is not the length of time spent in an institution, but the quality of the experiences that occur during that time combined with developmental and behavioural problems at the time of adoption that will affect a child's ability to form attachments (Judge, 2004).

Facilitating Attachment

Entering into a relationship with a child who has poor attachment can be frustrating and overwhelming for parents. Child rearing is typically a reciprocal experience. The parent provides attention and love to the child, and the child in return provides attention and love to the parent. Adoptive parents often realize that the reciprocal nature of their relationship with their child will take time. It does not always occur to a parent that their child may not be aware of what they are missing from not having a reciprocal relationship. In reality children may not have the same goals as their parents since they have never experienced a healthy attached relationship. It is often difficult for a parent in this scenario not to take the rejection from a child personally (Hughes, 1999).

Being informed about attachment is the first step in facilitating attachment for a child. This is where parental training and post-adoption supportive services become crucial elements to a positive adoptive experience. Being able to identify attachment related behaviours allows a parent to have an idea of what is going on with their child, and insight regarding the root of their attachment experiences (Perry, 2001). Misunderstanding a child's attachment behaviours can prevent a parent from getting their child the help they may need. It is also crucial that a parent understands that not all institutionalized children will have difficulties in the area of attachment. As an adoptive parent, it is important that attachment is well understood, but that it is not assumed that a child will struggle with attachment related difficulties (Hopkins-Best, 1997). If a parent has identified problematic attachment related behaviours in their child, it is vital that a qualified professional is consulted to determine if attachment difficulties are the root of the problem or if other components are partially responsible (Hughes, 1999). A professional can also suggest therapeutic interventions to help facilitate attachment if attachment is found to be the source of the child's troubles. If therapy is needed for the child, the parents must be participants since the goal is for the child to attach to her parents, not to the therapist.

It is necessary that families choosing to adopt internationally learn the circumstances of their child's birth. Having an understanding of the child's previous environment will help the family know what types of interventions may be needed once the child is in their family (Narad & Mason, 2004). When dealing with children who have spent time in an orphanage, it is important to take into consideration that in order to survive they had to depend on a variety of individuals to supply them with food and attention.

Due to this fact, the idea that one caregiver or one caregiver dyad will constantly meet their needs may be overwhelming, threatening and inherently hard to believe for a child. It is the responsibility of the caregiver to provide consistency and reliability over-time and to understand that building trust may require time since the child has to relearn what they know about caregivers and the world (Narad & Mason).

It is important not to over stimulate a child when you first bring them into your home. For a child coming into an American home from an overseas orphanage the change in people, language, food, and smells is understandably overwhelming. For a child who is not securely attached to a caregiver these experiences are fear provoking because they have no secure base to return to after their new experiences (Narad & Mason, 2004). Initially it is best for the child to spend individual time with their caregivers in the families' home. Initially, it is preferable that activities such as feeding, cuddling, and prolonged eye contact are reserved for only the parents or immediate family, since these activities are important in building attachment (Gray, 2000.) As attachment is formed and the child begins to adjust to the new environment it is then safe to integrate new activities and new people into the child's life (Hughes, 1999). New situations and changes in schedules may be difficult for insecurely attached children. Sensitivity to new situations may continue with these children as they grow older. New situations tend to bring children back to an uneasy state in which they become anxious and distressed. In order to make the child feel safe, it is important to keep schedules as consistent and predictable as possible.

Nurturance and increased bonding experiences are of utmost importance in developing secure attachments. Children who have experienced adverse environments, lacking in basic nurturance, have an unfulfilled need that adoptive parents cannot disregard. Such children need to be held, cuddled, rocked, and soothed with eye contact and face to face interactions. Since these experiences may be new to the child, or may be associated with painful experiences in the past, it is important to be sensitive to how the child is responding to the caregiver and to try to attune their needs with the caregiver's response (Perry, 2001).

The emotional age of a child is as important for an adoptive parent to know as the physical age of the child. Neglectful circumstances can produce emotional and social delays. In difficult situations, a child may regress to the place they were emotionally when they last received the care needed to feel safe and secure. Infants, who have never received such care, may need to revert to early infancy in order to have this need met in their new family (Perry, 2001). A three-year old child may respond positively to being wrapped up tight like a new born baby and rocked to sleep in the comfort and security of their mother's arms. Even if the child appears as a toddler, emotionally they may still have the needs of an infant.

Often adoptive parents fear placing strict boundaries and consequences on a child who appears to be struggling with attachment. The reality is that attachment takes time, and that regardless of the security of attachment, healthy boundaries and consequences are necessary for all children. For an adopted child it is important to realize that consequences may appear differently than those given under typical circumstances. Instead of time-outs, time-ins may be used to aid in building healthy attachments. For a poorly attached child, close proximity to the parent is necessary as often as possible and this should be considered when choosing consequences. Also, an adopted infant should never be left alone while crying. An infant needs to build trust to form attachments and when a parent responds to an infant's cry the infant begins to learn that they can depend on the parent, and trust begins to form (Fay & Fay, 2000.) It is also important that adoptive parents do not shy away from physical contact with their child due to the child's inability to receive love. For a child that has not been held and cuddled, initially this may feel overwhelming and uncomfortable.

Children need physical contact with their parents to grow emotionally, and to become well attached individuals, and an adoptive parent needs to know this even when the child does not. Parents must provide food, shelter, eye contact, touch, comfort and overall nurturance and security along with opportunities for the child to play and interact with others socially. Initially, an institutionalized child may not be able to accurately recognize or label their own needs, and may avoid the very things that will allow them to thrive and attach to their new family (Hopkins-Best, 1997).

Providing an education on the topic of attachment for prospective adoptive parents equips them with skills necessary to recognize and respond to any attachment based struggles that an internationally adopted child may encounter. This curriculum has been developed to meet this need of increased education for adoptive parents.

References

Ainsworth, M.D.S. (1969), Object relations, dependency and attachment: A theoretical review of the infant-mother relationship. *Child Development*, 40, 969-1025.

Ainsworth, M.D.S., Blehar, M.C., Waters, E & Wall, S. (1978), *Patterns of attachment: psychological study of the strange situation.* Hillsdale, NJ: Erlbaum.

Adoption UK (2000), *Making Sense of Attachments in Adoptive and Foster Families.* Banbury, Oxon: Adoption UK.

American Psychiatric Association (2000), *DSM-IV-TR*. Washington DC: American Psychiatric Association.

Bakermans-Kranenburg, M.J., Van IJzendoorn, M.H., & Juffer, F. (2003), Less is More: Meta-Analyses of Sensitivity and Attachment Interventions in Early Childhood. *Psychological Bulletin*, 129(2), 195-215.

Boris, N.W. & Zeanah, C.H., (1999), Disturbances and disorders of attachment in infancy: An overview. *Infant Mental Health Journal*, 20 (1), 1-9.

Bowlby, J. (1969), *Attachment.* New York: Basic Books.

Bowlby, J. (1970), *Attachment and loss, Vol. I*: Attachment. New York: Basic Books.

Condon, J.I. & Corkindale, C.J. (1998), The assessment of parent-to-infant attachment: development of a self-report questionnaire instrument. *Journal of Reproductive and Infant Psychology*, 16, 57-77.

Chapman, S. (2002), Reactive Attachment Disorder. *British Journal of Special* Education, 29(2), 91-95.

Erikson, E. (1959), Identity and the life cycle. *Psychological Issues*. 1(1) Monograph 1. New York: International Universities Press, Inc.

Erikson, E. (1963), *Childhood and society*. (2nd ed.) New York: W.W. Norton and Co. Feldstein, S., Hane, A.A., Morrison & B.M. Huang, K.Y. (2004), Relation of the Post-natal Attachment Questionnaire to the Attachment Q-Set. *Journal of Reproductive and Infant Psychology*, 22 (2), 111-121.

Fay, J. & Fay, C. (2000), *Love and Logic Magic for Early Childhood: Practical Parenting from Birth to Six Years.* Golden, Colorado: The Love and Logic Press.

Gray, D. D. (2002), *Attaching in Adoption.* Indianapolis, IN: Perspectives Press.

Gunnar, M.R., Bruce, J. & Grotevant, H.D. (2000), International adoption of institutionally reared children: Research and policy. *Development and Psychopathology,* 12, 677-693.

Hopkins-Best, M. (1997), *Toddler Adoption: The Weaver's Craft.* Indianapolis, Indiana: Perspectives Press.

Hughes, D.A. (1997), *Facilitating Developmental Attachment: the road to emotional recovery and behavioural change in foster and adopted children.* Lanham, Maryland: Rowman & Lettlefield.

Hughes, D.A. (1998), *Building the Bonds of Attachment: Awakening Love in Deeply Troubled Children.* Lanham, Maryland: Rowman & Lettlefield.

Hughes, D.A. (1999), Adopting Children with Attachment Problems. *Child Welfare,* 78(5), 541-561.

Isupova, O.G. (2004), The Relinquishment of Newborns and Women's Reproductive Rights. *Russian Social Science Review,* 45(3), 40-57.

Jenista, J. (2000), Preadoption review of medical records. *Pediatric Annals,* 29(4), 212-215.

Judge, S.L. (1999), Eastern European Adoptions: Current Status and Implications for Intervention. *Topics in Early Childhood Special Education,* 19(4), 244-252.

Judge, S.L. (2004), Adoptive Families: The Effects of Early Relational Deprivation in Children Adopted from Eastern European Orphanages. *Journal of Family Nursing,* 10(3), 338-356.

Juffer, F., Bakermans-Kranenburg, M. J., & Van IJzendoorn, M. H. (2005), The importance of parenting in the development of disorganized attachment: evidence from a preventive intervention study in adoptive families. *Journal of Child Psychology and Psychiatry,* 46(3), 263-274.

Karen, R. (1998), *Becoming Attached: First Relationships and How They Shape Our Capacity to Love.* New York: Oxford University Press.

Larsen, D., Attkisson, C., Hargreaves, W., & Nguyen, T. (1979), *Assessment of client/patient satisfaction: Development of a general scale, Evaluation and Program Planning,* 2, 197-207.

Leon, I.G. (2002), Adoption Losses: Naturally Occurring or Socially Constructed? *Child Development,* 73(2), 652-663.

Lihua, H. (2001), *Chinese Adoption: Practices and Challenges.* Washington D.C. Child Welfare League of America.

Marvin, R., Cooper, G., Hoffman, K. & Powell, B. (2002), The Circle of Security project: Attachment-based intervention with caregiver pre-school child dyads. *Attachment and Human Development,* 4(1), 107-124.

Meese, R.L. (2005), A Few New Children: Post-institutionalized Children of Inter-country Adoption. *The Journal of Special Education, 39*(3), 157-167.

Narad, C., Mason, P.W. (2004), International Adoptions: Myths and Realities. *Family Matters,* 30(6), 483-487.

Nickman, S. L., Rosenfeld, A. A, M.D., Fine, P.M.D., Macintyre, J. C., Pilowsky, D.J., M.D. & Howe, R.J.D. (2005), Children in Adoptive Families: Overview and Update. *Child Adolescent Psychiatry,* 44(10), 987-995.

O'Connor, T.G., Bredenkamp, D., Rutter, M. (1999), Attachment Disturbances and Disorders in Children Exposed to Early Severe Deprivation. *Infant Mental Health Journal,* 20(1), 10-29.

O'Connor, T.G., Rutter, M.D., The English & Romanian Adoptees Study Team (2000), Attachment Disorder Behaviour Following Early Severe Deprivation: Extension and Longitudinal Follow-up. *Journal of American Academy of Child and Adolescent Psychiatry,* 39(6), 703-711.

Oslon, B.N. & Kholmogorova, A.B. (2003), The Professional Foster Family as One Model for Solving the Orphan Problem in Russia. *Russian Education and Society,* 45(6), 26-44.

Parfitt, T. (2003), Care of learning-disabled Russian children condemned. *Lancet,* 362, 1291.

Perry, B.D. (2001), Bonding and Attachment in Maltreated Children. *The Child Trauma Academy,* 1-18.

Perry, B.D. (2003), *Understanding Maltreated and Traumatized Children Part III: how the brain develops: The Importance of Early Childhood.* Sherborn, M.A. Aquarius Health Care Videos.

Rapacholi, B. & Trapolini, T. (2004), Attachment and pre-school children's understanding of maternal versus non-maternal psychological states. *British Journal of Developmental Psychology,* 22, 395-415.

Rutter, M. (1995), Clinical Implications of Attachment Concepts: Retrospect and Prospect. *Journal of Child Psychology,* 36(4), 549-57.

Rycus, J.S., Hughes, R.C. (1998), Field Guide to Child Welfare: Placement and Permanence.Vol. IV. CWLA Press, Washington, D.C.

Shore, A.N. (2001), The Effects of Early Relational Trauma on Right Brain Development, Affect Regulation, and Infant Mental Health. *Infant Mental Health Journal,* 22, 201-269.

Stein, M.T., M.D., Faber, S., M.D., Berger, S.P., M.D., Kiliman, G., M.D. & Albers, L., M.D. (2004), International Adoption: A 4-Year Old Child with Unusual Behaviours Adopted at 6 Months of Age. *Pediatrics,* 114(5), 1425-1431.

Steltzner, D.M. (2003), Inter-country Adoption: Toward a Regimen that Recognizes the "Best Interest" of Adoptive Parents. *Case Western Reserve Journal of International Law,* 35, 113-130.

Weisner, T.S. (2005), Attachment as a Cultural and Ecological Problem with Pluralistic Solutions. *Human Development*. 48, 89-94.

Zeanah, C.H., Boris, N.W. & Scheeringa, M.S. (1997), Psychopathology in Infancy. *Journal of Child Psychology and Psychiatry*, 38(1), 81-99.

Zeanah, C.H. & Fox, N.A. (2004), Temperament and Attachment Disorders. *Journal of Clinical Child and Adolescent Psychology*, 33(1), 32-41.

4

The UK's Experience and Status on the Rights of Children

PETER SELMAN

Introduction

"Human rights are inscribed in the hearts of people; they were there long before law-makers drafted their first proclamation."

Mary Robinson, Former United Nations High Commissioner for Human Rights

Action in establishing children's rights is a recent development in the United Kingdom. Anyone familiar with the history of Britain in the 19th century will know that it is a sad story of child labour, street children and a bleak dependence on the workhouse for many poor children. Charles Dicken's *Oliver Twist* is a vivid portrayal of one aspect of this—the life of an orphan. Oliver's request "Please Sir, can I have some more?" was met with a sharp rebuff showing that in Dickensian Britain a child in a workhouse did not even have a right to ask for more food!

However, the last decade—especially during the period of "New Labour" government—has seen major progress with the passing in 1998 of the *Human Rights Act* and the introduction, in all four of the component countries (England, Wales, Scotland and Northern Ireland) of Children's Commissioners. These will be discussed in more detail in later sections of the paper.

Last year, Rosemary Sarri (2004) presented an excellent paper on "Human Rights of Children and Youth: Myths and Realities" and my aim will be to build on this by exploring the experience of the UK. I shall, therefore, not repeat the general background to the developing concern over Children's rights outlined in that paper and would advise anyone who has not read it to do so, alongside this presentation.

The UK is now one of the very richest countries of the world and we should be able to make Children's rights a central part of our agenda, but we still fall far behind many of our Western European neighbours. This paper will show that while we have made much progress there is still a long way to go and I believe that sharing our experience will identify many problems also facing you in Korea.

But we must not forget that the fight for Children's rights is worldwide and for many children the future must seem a very bleak one. As I type this introduction news is breaking of new famine in Niger and throughout Africa AIDS has created a new generation of orphans, while in parts of Eastern Europe and the former Soviet Union mortality rates have been rising and poverty growing.

Commitment to Children's Rights in the UK

The UK has shown its commitment in a formal sense by ratifying most of the key conventions relating to Children's Rights, notably:

- The European Convention on Human Rights (ECHR)
- United Nations Convention on the Rights of the Child (UNCRC)
- The Hague Convention on Inter-country Adoption 1993 (THC)

We have also passed some important legislation in the past 10 years:

- Human Rights Act, 1998—which largely implements the ECHR
- Adoption and Children Act, 2002

A referendum has yet to take place on the proposed EU Constitution, but if this is accepted it will introduce a new *Charter of Fundamental Rights.*

A Children's Commissioner/Ombudsman

One of the most important developments in respect of children's rights in the UK has been the appointment in all four component countries of Children's Commissioners. The first of these was appointed in Wales in 2001, followed by Northern Ireland (2003), Scotland (2004) and finally in England, where Al Aynsley Green started work at the end of July 2005 (Brooks, 2005).

Norway was the first country to establish an Ombudsman with statutory powers to protect children and their rights in 1981 and since then the office (with 15 employees and a budget of £ 530,000 a year) has worked continuously to improve national and international legislation affecting children's welfare. The Ombudsman has free access to all public and private institutions for children. Details of other European provision can be found on the web-site of the *European Network for Children Ombusdmen at* http://www.ombudsnet.org/

New Zealand was the first country to establish the post of Children's Commissioner—in 1989—and the current Commissioner, Cindy Kiro has recently visited the UK to "investigate policies affecting children and glean ideas to take home" (Ward, 2005).

In New Zealand the Commissioner's role, as defined in the *Children's Commissioner Act, 2003,* is seen as *"speaking out on behalf of all children to ensure their rights are respected and upheld"*. The Commissioner can inquire into any matter affecting children and young people in any service organisation and investigate the actions of the Department of Child, Youth and Family Services.

The Northern Ireland Commissioner describes his role as *"Promoting and safeguarding the rights and best interests of children and young people by listening to them and working with them to challenge and change the world in which they live!"* With an office of 26 staff, he is widely regarded as the best model within the UK.

Peter Clarke, the Children's Commissioner for Wales, says that and he and his team are there to help make sure that children and young people in Wales:

- are safe from harm and abuse
- get the opportunities and services they need and deserve

- are respected and valued
- have a voice in their communities and are able to play as full a part as possible in decisions that affect them
- know about their rights and the UN Convention on the Rights of the Child

His office also helps older young people who've been in care, and look into things that affected some adults while they were children.

There has been much criticism of the limited powers accorded to the Children's Commissioner in England (Batty, 2004). Following Government amendments to the Children Bill, 2004, his role has been downgraded from *"promoting and safeguarding children's rights to merely promoting their views and interests"* (Batty, 2004). This change was largely influenced by the new Minister for Children who argued that he should not get "bogged down" in "policing children's rights" like his Welsh counterpart. He will also have much lower funding per child than the other Commissioners.

The *European Network of Ombudsmen for Children* (ENOC) which has offices in 23 countries (with the UK represented by the other 3 Commissioners) has criticised the apparent lack of independence, having already indicated that the English Commissioner might not be eligible to join its ranks because the proposed powers were too weak.

The United Nations Convention on the Rights of the Child

> *"A century that began with children having virtually no rights is ending with children having the most powerful legal instrument that not only recognises but protects their human rights."*
>
> **Carol Bellamy**, UNICEF Executive Director

At the centre of any discussion about the rights of the child must be an awareness of the importance of the Convention on the Rights of the Child. The Convention was drafted over the 10 years—from 1979 to 1989—with the input of representatives from all societies, religions and cultures, and came into force in 1989. It has been ratified by 192 countries—only two countries have not ratified; the United States and Somalia, both of which have nevertheless formally signed the Convention.

Prior to or shortly after ratifying the Convention, States are required to bring their national legislation into line with its provisions – except where the national standards are already higher. In this way, child rights standards are no longer merely an aspiration but, rather, are nationally binding on States.

> *"The Convention is not only a visionary document. We are reminded daily that it is an agreement that works – and its utility can be seen in the everyday use to which I have seen it increasingly being put by country after country, in policy, in practice and in law."*
>
> **Carol Bellamy**, UNICEF Executive Director

The Convention on the Rights of the Child is the first legally binding international instrument to incorporate the full range of human rights – civil and political rights as well as economic, social and cultural rights. Two "Optional Protocols", on the involvement of children in armed conflict and on the sale of children, child prostitution and child pornography, were adopted to strengthen the provisions of the Convention in these areas. They entered into force in 2002.

Full details and commentary on the Convention can be found on the UNICEF web-site at http://www.unicef.org/crc

UN Committee on the Rights of the Child

The Committee on the Rights of the Child was established in 1991 in accordance with article 43 of the Convention. It is made up of members from different countries and legal systems who are experts in the field of human rights. These are not representatives of their countries and are "accountable solely to the children of the world. The Committee monitors the implementation of the Convention by reviewing the reports of *States Parties* to the Convention and reporting back to those States. The reports are published and can be obtained from the office of the UN High Commissioner for Human Rights.

In 1995, the Committee met with a delegation from the UK Government, described by the Committee as "uncooperative and arrogant", to discuss the UK's first report on its implementation of the CRC. Following their meeting, the Committee published a list of concerns and criticisms with a comprehensive set of recommendations on how the Government could better protect Children's rights. These criticisms were met with outrage by the UK press and politicians.

Seven years later in September 2002, a far more co-operative delegation met with Committee. The second Report noted that the New Labour Government was taking concrete steps to implement children's rights and was committed to making progress in the future. The Committee expressed disappointment that the UK Government had failed to act upon the majority of the 1995 recommendations and said that the UK lacked a 'rights-based approach', focusing instead on the welfare of children and service provision.

The Committee then identified certain key areas of failings (Harvey, 2002).

1. Child Poverty and Social Exclusion
2. Lack of Representation for Children
3. Corporal Punishment
4. Juvenile Justice

Child Poverty and Social Exclusion

Although the UK today has the fourth strongest economy in the world, in 2002 a third of its households were classified as living in poverty and a UNICEF study showed that in the last decade of the 20th century the UK had one of the highest rates of Child Poverty amongst developed nations—see Table 4.1—and also one of the higher rates of children in public care.

The Committee was extremely concerned at these figures, pointing out that poverty leads to a higher incidence of mortality, accidents, teenage pregnancies, poor housing and homelessness, malnutrition, educational failures and suicide. It welcomed the initiatives of the New Labour Government, but urged it to better co-ordinate these efforts to eradicate child poverty. Table 4.2 below presents some additional data on the UK, showing its relatively high rates of teenage pregnancy and child maltreat-ment, linked to a lower public expenditure and greater inequality.

Table 4.1: Child Poverty and the Incidence of Children in Public Care

Country	*GN1 Per Capita (2002)*[1]	*Under 5 Mortality (2002)*[1]	*% of Children in Poverty*[2]	*Children in Public Care*[3] *1998/99*	*% Adopted from Care*[4] *1998/99*
Australia	$19,740	6	12.6%	30	0.8
Sweden	$24,820	3	2.6%	50	0.2
Norway	$37,850	4	3.9%	30	0.7
Netherlands	$23,960	5	7.7%	24	N/A
UK	$24,250	7	19.8%[5]	55	4.0
USA	$35,060	8	22.4%	75	6.7

Sources: 1. UNICEF (2004) *State of the World's Children 2004* Table 1, New York: UNICEF.
2. UNICEF (2000) *A League Table of Child Poverty in Rich Nations,* Innocenti Report Card No. 1, June 2000; Florence: UNICEF Innocenti Research Centre.
3. Figures – per 10,000 aged 0-18: Selwyn J. & Sturgess W. *International Overview of Adoption: Policy and Practice:* University of Bristol, April 2000; Thoburn J. (2000) *A Comparative Study of Adoption,* University of East Anglia.
4. PIU (2000) *Prime Minister's Review of Adoption,* London: HMSO.
5. For further comments on UK figures see also Department of Work & Pensions (2003).

Table 4.2: Additional Data on the UK and Five other Countries

Country	*Teen births 1998*[1]	*Child Maltreatment*[2]	*Government Expenditure: % of GDP – 2000*[3]	*Inequalities 2001-2*[4]
Australia	18.4	0.8	36.0	0.305
Sweden	6.5	0.8	57.4	0.230
Denmark	8.1	0.8	54.8	0.217
Netherlands	6.3	0.6	45.3	0.255
UK	30.8	0.9	37.0	0.324
USA	52.1	2.4	33.6	0.344

Sources: 1. UNICEF Innocenti Report Card 3, 2001.
2. UNICEF Innocenti Report Card 5, 2003.
3. OECD.
4. The Gini co-efficient is a measure of income inequality developed as a number between 0 and 1, where 0 corresponds with perfect equality (where everyone has the same income) and 1 corresponds with perfect inequality (where one person has all the income, and everyone else has zero income). Source = Institute for Fiscal Studies 2001.

Child Poverty had increased during the long period of Conservative Government in 1980s and 1990s, and when New Labour was elected in 1997 one of its first acts was to pledge to end child poverty by 2020. It is hard to judge progress but recent work by Jonathan Bradshaw (DWP, 2003) indicates that seven years later things are getting better and that the UK now offers a better level of financial support to families than most other countries.

What is certain is that the elimination of child poverty must be central to any strategy of children's rights if those rights are to have any meaning in terms of the quality of life for children.

Lack of Representation for Children

Participation is one of the guiding principles of the Convention, as well as one of its basic challenges. Article 12 states that children *"have the right to participate in decision-making processes that may be relevant in their lives and to influence decisions taken in their regard – within the family, the school or the community."* The principle affirms that children are full-fledged persons who have the right to express their views in all matters affecting them and requires that those views be heard and given due weight in accordance with the child's age and maturity. It recognizes the potential of children to enrich decision-making processes, to share perspectives and to participate as citizens and actors of change. Adults are therefore expected to create spaces and promote processes designed to enable and empower children to express views, to be consulted and to influence decisions. Over the years, this general principle has taken on greater importance and has been recognised as vital in fully implementing and upholding children's rights.

The Committee acknowledged the efforts of the UK to enable children and young people to express their views freely, and for their views to be taken into account in the development of policies and services, but felt that participation initiatives were still on an *ad hoc* basis and recommended that the UK take steps to promote, facilitate and monitor systematic and meaningful participation of all groups of children in society.

But this is no easy challenge and we have far to go. School students outside of Scotland are not given any legal rights to participate in key decisions, including whether they are excluded. Often we make mistakes in encouraging participation:

> *"Too often children are expected to fit into adult ways of participating when what is needed is institutional and organisational change that encourages and facilitates children's voices"* (Prout 2003).

> *"Participation is serious...it's real and it's not consultation. Consultation means adults ask children, but children decide. Participation means children are actively involved in issues that affect their lives"* (Aynsley Green, quoted in Brooks 2005).

A special issue of the journal, *Adoption & Fostering* Spring 2005 on "Listening to Children" has a number of interesting articles on promoting children's rights in the field of child welfare (Cairns & Brannen, 2005; Clark & Statham 2005).

Corporal Punishment

> *"Children have the same basic human right as adults to be protected from any form of violence yet the laws of most countries extend far greater protection against being hit or humiliated to adults than to children"* (Penelope Leach (2001).

Leach goes on to argue that *"smacking, spanking, beating and any other physical punishments breach rights to respect for human dignity and physical integrity"* and that the special defences in state laws that protect parents, teachers and carers who do violence to children in the name of discipline breach the right to equal protection under the law.

The UN Convention on the Rights of the Child is the first international human rights instrument to expressly address this issue. Article 19 requires States Parties to take *"...all appropriate legislative, administrative, social and educational measures to protect the child from all forms of physical or mental violence, injury or abuse, neglect or negligent treatment, maltreatment or exploitation, including sexual abuse, while in the care of parent(s), legal guardian(s) or any other person who has the care of the child"*. The UN *Committee on the Rights of the Child* has made it clear that the legal and social acceptance of corporal punishment of children, whether in their homes or in institutions, is not compatible with the Convention. The Committee recommends prohibition of all corporal punishment, together with campaigns to raise awareness of its negative effects and to encourage the development of positive, non-violent child-rearing and educational practices.

14 European states and Israel have prohibited all corporal punishment of children:[1]

Supreme Court judgments in Italy and Portugal also prohibit all corporal punishment of children. This means that more than a third (16 out of 46) member states of the Council of Europe now give children equal protection from assault. However, the vast majority of member states of the United Nations allow at least parents to use it—see Table 4.3 below for examples.

Table 4.3: Prohibition of Corporal Punishment in Selected States

Country	*Prohibited in the Home*	*Prohibited in Schools*	*Prohibited in Penal Systems*
Afghanistan	No	No	No
Bulgaria	Yes	Yes	Yes
China	No	Yes	Yes
El Salvador	No	No	Yes
Ethiopia	No	Yes	No
India	No	No	No
Israel	Yes	Yes	Yes
New Zealand	No	Yes	Yes
Norway	Yes	Yes	Yes
Oman	No	Yes	No
South Korea	No	No	Yes
United Kingdom	No	Yes	Yes
United States	No	No	No

Source: http://www.endcorporalpunishment.org[1]

Corporal Punishment in the UK

In the UK corporal punishment is no longer allowed in schools, children's homes or by child-minders but "reasonable chastisement" by parents is permitted. Likewise in New Zealand parents are allowed to use "reasonable force" when disciplining children. But increasingly both countries are seen as failing children in this respect, as more and more Western European countries make it illegal for parents to use physical force in disciplining their children.

In its 2002 report, the Committee on Children's Right was critical of the UK position, arguing that the lack of implementation of *CRC* and lack of respect for children's rights was exemplified by the retention in domestic legislation of the 'reasonable chastisement' defence which allows parents to use physical violence against their children. Despite the Committee's 1995 recommendation that corporal punishment be prohibited, and the ruling by the European Court of Human Rights that the defence of reasonable chastisement violated Article 3 *European Convention on Human Rights,* the Government had not taken any action to prohibit corporal punishment in the family, or to remove the defence of reasonable chastisement. The Committee recommended that the UK "urgently adopt legislation that removes the defence of 'reasonable chastisement', prohibit all corporal punishment in the family, and promote non-violent forms of discipline and respect for children's equal right to human dignity and physical integrity". The Committee recognised that UK public opinion was currently against a ban on corporal punishment because it is believed that it would be unenforceable, would violate parent's rights and would criminalise parents for smacking their children, but emphasised that public opinion did not override the UK's obligation to implement and protect children's rights. Subsequent attempts by private members' bills to remove the clause have failed.

Corporal Punishment in Korea

The UN Committee on the Rights of the Child has also raised the issue of corporal punishment in Korea in its two reports in 1996 and 2003. In a "supplementary report" to Korea's second periodic report on the implementation of the UNCRC, the Korean Civil Rights Group (2002) notes that children are regularly subjected to corporal punishment at school and in the home—a government report in 2000 found that over half the schools surveyed allowed corporal punishment and that 7 out of 10 teachers had administered it. However, as in the UK, it is the right of the parent to use physical punishment as a means of discipline that is most strongly defended.

Leach (2001) reports that a survey by the Child Protection Association found that 97 per cent of children had been physically punished, many very severely. Certainly an excess use of physical chastisement by some parents has received much publicity outside Korea, particularly the case of a Korean living in Canada (Fong 2005), where a father pleaded guilty to assault with a weapon and assault causing grievous bodily harm, after reportedly hitting his 16-year old son more than 100 times. In his defence he said that caning was "traditional Korean culture" and that parents buy a "cane of love".

The supplementary report concludes that "banning corporal punishment in homes can develop only through banning corporal punishment in public schools", adding that "Banning corporal punishment has to be developed not from the opinions of adults who accept it as natural but from the perspective of protecting the human dignity of children" (Korean Civil Society Groups, 2002, p. 16).

Conclusion

I shall end this section with a quote from Mary Robinson speaking at the launch of a global initiative to end corporal punishment.

> *"The recourse to physical punishment by adults reflects a denial of the recognition, by the Convention on the Rights of the Child, of the child as a subject of human rights. If we want to remain faithful to the spirit of the Convention, strongly based on the dignity of the child as a full-fledged bearer of rights, then any act of violence against him or her must be banned, in accordance with articles 19 and 28.2."*
>
> **Mary Robinson**, Former United Nations High Commissioner for Human Rights

Juvenile Justice

There is a long history in the UK of attempts to reform the juvenile justice system – with a constant tension between an approach that held the child's interests at the centre and the concerns of the wider public about the threat of youth – manifested on many occasions by what has been called "moral panics"(see Selman, 2003).

Although some of our old punitive establishments like the "approved schools" have been abolished there are constant calls for new ones and for a "short, sharp, shock" – with many people arguing that we should follow the US example of a "boot camp". Just as the UK has the highest adult prison population in Europe, it also has the highest number of children in detention of any Western European country. There has also been much concern recently about the suicide of young people remanded in adult prisons. A further problem is arising over was the treatment, and in particular the detention, of refugees and asylum seekers under the age of 18 (Amnesty International, 2002).

The Committee on the Rights of the Child criticised the UK for the lack of a child-centred and rights-based approach to the juvenile justice system and the punitive attitude currently prevailing. In its 1995 Report the Committee had recommended that the UK's low age of criminal responsibility (14 years) should be raised and the Committee noted that, not only had the age not been raised, but that it had effectively been lowered to 10 (8 in Scotland).

For those of you particularly interested in the rights of children in the Juvenile and Criminal Justice systems, I would commend Rosemary Sarri's paper presented at last year's conference which looks in detail at the situation in the United States (Sarri, 2004, pp. 11-18).

ASBOs (Anti-Social Behaviour Orders)

Anti-Social Behaviour Orders were a key part of the Crime and Disorder Act, 1998 and came into force on 1 April, 1999. Since modified, by the Police Reform Act, 2002 and the Anti-Social Behaviour Act, 2003, orders ban individuals from entering certain areas or carrying out specific acts for a minimum period of two years. Anti-social behaviour is defined as:

> *"Behaviour which causes or is likely to cause harassment, alarm or distress to one or more people not in the same household as the perpetrator."*

They are "civil" orders and are not designed as punishment, but often seem to be used as such. They also depend on local people collecting evidence, which has been another source of tension. Critics argue that ASBOs criminalise non-criminal behaviour. Home Office guidelines for the Crime & Disorder Act stated that *"ASBOs will be used mainly against adults"*, but in practice they are increasingly used on children as young as ten, who are subsequently "named and shamed".

In a recent highly publicised case in July of this year a 15-year old boy won a landmark High Court challenge to the legality of curfew zones used by Richmond Council to reduce anti-social behaviour. Unaccompanied under-16s found in the zones, introduced under the 2003 Anti-Social Behaviour Act, could be held and escorted home, whether badly behaved or not. The Children's Commissioner for England was criticized for not supporting the appeal, which was backed by the Civil Rights Group Liberty.

The teenager argued that the zones breached his rights under the European Convention on Human Rights. The High Court ruled that the law did not give police the power of arrest and officers could not force a young person to go with them. Giving judgement, Lord Justice Brooks said: "*.... All of us have the right to walk the streets without interference from police constables...unless they possess common law or statutory powers to stop us.*"

The Northern Ireland Commissioner for Children & Young People was refused a judicial review of the introduction ASBOs in June 2004, but a High Court Judge in Northern Ireland has now set a date in September 2005 for a full court hearing regarding Anti-Social Behaviour Orders (ASBOs), based on allegations that the Northern Ireland Office overlooked equality duties in its introduction of the legislation.

Looked after Children in the UK

The UK has one of the highest rates of children in public care of all Western European countries (Selman & Mason 2005: see Table 4.1) and the evidence from research shows that they are a particularly disadvantaged group, drawn disproportionately from families of lower socio-economic background. Many of the issues raised already apply to this group. Not only do they come from a poor background but after leaving care they are more likely to leave school early (with the young women more likely to become teenage mothers and the young men to become offenders), less likely to get a job and seem destined to a future life of poverty and homelessness. Similar findings emerge in a study of young Swedes (Hjern *et al.* 2004) which showed a much increased risk of suicide in child welfare recipients, and especially a sub-group defined as in long-term foster care, who were found to be also at risk of other "avoidable deaths" (e.g. homicide; deaths related to substance and alcohol misuse). One factor was likely to be the foster children's background – 41 per cent had parents who had been admitted to hospital for alcohol or substance misuse or psychiatric disorder. However, a key aspect of the findings was that such deaths were most likely to occur over the age of 18 "highlighting the difference of being a permanent and transitory members of a substitute family". American studies have also identified deaths in "looked after" children as restricted to time after care (Barth 1998; Thomson, 1995).

These findings are an indictment of society's ability to care for children deprived of a normal family life and have led the UK, following in the steps of the US, to seek adoptive families for children in long-term care (Selman & Mason, 2005). This is being encouraged through adoption allowances to those who take a "looked after" child, especially one with special needs and by the establishment of an "adoption register" to match hard to place children with adoptive parents.

The number of children placed for adoption from care in England has risen from 1,900 in 1997 to 3,700 in 2004 (an increase of over 80%), but the impact has been lessened by a rise in the total number of looked after children, so that the proportion adopted has risen by only 57 per cent from 3.7 to 5.8 (see Table 4.4 below).

Table 4.4: Looked after Children in England 1997-2004

Year	*Total in Care*	*Rate per 10,000 Aged 0-18*	*Number Fostered*	*Number Placed for Adoption*	*% of Looked After Children*
1997	51,200	47	33,500	1,900	3.7
1999	55,500	50	36,200	2,200	4.0
2001	58,900	53	38,300	3,100	5.3
2003	60,800	55	41,000	3,500	5.8
2004	61,100	55	41,600	3,700	6.1

Source: DfES/DH Statistics for *Children Looked after in England* for year ending 31st March.

Despite over 16,000 children leaving care to join adopted families between 1999 and 2003 the total number of looked after children has risen by over 5,000. The impact of adoption in terms of securing a permanent future for children is limited without a parallel drive to reduce the numbers entering care.

The policy has also raised another question about women's rights as a majority of the children are placed for adoption without the consent of their parents, a practice not found in most other countries in mainland Europe, where as a consequence adoption is now very rare. Studies of the parents who lose their children in this way through what we call "contested" adoptions indicate that the birth parents subsequently receive very little support (Mason & Selman, 1997).

Children's Rights in Inter-country Adoption

The United Kingdom (population 59,250,000 in 2003) has the lowest number of inter-country adoption (per 1,000 population) of all major receiving States, a total of only 300 in 2003, compared to 3,995 in France which has a similar population size (60,144,000 in 2003) – see Selman (2002 and 2005) and Table 4.5 below:

Table 4.5: Number of Inter-country Adoptions in Receiving States 1998-2003—by Rank in 1998

Country	*1998*	*1999*	*2000*	*2001*	*2002*	*2003*
US	15,774	16,363	17,718	19,237	20,099	21,616
France	3,777	3,597	2,971	3,094	3,551	3,995
Italy	2,233	2,177	346*	2,225	2,225	2,772
Canada	2,222	2,019	1,866	1,874	1,891	2,181
Spain	1,487	2,006	3,062	3,428	3,625	3,951
Sweden	928	1,019	981	1,044	1,107	1,046
Germany	922	977	854	798	884	674
Netherlands	825	993	1,193	1,122	1,130	1,154
Switzerland	686	582	478	457	474	366
Norway	643	589	589	713	747	714
Denmark	624	697	716	631	609	522
New Zealand	371	356	290	358	263	278
UK	258	312	351	326	285	300
Total (20 States)	31,720	32,650	32,527	35,903	38,139	40,791

But Britain itself has an earlier experience of sending children far from their homeland to Canada and Australia. These so-called "child migrants" have been returning in the years since, revealing many bad experiences and searching for their families, finding in many cases that their parents had not fully consented to them going away or had been persuaded by care workers that it was in their best interests (Bean & Melville, 1989).

In the same year Korea (population 47,700,000 in 2003) sent 2,287 children for inter-country adoption and is the fourth largest source: the two top countries being China and Russia with much larger populations. In 1988 Korea was the largest supplier of children, sending 8,837. Since the Seoul Olympic Games of 1988 there has been constant talk of reduction and eventual end to ICA, which started in the aftermath of the Korean War. In 1989, the Ministry of Social Affairs proposed a schedule which would have reduced the number of inter-country adoptions to 1,700 by 1995 and raised the number of domestic adoptions to 3,500. However, by 1998 ICAs were still above 2,000 a year and domestic adoptions less than 1,500.

Table 4.6: Inter-country and In-country Adoptions Korea 1958-2003

Year	*Inter-country Adoptions*	*In-country Adoptions*	*Children in Institutions*
1958	930	N/A	51,630
1976	6,597	1,386	39,844
1985	8,837	2,885	25,424
1992	2,045	1,190	21,293
2003	2,287	1,564	18,818
1958-2003	153,386	18,818	

The Committee on the Rights of the Child have raised concerns about the level of inter-country adoption in Korea (Table 4.7) and has called on the government to ratify the 1993 Hague Convention on Protection of Children and Co-operation in Respect of Inter-country Adoption. They have also pointed to the low level of in-country adoption and that. Korea has one of the highest rates of institutionalised children in developed countries (Table 4.6). Likewise, in their supplementary report to Korea's second periodic report on the implementation of the UNCRC, Korean civil rights groups make a strong case for the reform of adoption law and address the problems of institutional care (Korean Civil Society Groups, 2002). They point out that there is no effort to keep adoption abroad as a last resort in line with the principle of subsidiarity enshrined in the 1998 Hague Convention and the UNCRC.

Table 4.7: Inter-country and In-country Adoptions: India and Korea 1989 to 2004

Year	*India Adoptions*		*Korea Adoptions*	
	Inter-country	*In-country*	*Inter-country*	*In-country*
1989	1,213	757	4,191	1,872
1996	990	1,623	2,080	1,229
2000	1,364	1,890	2,360	1,686
2004	1,021	1,707	2,258	1,641
Population 2003	1,065,462,000		47,700,000	
Live Births 2003	25,052,000		562,000	
Ratio (per 1,000 births)	0.044	0.078	4.1	2.8

Source of demographic data: State of the World's Children 2005, NY: UNICEF.

On April 12, 2005 the National Human Rights Commission stated it will recommend to the Prime Minister and the Ministry of Foreign Affairs to withdraw the reservation to article 12 para (a) of the UNCRC; to ratify the Hague Convention; and to revise the current adoption process and strengthen policies to promote domestic over inter-country adoption.

South Korea today is a prosperous country with an high level of education and a low birth rate (Table 4.8), but there is a continuing problem over stigma of unmarried parenthood and in the absence of a comprehensive welfare system, it is impossible for a poor single mother to keep her child (Rahn 2005). Sarri *et al.,* (1998) argue that ICA has discouraged Korea from developing an adequate child welfare programme. There are a growing number of critical accounts of the Korean adoption programme, many written by young people adopted from Korea in the 1970s and 1980s (Hubinette 2004; Kim 2003, 2004).

The Rights of Women, with special reference to Young Unmarried Mothers

> *"The human rights of women and the girl child are an inalienable, integral and indivisible part of universal human rights: the eradication of all forms of gender discrimination are priority objectives for the international community and equal status of women and their human rights should be integrated into the mainstream of UN activity".* —Fourth Conference on Women 1995.

To deal with the rights of women as well as children would require another paper and this one is already in danger of becoming too long, but I would like to look at just one area where the rights of women and children become one. The area is that of unmarried teenage (under 18 years old) mothers, who are themselves "children" in the definition of the UNCRC and much UK legislation but find themselves with the responsibility for their own much younger children.

History of Unmarried Mothers in Britain

The story of the treatment of young single mothers in the UK is a sad one in which they and their children have been the subject of much hostility and neglect. In the 19th century an unmarried mother and her child would usually end up in the dreaded workhouse or surrender their child to "baby farmers", who often let them die. The number of young single mothers increased after both World Wars and it was this increase in "illegitimacy" that influenced the introduction of adoption legislation in England and Wales in 1926, but the biggest rise came in the 1960s when the number of extra-marital pregnancies rose every year. Many of these ended as legitimate births following a "shot-gun marriage" but more than one in five of those young women who did not marry gave their child up for adoption. At that time there was considerable stigma attached to unmarried parenthood and little government support so that many women ended up in "mother and baby" homes where they were often badly treated and pressured to "do the right thing" by relinquishing their baby for adoption.

Teenage birth rates peaked in the 1960s but then began to fall in the 1970s following the introduction of the 1967 Abortion Act and the provision of free oral contraception on the NHS (Selman, 1996). The number of babies offered for adoption also fell as the stigma attached to single parenthood lessened—as a consequence the number of single parent families increased. Fewer women felt the need to "get married" and many lived with their baby's father. In the 1980s, when teenage pregnancy rates were continuing to fall in most other European countries, such as Sweden, France and the Netherlands, the rate in the UK and the USA rose—a fact which has been linked to the growing inequalities during the Reagan and Thatcher governments. During this time teenage mothers were subject to much hostility (Selman, 2003), partly because they were seen as a welfare burden.

When the New Labour government was elected in 1997 one of its first act was to establish a Social Exclusion Unit and at an early stage they were asked to look at the issue of teenage pregnancy. Their subsequent report (SEU, 1999) set targets to halve the number of teenage pregnancies by 2010, but a second goal was "getting more teenage parents into education, training or employment to reduce their risk of long term social exclusion". With colleagues at the Universities of Bristol and Newcastle, I have been researching the outcomes of this strategy and we have just produced our final report, which builds on an earlier study on the same topic (Hosie and Dawson, 2005; Selman *et al.*, 2001). One of our key findings was that many of the school-age mothers had been poor attenders long before their pregnancy so that the original aim of reintegrating them into mainstream schooling proved difficult. However the introduction of specialist "Re-integration" Officers and the availability of specialised educational units where the young women could place their young babies in an on-site nursery led to some remarkable changes with many of those young women with the worst attendance records improving to the extent that they took and passed several GCSEs (Hosie & Selman, 2001; 2003). Despite the evidence that these young women were not hopeless cases, hostility to young single mothers continues and the support policies have been attacked as encouraging girls to get pregnant!

Teenage mothers continue to have fewer rights than their older counterparts – lower welfare payments (or none if she is under 16); no right to a council house; and an expectation that they attend school or work. However her rights as a "child" are also curtailed—these being seen as now transferred to her own "unfortunate" offspring and the mothers we interviewed lived in constant fear that their baby would be taken away from them.

Unmarried Mothers and their Children in Korea

The situation of single mothers in Korea today seems to have many similarities to the UK in the 1960s. In an article in the *Korea Times,* Rahn (2005) discusses the situation of unmarried mothers for whom "government support remains inadequate... forcing many to give up their babies for adoption." This continuing lack of support for single parents was criticised by the Committee on the Rights of the Child in its 2003 report. Government support for these women remains inadequate and society often treats them as second-class citizens, forcing many to give up their babies for adoption.

Birth Mothers – the Hidden Dimension

The unmarried mothers who relinquish their children for adoption— whether in-country or inter-country – have few rights. It has taken us a long time to recognise the pain experienced by birth parents in the UK and to acknowledge how little choice many have had in their "decision" to relinquish a child. In England the Adoption and Children Act, 2002 gives new rights to birth relatives to gain information about the fate of the children they relinquished and make contact if the adopted person agrees. The Adoption and Children Act, 2002 gives new rights to birth relatives to gain information about the fate of the children they relinquished and make contact if the adopted person agrees. But little attention has been paid to the situation of the birth parents in inter-country adoption—partly due to what Gailey (2000) has called the "orphan myth" – and there is need for more exploration of the views of mothers in sending countries such as Korea or China (Haworth & Selman, 2005; Johnson, 2004).

Conclusion

In the UK today, children's rights are accepted, but not fully implemented. We have made some important moves forward in recent years with the appointment of Children's Commissioners in all four component countries and the establishment of a Minister for Children and new Children's Trusts. The Adoption and Children Act, 2002 holds out much promise for a better deal for looked after children.

But there continue to be many issues to be addressed— continuing child poverty; the use of corporal punishment in the family; the lack of rights for unaccompanied asylum seekers; the lack of children's representation in education. In some of these areas a central problem is the apparent clash between the rights of children and the rights of parents (Henricson & Bainham, 2005a and b). In child care and adoption the best interests of the child are now "paramount", but in areas such as education and the defence of "reasonable chastisement", the rights of parents seem to predominate and in the area of criminal justice the needs of adult "society" override some basic rights for young people. Henricson & Bainham, (2005a) argue that there is a need to integrate a rights approach into government thinking and practice, because,

> *"Rights provide a framework and point of reference for handling competing interests. They make individual and collective entitlement transparent and engender an expectation that interests will be balanced."*

I want to end with another quotation from Carol Bellamy made 10 years after the Convention came into operation. Although I have concentrated on some rather specific areas where the UK has failings, the important thing is to retain a vision of why we believe in the importance of progressing children's rights in every country—to achieve, as Bellamy says—a world where the best interests of the child always comes first.

> *"It is not too much to imagine a world where every child's right to health, good nutrition and quality education, especially for girls, is championed by families, by communities and by governments; a world where safe motherhood, gender equality and adequate water and sanitation are available to all—where millions of children don't fall victim to preventable ailments and diseases like polio are finally eradicated; a world where special protection is assured for the most disadvantaged and disabled of our children—including those caught up in armed conflict, natural disasters, extreme poverty and all forms of violence; a world where child-rearing and nurturing is an ongoing, comprehensive process and where the right of adolescents to health and development is given the close attention it deserves. A world, in short, where the best interests of children always come first."*

Carol Bellamy, UNICEF, Executive Director

Note: The Paper was presented in a conference on the Rights of the Child, Seoul, South Korea, August 27th, 2005.

Note

1. Austria (1989); Croatia (1999); Cyprus (1994); Denmark (1997); Finland (1983); Germany (2000); Israel (2000); Latvia (1998); Norway (1987); Sweden (1979); Iceland (2003), Hungary (2004), Romania (2004) and Ukraine (2004).

References

Amnesty International (2002), *UK: The Committee on the Rights of the Child issues its Concluding Observations on the UK's implementation of the Convention on the Rights of the Child,* London: Amnesty International.

Barth, R.D.B. (1998), "Death rates among California's foster care and former foster care populations", *Children and Youth Services Review* 20: 577-604.

Batty, D. (2004), "Concern over 'toothless' children's champion", Society Guardian, November 10, 2004—available at: http://society.guardian.co.uk.html

Bean, P. & Melville, J. (1989), *Lost Children of the Empire.* London: Unwin Hyman.

Brooks, L. (2005), "Balance of power; interview with new children's commissioner for England" *Society Guardian* 27.07.05, pp. 6-7.

Cairns, L. & Brannen, M. (2005), "Promoting the human rights of children and young people: the 'Investing in Children' experience. *Adoption & Fostering* 29-1, pp. 78-87.

Clark, A. & Statham, J. (2005), "Listening to young children: experts in their own lives" *Adoption & Fostering* 29-1, pp. 45-52.

Department of Work & Pensions (2003), *Measuring Child Poverty*: London: DWP Fong P (2005) "A Korean father's lesson on raising cane", Globe & Mail, Canada, March 12, 2005.

Gailey, C. (2000), "Race, Class and Gender in Inter-country Adoption in the USA" in P. Selman (ed.) *Inter-country Adoption; Developments trends and perspectives,* London: British Agencies for Adoption & Fostering.

Harvey, R. (2002), "The UK before the UN Committee on the Rights of the Child", *Child Right,* October Issue No. 190.

Haworth, G. & Selman, P. (2005), "Post-adoption support and services in inter-country adoption", Paper presented at 3rd International Conference of Adoptive Families of Filippino Children, Manila, August 15-16, 2005.

Henricson, C. & Bainham, A. (2005a), *The Child and Family Policy Divide: Tensions, Convergence and Rights,* York: Joseph Rowntree Foundation.

Henricson, C. & Bainham, A. (2005b), "Human rights obligations and policy supporting children and families", Joseph Rowntree *Findings.*

Hjern, A., Vinnerljung, B. & Lindbald, F. (2004), "Avoidable mortality among child welfare recipients and inter-country adoptees; a national cohort study", *Journal of Epidemiology and Community Health,* 58, 412-417.

Hosie, A. & Dawson, N. (2005), with Meadows S., Selman P. & Speak, S. *The Education of Pregnant Young Women and Young Mothers in England,* final report to the Teenage Pregnancy Unit; Universities of Bristol & Newcastle upon Tyne.

Hosie, A. & Dawson, N. (2005), with Meadows, S., Selman, P. & Speak, S. *The Education of Pregnant Young Women and Young Mothers in England,* final report to the Teenage Pregnancy Unit.

Hosie, A. & Selman, P. (2001), *Teenage Pregnancy in Young Women of School age: an exploration of disengagement from the education system,* paper presented at 34th Annual Conference of the Social Policy Association Annual Conference, Queen's University, Belfast.

Hosie, A. & Selman, P. (2003), *The Education of School Age Mothers: social exclusion, reintegration and the need for childcare,* Paper presented at 36th Annual Conference of the Social Policy Association, Teesside University, July 15-17.

Hubinette, T. (2004), "Adopted Koreans and the development of identity in the 'third space'" *Adoption & Fostering,* 28-1, pp. 16-24.

Johnson, K.A. (2004), *Wanting a Daughter, Needing a Son: Abandonment, Adoption, and Orphanage Care in China,* St. Paul, Minnesota: Yeong & Yeong Book Company.

Kim, E. (2003), "Wedding Citizenship and Culture: Korean Adoptees and the Global Family of Korea" *Social Text,* 21-1, Spring 2003.

Kim, E. (2004), "Gathering 'Roots' and Making History in the Korean Adoptee Community" in M. Checker and M. Fishman (eds.) *Local Actions: Cultural Activism, Power and Public Life,* Columbia University Press.

Korean Civil Society Groups, (2002), *Supplementary Report to the Republic of Korea's Second Periodic Report on the Implementation of the Convention on the Rights of the Child.*

Leach, P. (1999), *The Physical Punishment of Children,* London: NSPCC.

Leach, P. (2001), *Corporal punishment at home: an issue for Children's Rights.* Paper presented at the 3rd World Congress on Family law and the Rights of the Child, Bath, England, 20-22 September http://www.lawrights.asn.au/docs/leach2001.pdf.

Mason, K. & Selman, P. (1997), "Birth parents' experiences of contested adoption", *Adoption & Fostering,* 21-1, pp. 21-28, (Reprinted in M. Hill and M. Shaw, *Signposts in Adoption,* London: BAAF, 1998, pp. 273-287).

Prout, A. (2003), "Participation, policy and the changing conditions of childhood", paper presented at ESRC seminar, Glasgow.

Rahn, K. (2005), "Single Mothers Face Discrimination", *The Korea Times.*

Sarri, R., Bail, Y. & Bombyk, M. (1998), "Goal Displacement and Dependency in South Korean-United States Inter-country Adoption" *Children & Youth Services Review,* Vol. 20, pp. 87-114.

Sarri, R. (2004), *Human Rights of Children and Youth: Myths and Realities,* paper presented at conference in Seoul, August 2004.

Selman, P. (1996), "Teenage Motherhood Then and Now: a comparison of the pattern and outcome of teenage pregnancy in England & Wales in the 1960s and 1980s" In J. Millar and H. Jones (eds.), *The Politics of the Family,* London: Avebury, pp. 103-128.

Selman, P. ed. (2000), *Inter-country Adoption; Developments trends and perspectives,* London: British Agencies for Adoption & Fostering, 2000.

Selman, P. (2003), "Scapegoating and Moral Panics: Teenage Pregnancy in Britain and the United States" In S. Cunningham-Burley & L. Jamieson (eds.), *Families and the State: Changing Relationships,* Basingstoke: Palgrave.

Selman, P. (2004), "Adoption—a cure for (too) many ills?" in F. Bowie (ed.) *Cross Cultural Approaches to Adoption,* London: Routledge.

Selman, P., Richardson, D., Hosie, A. & Speak, S. (2001), *Monitoring of the DfES Standards Fund, Teenage Pregnancy Grant,* Final Report to DfES.

Selman, P. (2002), "Inter-country Adoption in the new millennium: the silent migration revisited", *Population Research & Policy Review,* 21.

Selman, P. (2005), *The Quiet Migration in the New Millenium: trends in inter-country adoption 1998-2003,* Paper to be presented at the 8th Global Consultation on Child Welfare, Manila, Philippines, August 10-12.

Selman, P. & Mason, K. (2005), *Alternatives to Adoption for Looked after Children,* report to Adoption Law review Group of Scottish Executive, January 2005; published as Annex C to Better Choices for Our Children, Report to Scottish Executive on Phase II of the Adoption Policy Review.

Thompson, A.H. & Newman, S. (1995), "Mortality in a child welfare population; implications for policy", *Child Welfare,* Vol. 24, 843-57.

Ward, L. (2005), "Two-way mirror", *The Guardian,* 20th October.

Part II

ADOPTION: SOME GLOBAL ISSUES

5

Open Adoption

An Innovative Practice Option

PAUL SACHDEV

In his book, *Shame,* Salmon Rushdie suggests that history is best understood as a struggle between "the epicure" and "the puritan". (Cited in Gritter, 1997:265). This description certainly fits the current adoption scene. The pendulum has swung dramatically from the 'don't ask/don't tell' nature of the past practice to (the emerging approach that involves) full disclosure with ongoing contact. During the past 15 years, the shift from the traditional practice characterized by restraint or secrecy towards (almost unimpeded) permission for openness has been so fast that the changes are dizzying even the most active participants, especially adoptive parents and those considering adoption. The concept of open adoption is understood and practiced differently by different agencies. Some agencies provide a limited degree of openness, while others practice this model more liberally. In one study by McRoy (1991), the wide variations in terminology was evident where thirty different interpretations of openness and contact were required to accurately identify the variety of possible arrangements. Most experts agree that openness in adoption is a continuum of information sharing options between the birth and adoptive families that range from *confidential* adoptions in which non-identifying information is shared indirectly at the placement or shortly thereafter, to *mediated or semi-open* adoptions in which non-identifying information via letters, pictures or gifts is shared between parties through agency personnel, to *fully disclosed* adoptions which involve birth parents choosing adoptive parents from pre-selected non-identifying files, and having ongoing personal contact with them and the child. The frequency and the form of contact (letters or visitations), however, are mutually determined by the parties involved in each particular case (Silber and Doner 1989; Rappaport 1992). These adoptive arrangements are subject to change over time (Brodzinsky *et al.*, 1998; Grotevant and McRoy 1998; Mendenhall *et al.*, 2004; Miall & March 2005). In a more broadened definition of open adoption the birth family is treated like an extended family or relatives like other relatives within the adoptive family of the child. Whatever the definition of the concept, adoptive parents retain legal rights to the child and they are the child's real parents.

Forces Contributing to Change

Several forces such as agencies dissatisfaction with closed adoption, recognition of adoptees' 'genealogical bewilderment,' the search movement, the growing pressure for full information about adoptees and birth families and recognition of blood ties converged to transform the traditional practice. The cumulative research showed that the belief system behind confidential adoptions that took the "happily-ever-after" stance proved wrong, especially for adoptees and birth mothers (Fravel *et al.*, 2000; Sachdev 1989: 498). The predominant factor that provided as 'jet fuel' for the openness movement was the limited availability of newborn babies due to the combined effects of greater acceptance of contraception, legal abortion and single parenthood. This led to the steep rise in demand for newborn giving birth mothers a sense of power to pick new parents for their babies and shape their adoption arrangements. Regardless of how agencies felt about openness, many moved to offer birth mothers this as an option in order to remain competitive especially with independent adoption agencies. Coupled with these factors was the belief and experience of agency staff regarding the benefits of open adoption for triad members that drove many agencies to change their practices. Currently, this belief drives many openness practices as agencies use their influence in "encouraging," preparing and educating triad members about openness (Henny *et al.*, 2003; Sobol *et al.*, 2000). Some agency staff support open adoption with almost missionary zeal and proudly profess their bias as the authors of one of the popular books : *Dear Birthmother* states in the introduction: "*There have been no long-term psychological studies, no clinical investigations to prove us right, yet we are today committed advocates of a new approach to adoption"*, Silber & Speedlin (1982:5). In the words of Adam Pertman, "despite the uncertainty, the confluence of all these events has created a heady, hopeful time for birth parents and adoptees and confusing one for adoptive parents........" (p. 131). Henney, McRoy and Grotevant (2003) interviewed professional staff from 31 private agencies in 15 states to find out the relative preference for the type of openness by members of the triad. Interestingly, contrary to the belief that birth mothers would more likely prefer fully open adoption, a little more than half (57%) of them chose fully disclosed adoption with contact as their first choice, while 43 per cent chose agency-mediated adoption. Adoptive parents, generally, felt threatened by open records as overwhelmingly—60 per cent preferred mediated adoption; only one quarter chose fully open adoption and 15 per cent chose closed adoption. A British study by Lowe *et al.*, (1999) found among 226 adoptive families that adoptive parents' experience was in many instances, "notably", "poignant". According to Logan and Smith (2005) adoptive parents "tolerate" openness because they fear that failure to adhere to the written terms could jeopardize their adoptions. (p. 47). Sachdev (1989) in a randomly selected sample of 300 adoptive parents, birth mothers and adult adoptees, examined their attitudes towards unsealing of adoption records. The author found that adoptive parents were commonly apprehensive and least favourable towards the disclosure policy (see also, Sachdev 1992; 1992b). That birth mothers do not necessarily desire a fully open adoption arrangement with direct contact, was also reported by Cushin *et al.*, (1997) in a study of 171 American birth mothers who were followed up at four years post-relinquishment. The authors reported that "a large majority" of the sample birth mothers chose moderate or semi-open arrangements, i.e. receiving letters or pictures; "only 19 per cent " wanted to have direct contact with the adopted child and "about half" of them would have liked to meet the adoptive couple before relinquishing the child (p.16).

Lack of Agreement

Growing number of children are being placed in some form of open arrangement as standard practice, yet there is no universal agreement regarding which type of adoption arrangement best serves the interests of the adopted child, the birth parents, or the adoptive parents (Brodzinsky *et al.*, 1998; Logan & Smith 2005; Mendenhall *et al.*, 2004; Rosenberg 1998; Siegal 2003). In the words of Grotevant and McRoy (1998) the views about open adoption have "polarized the adoption community" (p. 1). Open adoption has both avid supporters and critics who continue to offer conflicting evidence about whether openness facilitates or impedes birth mother's grieving the loss of child, enhances or obstructs adoptees' identity formation, promotes or inhibits the bonding between the child and the adoptive parents, diminishes or enhances the adoptive parents' sense of entitlement and insecurity (Austin 1979; Derdeyn 1979; Kraft *et al.*, 1985; Reitz & Watson 1992; Siegel 2003; Logan & Smith 2005; Zeilinger 1979).

The proponents of open adoption assert that unlike traditional closed adoption, the open process helps birth mother gain self-esteem and grieve for the child by being actively involved in making adoption plan and thus accepting the reality of the loss. Also, she has a real peace of mind when she has knowledge of child's well-being and the opportunity for answers and information over the years. It facilitates adoptive parents coming to terms with their infertility through acknowledgement of the existence of the child's birth parents. Also, "permission" given to adoptive parents by birth relatives to be the child's real parents helps them accept the child as their own; they no longer have to have a fantasy that they had given birth to this child (Berry 1991, 1993; Chapman *et al.*, 1986, 1987a, 1987b; Rappaport 1992; Silber & Dorner 1990). Continued contact with the birth parents helps the adoptive parents acknowledge the difference between parenting by adoption and parenting a child hy birth, communicate more actively with the adopted child regarding adoption issues, show empathy for the birth parents and recognize the adopted child's need for connection to his/her birth family (Kirk 1964, 1981; Grotevant *et al.*, 1994; Silverstein & Demick 1994). These authors also claim that adoptive parents involved with open adoption develop understanding and trust of the birth parent, and feel reassured that birth mother has no intention of attempting to reclaim the child. They are better prepared to accept the prospect of their child searching someday, and these attitudes facilitate adoptive parents' feelings of entitlement to their child. Claims are also made for adoptees who benefit from open adoption, not usually available in traditional closed adoption. Having knowledge of their biological heritage allows adoptees to resolve identity issues and helps dissolve their normal developmental crisis. Open adoption forces adoption professionals to closely examine their reluctance to allow members of the triangle to make their own decisions which means relinquishment of their power and control over options that are permitted by social workers under the system of closed adoptions (Caplan 1990; Groth *et al.*, 1987; Lindsay 1987).

Critics of open adoption point out that this approach raises a few serious concerns. First, continued contact between adoptive parents, and the birth parent can complicate the responsibilities and rights of both, may undermine the adoptive parents' feelings of entitlement to the child and lead to confusion about the role that each is to play. Presence of the birth mother could make adoptive parents jealous of her fertility and serve as a painful reminder of their inability for not having given birth to this child. Second, access to the adoptive family by the child's "other mother" may confuse the child as to who is his/her "true" parent—the one who has the biological ties or the one who is involved in the day-to-day parenting (Reitz & Watson 1992). Third, in the new kinship network linking together the adopted child's two families, the members will be unsure where to draw the boundaries and what is expected of the new family system. Fourth, the contract or agreement about ongoing contact is not legally enforceable, and, therefore, its compliance depends on the good faith of those involved. Besides, an agreement is drawn based on conjecture and sincere promises, and is open to violation of its terms by either party because the circumstances, needs, or attitudes of the parties might change over time. Such situations are potentially fraught with the possibilities of tensions in the mutual relationship and may lead to adversarial procedures. The child is particularly vulnerable to such changes and may blame him/herself for the problems. It may prove detrimental to the child if the contact is not available when he/she is at the stage that such contact is highly crucial for his/her developmental needs. Fifth, continued contact by the child's birth parent may make adoptive parents feel that someone is looking over their shoulder, which may interfere with the process of attachment to the adopted child. The visits may precipitate ambivalence in the birth mother about her decision to surrender parenting of her child. As well, ongoing contact with the child would serve as a constant reminder of the child's existence and fuels fantasies of some day reuniting with him/her and thus could impede the birth mother's grieving process. Craft *et al.* (1985,1986) argue that the young adolescent mother is emotionally or cognitively not capable of assessing the consequences of a decision whether or not to maintain contact with the child. Sixth, open adoption also creates a dilemma for the adoption agency whether it should continue or cease its involvement after the adoption has been legally consummated. The finalisation of adoption involves a guarantee that adoptive parents have the right to parenting without outside interference.

Past Research

Earlier studies were largely anecdotal guided by personal beliefs and impressions. Although these authors address some of the psychological issues involved and provide increased awareness of the variety of adoptive experience, they do not provide the professionals with clinical or research material on which to base policy changes. One of the earliest independent adoption practitioners, Dr. Bruce Rappaport made a frank admission of his personal belief that guided him to embrace open adoption as a new practice model. In the introductory comments of his book: *The Open Adoption Book: A Guide to Adoption Without Tears,* he thus writes: "*In this book the problems and difficulties of open adoption will not be ignored, yet the focus will be on the positive side of open adoption. In choosing* this as the focus, I realize that I open myself to accusations of being a Pollyanna or a propagandist... " (Rappaport, 1992: 2-3). James Gritter (1997), an open adoption advocate, acknowledges the absence of empirical research in this area in the early days, but for him and his colleagues "open adoption was a novel foray into exotic territory....and a journey into a wilderness of uncounted possibilities"(pp. 4 & 5).

Despite nearly decade and a half old debate about the implications of open adoption, only recently have empirical studies using systematic inquiry appeared in the literature and their number is extremely small. Besides, there is no consistency in their findings. For example, a few authors have reported that birth and adoptive parents were very satisfied, for the most part, with open adoptions (Cushman *et al.*, 1997; Etter 1993; Gross 1997). However, recent comparative studies indicated no differences in levels of satisfaction between open and confidential adoptions (Berry *et al.*, 1998; Grotevvant *et al.*, 1999; Siegel 2003). There were also no differences reported between open and confidential adoptions on measures of children's adjustment (Berry *et al.*, 1998; Grotevant & McRoy 1998). Cushman *et al.* (1997) examined the experience of 171 young American birth mothers with regard to open and moderate or semi-open adoption arrangements at four years post-relinquishment. The authors measured the outcomes in terms of their current levels of grief, regret regarding the adoption decision, worry about the child, feelings of sadness and relief and found no difference in the positive outcomes for birth mothers in either of the adoption arrangements. Logan and Smith (2005) also observed lack of unequivocal research evidence regarding the *presumed* benefits of direct contact, particularly in relation to long-term outcomes for children. (*Italics added*). Reitze and Watson (1992) who argue against fully open adoption admit that "there is as yet no empirical evidence to support or refute open adoption...." (p. 260).

Almost all studies report adjustment outcomes over a limited time period, one year to a maximum of 7 years, when adopted children were toddlers or in their early adolescent period (See, Siegel, 2003; Grotevant & McRoy, 1998). It is evident that life circumstances of the members of the adoptive family system change over time and consequently their adjustment of contact. Clearly, the limited time research is not likely to capture the factors that account for these changes and the ability of the family members to negotiate and maintain their relationships and resolve problems, if any. Similarly, it is doubtful if a researcher can gain meaningful information about socio-emotional outcomes from toddlers or pre-adolescent children except the subjective interpretation of the adoptive parents. Only one study undertaken by Mendenhall *et al.*, 2004) involved adolescent children ranging in ages 11 years to 21 years and presented equivocal results. The authors found that overall, adolescent having no contact were satisfied, while those having contact were dissatisfied. There were no differences by age or gender. The authors concluded that all adopted persons did not desire contact. As well, they could not explain how much contact is required to reach plateaus level of satisfaction. Another study by Grotevant & McRoy (1998) found no differences between different forms of openness (i.e. no contact, time-limited or indirect contact, and direct contact) and their impact on children's self-esteem, curiosity and socio-emotional adjustment (p.102). Their children were aged between four and twelve at follow-up. Logan and Smith (2005) reviewed research studies conducted in the U.S.A. and New Zealand and their observations were consistent with the findings of above two studies. The authors concluded that while birth mothers benefited the most from direct contact, adopted children found the contact uncomfortable and distressing. Having reviewed the literature on the experience of birth mothers in open and moderately open arrangements Berry (1993), also, found that birth mothers commonly view open adoption positively as they perceive the benefits of knowing about the adoptive family and the child, while adopted children have shown mixed reactions to openness. McRoy and Grotevant's (1991) interview study of adolescent children revealed that "some embrace contact and some are frightened or confused by it." (p. 10). The authors also found no evidence that information sharing helped these children avoid the consequences of "genealogical bewilderment".

With the exception of a few (e.g. Cushman 1997; Grotevant & McRoy 1998, 1999), most studies examined the experience of the triad who were involved in only open adoption and thus excluded comparison between varying modes of openness. Without comparison no conclusion can be drawn with respect to the relative levels of satisfaction in the context of varied adoption alternatives. Moreover, most research studies focused mainly on post-placement satisfaction of adult members with the arrangement, while understanding of children's experience was left to the subjective interpretation of others. In this context these research studies were plagued with two serious shortcomings. First, they ignored the adoption agencies' primary focus on the 'best interest of the child'. Berry (1993) in her review of the literature noted that the research to date has failed to illuminate "the benefit of any contact or relationship with biological parents" for the child (p.133). Second, researchers did not explain the meaning of the terms "satisfaction," or "positive consequences". used to measure outcomes (Gross 1997; Grotevant *et al.*, 1999; Sobol *et al.*, 2000).

Children with Pre-adoptive Risks

Almost all studies included children who were relinquished as infants and thus had not experienced pre-adoptive risks such as poor parenting, parental abuse, previous foster placements, older children, adoptions made as a result of involuntarily termination of parental rights or special need children. Inevitably, these children and their birth families are not problem free and therefore are likely to affect the quality of relationships among the adults and consequently their impact on the child's socio-emotional outcomes. Kadushin and Martin (1988) warn that children with pre-placement history present additional challenge if contact is involved. Two studies in Britain by Fratter (1996) and Lowe *et al.*, (1999) involved older children who experienced both direct and indirect contact. The studies revealed benefits of contact, "in some form, for the majority of adoptive families." Yet, the investigators were cautious in affirming the efficacy of the type of contact arrangements, which will facilitate particular benefits. Lowe *et al.*, (1999) asserted that they were "by no means committed to the view that any form of contact between the child and birth family is always in the child's best interest irrespective of individual circumstances" (p. 323). Older children who have been exposed to physical abuse, substance abuse or domestic violence before they were adopted may be left with the residual scars of these trauma. Any contact with the birth family is likely to trigger painful memories making the resolution of the experience difficult. Parker (1999) studied relationship between contested adoptions and adults' and children's experience with face to face contact. He discovered that direct post-adoption contact with contesting birth mothers was not beneficial for children. As well, the adopters' relationship with birth mothers was problematic. However, indirect contact by exchanging letters and cards between the child and birth mother worked reasonably well. Interestingly, children preferred to have direct contact with maternal grandparents and birth siblings. In light of these findings with respect to adopted children with pre-placement antecedents, Kadushin and Martin (1988) recommend that changes from traditional adoption to open adoption should apply with caution to especially those adoptions made as a result of involuntary termination of parental rights. In such adoptions, the birth mother may not feel friendly towards adoptive parents and therefore may actively seek to disrupt relationship between the adopted child and adoptive parents. If contact is permitted, the birth mother may actively encourage feelings of conflict in the child and turn him/her against the adoptive parents. In instances of severe neglect, abuse or pathology in birth parents, the information about origins may be difficult for adoptee to handle. Thus, social workers may bear in mind that determination of post-placement arrangements begins in the context of pre-placement circumstances or experiences of the child.

Factors Facilitating Relationship

As the review of the literature on open adoption shows the investigators focused mainly on post-placement satisfaction of adults with the arrangement as a primary indicator of the relative success of adoption. I maintain that there is no simple cause and effect relationship between openness and satisfaction. It is possible that several factors determine openness level that adoptive and birth parents find acceptable and these factors in turn contribute to adoptive parent-birth mother relationship and therefore satisfaction. In essence, open adoption is at heart a *relationship* and the following factors are believed to be associated with adoptive relationship and thus parents satisfaction in adoption. These factors may include: free choice of the degree of openness, comfort level of the participants with the openness level, planned contact (which can provide adoptive parents with a sense of control over the birth parent's involvement), belief that unimpeded communication between the parties would benefit the child, empathic view of the birth mother, faith in birth mother's intentions, adoptive parent's sense of entitlement to act as the child's "real" parent; positive attitude towards adoption reflected in communication with the child about adoption, acknowledgement that adoptive parenting is different from biological parenting; acknowledgment of child's need for connectedness to his/her birth family, understanding of the birth parent's need for information, and pre-adoption counselling. The above concept is depicted in the Figure attached.

Factors Contributing to Relationship and Satisfaction

- Free choice of the degree of openness

- Comfort level of the participants with the openness level
- Planned contact (provide AP with a sense of control over the birth mother's involvement)
- Belief in unimpeded communication between parties
- Empathic view of the birth mother
- Faith in BM's intentions
- AP's sense of entitlement to act as the child's "real" parents
- AP's positive attitude towards adoption as reflected in communication with the child about adoption
- Acknowledgement that adoptive parenting is different from biological parenting
- Acknowledgement of child's need for connectedness to his/her birth family
- Understanding of birth parent's need for information
- Pre-adoptive counselling

Relationship is a dynamic process, changing and evolving as individual needs and wishes alter over time. As individual's needs for more or less openness change, which may not be in agreement with the needs of others, individuals engage in process of negotiating and compromising until they reach a mutually 'comfort zone of contact' (Gross, 1997; Mendenhall *et al.*, 2004). Thus, adoption arrangements established at the time of placement very often change over time and the shift from less to more openness or the reverse can occur for many complex array of reasons that include apprehension, ambivalence, rational or irrational fears or perception of motives. The process of what Grotevant *et al.*, (1999) call a *relationship dance* is not problem free. In reality, for healthy functioning of family life it is expected of its members to make adjustments and compromises. When the concept of adoption is added to the already delicate balance of familial relationships, problems inevitably arise (Cynthia Crosson-Tower 2004:349). It takes time to develop positive feelings about one another, especially when adoptive and birth mothers get to know each other well.

Conclusion

The few systematic studies that have been published offer contradictory conclusions and offer agencies little guide in making choices about where their policies should fall along the openness continuum. Disagreement remains about how far research evidence supports the presumed benefits of direct contact particularly in relation to long-term outcomes for late adolescent or early adult children. A few investigators who were lead to believe that 'adoption with some sort of contact could work well,' had this warning: *"It is a wrong assumption that contact is appropriate, irrespective of individual circumstances, or that any one form of contact is likely to be more beneficial than another" (Fratter 1996: 5 & 92).* Even Grotevant and McRoy (1998) did a comprehensive study and noted beneficial effects for the triad had these cautionary words: *"Neither confidential nor open adoption is best for everyone. The degree of contact should be decided on a case-to-case basis."* In other words, the authors warn: *'avoid a one-size-fits-all approach.'*

While it is unlikely that anyone would suggest that children and birth parents should not have knowledge about each other. It is, therefore, acknowledged that practitioners must still make judgements about individual children in the context of their particular socio-emotional needs, pre-adoption experiences, mental and emotional health of the parties and birth family functioning. Given the current state of knowledge, in most cases it should probably be left to the wisdom and instincts of the practitioner involved. Research to date provides some information about how birth and adoptive parents experience openness, but much more rigorous research is needed to understand the effects of openness on children's social and emotional outcomes and family relationships. Longitudinal research studies may eventually identify relationships between specific types of contact across openness level, and associated outcomes for birth families, adoptive parents and children.

Research is beginning to provide some evidence that openness may help birth mothers to feel more comfortable about their adoption decision than in closed arrangement and adoptive parents feel comfortable with openness provided they feel a sense of control over contacts and 'entitlement' to their adopted child. The birth relatives are, by and large, are satisfied with contact arrangements and can identify advantages for themselves and for their children (Berry, 1993; Logan & Smith, 2005). However, the limited research with adopted children shows that direct contact may be uncomfortable for some children (Thomas & Beckford,

1999; Macaskill, 2002). Research evidence also suggests that the adopted child is psychologically present in every birth mother's heart and mind, but its severity varies with the level of openness. Also, for many birth mothers, psychological presence is both positive and negative; "sometimes it causes pain and sometimes it causes joy" (Frvel *et al.*, 2000). In view of these research findings, practitioner should bear in mind that since not much is known about what accounts for the variations in birth mothers' feelings towards the child, the decision-making regarding choice of openness level should be taken with substantial caution. As Grotevant & McRoy (1998) suggest "there is not a single level of adoption openness best for every birth mother."

Some adoption professionals suggest that open adoption is not appropriate for adoptive parents who may be apprehensive about the consequences of continued contact, and for birth mothers who are ambivalent about relinquishing their children (Groth *et al.*, 1987; Reitz & Watson, 1992). Research evidence also suggests that adolescent birth mothers are not usually developmentally ready to assess the long-term implications of openness, but only consider the short-term benefits. Developmentally immature birth mothers are found overly dependent on adoptive parents (Kallen *et al.*, 1990). Also, contact by the birth mother may not be beneficial to an infant or a very young child whose primary need at this developmental stage is to form a bonding with the adoptive parent which may be disrupted by precipitating a break in the parent-child attachment (Kraft, 1985). In view of these findings, some experts suggest that the process of relationship may be started after a period of exclusive bonding between adoptive parents and their children (Pertman, 2000).

Role of Agency

As the current trend towards greater openness in adoption continues, there is a need for more developed pre and post-placement services and longer agency involvement is more apparent than ever before. In the new kinship network linking together the adopted child's two families long-term adjustment issues are likely to arise. The members could be confused about their respective boundaries, roles and responsibilities. There may be problems that may arise from the interpretation or lack of compliance by either party of the contract or original agreement. Changes in adoption arrangement might be required by either party because of the changes over-time in the circumstances, needs or attitudes of the parties. Such situations are potentially fraught with the possibilities of tensions in the mutual relationship. Agencies role does not cease with the consummation of adoption as used to be the case in practice of closed adoptions. As the nature of adoption practice has changed to openness with ongoing contact so has the role and responsibility of agencies. Since adoption is recognized as a lifelong experience agencies need to be available to assist their clients with long-term adjustment issues. They need to facilitate and help clients negotiate changes in openness arrangements. Agencies are obligated to help parents deal with problems that are unique to openness. They may offer counselling, mediation and supportive services. It is imperative that agencies prepare triad members adequately for openness and the potential problems that are associated with it. Unfortunately, the enhanced services that are made obligatory by the more open approach to adoption have a price in terms of funding and staffing. Agencies are likely to feel pressure to hire more staff and seek additional sources of funding in order to provide a variety of services to families not only before placement of a child but also long after the adoption is completed.

References

Anderson, Carole, M.S.W., J.D. (1987), *Comments on Open Adoption*. Des Moines, IA: Concerned United Birthparents, Inc.

Belbas, N. (1987), Staying in touch: Empathy in open adoption. *Smith College Studies in Social Work*, Vol. 57, 184-198.

Berry, M. (1991), "The Practice of Open Adoption Findings from a Study of 1396 Adoptive Families." *Children and Youth Services*, Vol. 13, 379-395.

Berry, M. (1991), "The Effects of Open Adoption on Biological and Adoptive Parents and their Children: The Arguments and the Evidence." *Child Welfare*, Vol. 70, No. 6, 637-651.

Berry, M. (1993), "Adoptive Parents' Perceptions of, and Comfort With, Open Adoption." *Child Welfare*, Vol. 72, No. 3, 231-253.

Berry, Marianne (1991), "The Effects of Open Adoption on Biological and Adoptive Parents and the Children: The Arguments and the Evidence." *Child Welfare*, Vol. 70, No. 6 (Nov./Dec.), 637-52.

Berry, Marianne (1993), "Risks and Benefits of Open Adoption." *The Future of Children Adoption*, 3(1), 125-38.

Berry, M. *et al.*, (1998), "The role of open adoption in the adjustment of adopted children and their families." *Children & Youth Services Review*, 20: 151-171.

Blanton, T., & J. Deschnel (1990), "Biological Mothers' Grief: The Post Adoptive Experience in Open Vs. Confidential Adoption." *Child Welfare*, Vol. 69, No. 6 (Nov./Dec.), 525-535.

Brodzinsky, David M. & Anne B. Brodzinsky (1992), "The Impact of Family Structure on the Adjustment of Adopted Children." *Child Welfare*, Vol. 71, No. 1 (Jan./Feb.), 69-76.

Brodzinsky, D.M., Smith, D.W., Brodzinsky, A.G. (1998), "Children's Adjustment to Adoption." *Developmental Clinical Psychology and Psychiatry*, 38, 79-88.

Butler, I. & Williamson, H. (1994), *Children Speak: Children Trauma and Social Work.* London: Longman.

Caplan, Lincoln (1990), *An Open Adoption.* New York: Farrar, Strauss and Giroux.

Corcoran, Ann (1988), "Open Adoption: The Child's Right." *Adoption and Fostering*, Vol. 12, No. 3, 39-41.

Crosson-Tower, C. (2004), *Exploring Child Welfare; A Practice Perspective. 3rd ed.* Toronto: Pearson Education.

Curtis, Patrick (1986), "The dialectic of Open Vs. Closed Adoption of Infants," *Child Welfare*, LXV(5).

Cushman, L., Kalmuss, D., Namerow, P. (1997), "Openness in Adoption: Experiences and Social Psychological Outcomes Among Birth Mothers. *Families and Adoption*, 7-18.

Demick, J., Adaption of marital couples to open Vs. closed adoption: A preliminary investigation (pp. 175-201). In J. Demick, K. Bursik, & R. DiBiase (eds.), *Parental development.* Hillsdale NJ: Lawrence Erlbaum Associates.

Deykin, Eva, Y., Ph.D., Lee Campbell, M.Ed., and Patricia Patti, B.S.N. (1984), "The Post-adoption Experience of Surrendering Parents." *American Journal of Orthopsychiatry*, Vol. 54, No. 2 (Apr.), 271-80.

Etter, J. (1993), "Levels of Cooperation and Satisfaction in 56 Open Adoptions." *Child Welfare*, Vol. 72, No. 3, 257-267.

Fratter, J. (1996), *Adoption with Contact: Implications for Policy and Practice.* London: British Agencies for Adoption and Fostering.

Fravel, D.L., McRoy, R.G., Grotevant, H.D. (2000), Birthmother Perceptions of the Psychologically Present Adopted Child: Adoption Openness and Boundary Ambiguity, *Family Relations*, 49, 425-433.

Garrett, Diane (1989), "More Options for Adoption." *Main Line Times Sunday Magazine* (Nov. 123).

Gritter, J.L. (1997), *The Spirit of Open Adoption.* Washington: CWLA Press.

Gross, H.E. (1993), "Open Adoption: A Research Based Literature Review and New Data", *Child Welfare*, Vol. 72, No. 3, 269-284.

Gross, H.E. (1997), "Variants of Open Adoptions: The Early Years." *Marriage & Family Review*, 25(1/2) 19-42.

Grotevant, H. *et al.*, (1994), "Adoptive Family System Dynamics: Variations by Level of Openness in the Adoption." *Family Process*, Vol. 33.

Grotevant, H.D. & McRoy, R. (1998), *Openness in adoption: Exploring family connections*, Thousand Oaks, CA. Sage.

Grotevant, H.D. *et al.*, (1999), "Adaptive Behavior in Adopted Children: Predictors from early Risk, Collaboration in Relationships within the Adoptive Kinship network, and Openness Arrangements." *Jr. of Adolescent Research*, 14(2), 231-247.

Haugaard, J., Moed, A., West, N. (2001), Outcomes of Open Adoptions. *Adoption Quarterly*, 4(3), 63-65.

Henney S. M. *et al.*, (2003), "The Impact of Openness On Adoption Agency Practices: A Longitudinal Perspective." *Adoption Quarterly*, 6(3), 31-51.

Hollenstein, T. *et al.*, (2003), "Openness in Adoption Knowledge of Birthparent Information, and Adoption Family Adjustment." *Adoption Quarterly*, 7(1), 43-52.

Huges, Beverely, (1995), "Openness and Contact in Adoption: A child-centered Perspective," *British Journal of Social Work*, 25, 729-747.

Kadushin, A., Martin, J. (1988), *Child Welfare Services*, 4th ed. New York: Macmillan.

Kahn, R. & Cannell, C. (1957), *The Dynamics of Interviewing*. New York: John Wiley & Sons, Inc.

Kallen, D.J. Griffore, R.I., Popovich, S., & Powell, V. (1990), Adolescent Mothers and their Mothers View of Adoption. *Family Relations*, 39: 311-16.

Kantrowitz, Barbara and Elisa Williams (1986), "Life With Two Mothers." *Newsweek*, Vol. 107, No. 2 (May 12), 86.

Kasper-Glass, Suzanne (1992), "Open Adoption Research: What we Now Know." *OURS*, Vol. 25, No. 2 (Mar./Apr.), 15-16.

Kirk, D. (1964), *Shared Fate*, New York: The Free Press.

Kirk, D. (1981), *Adoptive Kinship*. Toronto: Butterworths.

Kreuger, L.W. & Neuman, W.L. (2006), *Social Work Research Methods*. New York: Allyn & Bacon.

Lindsay, Jeanne Warren (1987), *Open Adoption: A Caring Option*. Buena Park, CA: Morning Glory Press.

Logan, J. & Smith, C. (2005), "Face-to-Face Contact Post Adopton: Views from the Triangles." *British Jr. of Social Work*, 35, 3-35.

Loos, Shelly (1994), *Dealing with Grief: A Survey of the Birthmothers*. A Masters Thesis, University of Kentucky.

Lowe, N., *et al.*, (1999), *Supporting Adoption: Reframing the Approach*. London: British Agencies for Adoption and Fostering.

McRoy, R. *et al.*, (1998), *Openness in Adoption.* New York: Praeger Press.

McRoy, R.G. and Groevant, H.D. (1991), American Experience and Research on Openness. *Paper Presented to the International Conference on Adoption,* September 19, Edinburgh, Scotland.

Melina, Lois, (1987), "Speaker Outlines Why Adopting is Different and Marriage Stress by Arrival of New Child." *Adopted Child,* Vol. 6, No. 7, (Jul.), 1-4.

Melina, Lois (1988), "Open Adoptions Require Building Relationships." *Adopted Child,* Vol. 7, No. 9 (Sep.), 1-4.

Mendenhall, T.J. *et al.*, (2004), "Adolescents' Satisfaction with Contact in Adoption." *Child and Adolescent Social Work Journal,* 21(2), 175-190.

Miall, C. E., March, K. (2005), "Open Adoption as a Family Form: Community Assessments and Social Support" *Jr. of Family Issues,* 26(4), 380-410.

Morris, Rebecca (1990), "Giving Up Devin", *The Sunday Oregonian Magazine* (Jan. 14), 8-14.

Macaskill, C. (2002), *Safe Contact: Children in Permanent Placement and Contact with their Birth Relatives.* Dorcet: Russell House Publishing.

Mullender, A. (1999), "Sketching in the Background", in A. Mullender (ed.), *We are Family Sibling Relationships in Placement and Beyond.* London: British Agencies for Adoption and Fostering, 1-18.

National Committee for Adoption. *Adoption Factbook.* Washington, DC: National Committee for Adoption, 1989.

Parker, R. (1999), *Adoption Now: Messages from Research.* Chichester: John Wiley and Sons.

Pertman, Adam (2000), *Adoption Nation.* New York: Basic Books.

Rappaport, Bruce M., Ph.D. (1992), "Semi Open Vs. Fully Open Adoption." *Open Adoption Magazine,* Vol. 2, No. 1, (Winter): 4, 22.

Ryburn, M. (1996), "A Study of Post Adoption Contact in Compulsory Adoption," *British Journal of Social Work,* 26(5), 627-646.

Sanders, C., Mauger, P. and Strong, P. (1985), *A Manual for the Grief Experience Inventory.* Palo Alto, CA: Consulting Psychologists Press, Inc.

Silber, K. & Dorner, P.M. (1990), *The Children of Open Adoption.* San Antonio, TX: Corona.

Swanson, Jo Anne (1989), *The Adoption Machine.* Gladstone, MI: Birco Publishing Company.

Sachdev, Paul (1981), "Unlocking the Adoption Files: A Social and Legal Dilemma." In Paul Sachdev (ed.) *Adoption: Current Issues and Trends.* Toronto: Butterworths.

Sachdev, Paul (1989), *Unlocking the Adoption Files.* Lexington, MA: DC Health.

Sachdev, Paul (1991a) "The Birth Father: A Neglected Element in the Adoption Equation." *Families in Society,* Vol. 72, No. 3, 131-139.

Sachdev, Paul (1991b), " Achieving Openness in Adoption: Some Critical Issues in Policy Formation." *American Journal of Orthopsychiatry,* Vol. 61, No. 2, 241-249.

Sachdev, Paul (1991c), "Birth Mothers and their Reunion Experiences: A study of 37 U.S. States." Paper presented at American Adoption Congress, Garden Groves, CA, Sept., 3-7.

Sachdev, Paul (1992), "Adoption Reunion and After: A study of the Search Process and Experiences of Adoptees." *Child Welfare,* Vol. 71, No. 1, (Jan./Feb.), 5368.

Sachdev, Paul (1993), *Sex, Abortion and Unmarried Women.* Westport, CT: Greenwood.

Seigel, Deborah H. (1993), "Open Adoption of Infants: Adoption Parents' Perceptions of Advantages and Disadvantages." *Social Work,* Vol. 38, No. 1, (Jan.): 15-25.

Siegel, D.H. (2003), "Open Adoption of Infants: Adoptive Parents' Feelings Seven Years Later." *Social Work,* 48(3), 1-14.

Silber, Kathleen, M.S.W., A.C.S.W. (1991), "Risks in Adoption." *Open Adoption Magazine,* Vol. 1, No. 3 (Dec./Jan.), 9-10.

Silber, Kathleen and Phyllis Speedlin (1982), *Dear Birthmother: Thank You for Our Baby.* San Antonio, TX: Corona Publishing.

Silverstein, Debrah *et al.* (1994), "Toward on Organisational Relations Model of Open Adoption." *Family Process,* 33 (June).

Smith-Pliner, Dawn & Deborah H. Seigel (1992), "Successful Open Adoption: Advice for Adoptive Parents." *OURS,* Vol. 25, No. 1, (Jan./ Feb.), 15-17.

Sobol, M.P., Daly, K.J., Kelloway, K. (2000), "Paths to the Facilitation of Open Adoption,"*Family Relations,* 49: 419-430 (October).

Thomas, C. & Beckford, V. (1999), *Adopted Children Speaking.* London British Agencies for Adoption and Fostering.

6

Adoptions in and to the United States

JOSEPHINE A. RUGGIERO

Introduction

Adoption is a controversial subject both within and among societies.[1] In some societies, such as Hindu India, the Gilbert Islands, and Polynesia, and among some ethnic groups like African Americans, Native Americans, and Eskimos, for example, adoption is viewed positively and may even be a preferred way of raising children and of strengthening the extended family unit.[2] Among the Inuit of Northern Canada, children are both "adopted in" and "adopted out" with little or no fanfare. Adopted children know who their biological mother is. They probably interact with her on a regular basis but in the social role of "sister" or "aunt."[3] In other societies, like those based on Islam, for example, there may be historical and religious opposition to adoption.

Adoption in the United States

Views about the legitimacy of adoption also may vary within a society over time. The United States is a good example of such a society. During colonial times, for example, adoption was practiced on a limited basis and occurred both formally and informally.[4] Informal adoptions took place without involving legal proceedings. In such cases, dying parents might request that their child be raised by a family friend, Godparent, or a neighbour. Biological kinship did *not* hold the importance that it began to assume in contemporary America.

Current adoption policies and regulations in the United States make it much more difficult than in earlier times for a couple or individual to adopt a non-biologically-related child or children. Domestic adoptions are now regulated by law and are under the purview of social workers. The process has been known to be a long and cumbersome one that may tie up prospective adopters' plans to adopt in years of delays and red tape.

Although birth parents may give up legal rights to a child or children, or have their parental rights severed by the courts, many people still view the blood relationship between parent and child as indissoluble[5] whereas the tie between adoptive parents and their child is viewed as more tenuous. Despite the view about blood ties being stronger than kinship ties established by choice or law, Benet contends that adoption was accepted more readily in the United States than it was in Europe, where the hereditary notion of status was strong.[6]

In fact, in the title of his book on adoption, Adam Pertman, Executive Director of the Evan Donaldson Institute, refers to the United States as an "adoption nation."[7] It is certainly true that adoption has been a popular way to add a child or children to families—both for people who do not have biological children as well as for some who do. Still, according to statistics from research cited by the Evan B. Donaldson Institute, it is fair to say that adopted children currently comprise a very small percentage (N = 1.5 million, or just over 2%) of all children in the United States.[8]

Just when did adoption begin to be popular in the United States? In her recent book, historian Barbara Melosh provides the background information to answer this question.[9] She writes that, although affluent Americans adopted non-related infants in relatively small numbers as far back as the early decades of the 20th century, adoption became both more popular and under the purview of state supervision by the Second World War. Melosh states that, at that time, adoption became viewed as the "best solution" policy and was widely accepted as a legitimate, alternative way to form families. This "best solution" policy received the support of unprecedented numbers of white, middle-class families.

During the post-World War II years and the decades that followed, domestic adoptions increased dramatically. Melosh reports that, during the 1950s and 1960s, "... adoption gained new credibility as a kind of social engineering that appealed to American dreams of upward mobility and self-invention."[10] The economic and other changes that occurred in American society during those decades helped to fuel the "popular and professional embrace of adoption" as "a 'legitimate' response to illegitimacy."[11] Families created through adoption and comprised of strangers became accepted legally as kin. The courts could and did decree it.

The historical peak for domestic adoptions occurred in 1970, when 175,000 adoptions took place.[12] Between 1973 and 1995, the percentage of women who adopted in the United States declined from 2.1 per cent to 1.3 per cent.[13] In 1995, only one in five of the women who were interested in adopting applied to an adoption agency.[14]

What accounts for the decline reported in the number of domestic adoptions? It is difficult to believe that people's desire to adopt lessened. Rather, it seems that there were social forces at work which limited people's opportunity to adopt a child or children domestically. Finding adoptive families for "waiting children" in state care did not seem to be a major priority. To wit, reliable numbers for domestic adoptions in the United States apparently have *not* been "available" since 1992.[15] In that year, almost 127,000 adoptions took place.[16] Other social forces were also at work and resulted in reduced opportunities for would-be adopters to succeed.

International Adoption of Children to the United States

During the post-World War II period, adopting children born in other countries also became a way for Americans to build families. International adoption is similar to domestic adoption in that both are personal, familial experiences regulated by politics and policies. However, the two types of adoption differ in that international adoption *always* adds a cultural, and *often* an inter-racial, dimension to the adoption experience.[17]

Using data provided to me by the U.S. Citizenship and Immigration Service (USCIS), formerly known as the U.S. Immigration and Naturalisation Service (USINS), I examine the trends in international adoptions by Americans from the earliest (1957-1963) aggregated statistics to the most recent yearly total (2003) for which these data were available for analysis. I focus especially on changing trends in major sending countries. Where available, I also analyze the ages and gender of the children Americans adopted from major sending countries. It is worth noting here that many researchers use the number of Immigrant Visas granted to orphans entering the United States as equivalent to adoption figures. I have examined the figures from both sources over time and have found the Visa numbers, while easier to obtain, overestimate, to some extent, the actual number of children adopted into the United States from sending countries. Visa figures include children entering the U.S. for purposes other than adoption, such as for medical treatment, and children who come to the U.S. through the KidSave Program. Although, many of the KidSave children who spent time with host families do end up being adopted, all of these children go back to their home country prior to being adopted and enter the U.S. again, this time counted as adoptees.

General Trends

1. *Size*

Adopting a child or children born outside the United States is a trend that has grown dramatically and in interesting ways over time. Over the years, between September 11, 1957 and June 30, 1969, over twenty thousand (N = 20,668) children born outside the United States joined American families through adoption.

In the next 13-year period, between 1970 and 2003, statistics from the INS/CIC show that more than 300 thousand (N = 307,407) immigrant orphans entered the United States for the purpose of being adopted or as adoptees.[18] Decade totals reveal dramatic changes in numbers: Between 1970 and 1979, just under 50,000 (N = 47,796) immigrant orphans entered the United States. Between 1980 and 1989, this number jumped to 77,606—reflecting a positive rate of change of 62.4 per cent. The 1990s decade total showed a further numerical increase to 102,378 immigrant orphans adopted, a 32 per cent increase over the 1980s' decade total. Between 2000 and 2003, the most recent three years for which statistics are available at this writing, Americans adopted more children internationally (N = 79,627) than they did during the entire decades of the 1970s or 1980s. These data suggest that, all other things being equal, when the opportunity to do so is present, the trend toward Americans adopting a child or children internationally will continue to increase.

2. *Sending-Country Trends of Adoptees to the United States*

(a) Western Europe

Between 1957 and 1969, three in ten (28%, N = 5,781) international adoptees to the United States came from countries typically considered "Western" Europe. Listed in order of number of adoptees from each of these sending countries, the countries included Germany (N = 2,078), Italy (N = 2,212), Spain (N = 303), the United Kingdom (N = 282), France (N = 209), Portugal (N = 186), Austria (N = 128), Switzerland (N = 61), Ireland (N = 49), Finland (N = 47), Malta (N = 43), Luxembourg (N = 16), Denmark (N = 12), Netherlands (N = 10), Norway (N = 3), and Belgium (N = 1). Prior to 1970, almost three quarters of the Western European adoptees to the United States came from only two sending countries: Italy (38%) and Germany (36%).

Between 1970 and 2003, the number of Western European adoptees to the United States declined overall. More than 1600 hundred (N = 1,659) German-born adoptees joined American families through 1985, but they did so in noticeably smaller numbers annually, beginning in the late 1970s. Only 155 adoptees born in Italy arrived between 1970 and 2003.

(b) Asia

1. *Korea*

The emigration of Korean children to the United States for the purpose of adoption has a long history. Over the years between 1957 and 1969, more than half (56.6%, N = 11,697) of all international adoptees to the United States came from Asia. More than half of the Asian adoptees (56.5%, N = 6,603) were born in Korea. Between 1957 and 1963, Korean children comprised one-third (33.6%) of all international adoptees to the United States. Until 1963, more than nine out of ten (94.5%) Korean children adopted by Americans were adopted in Korea.[19]

Between 1964 and 1969, three in 10 of all inter-country adoptees who entered American families came from Korea. However, in just under one-third (32.3%) of these cases, the adoption took place *in the children's birth country.*[20] This shift in country of *adoption* for Korean-born children that joined American families continued to grow in the years between 1970 and 2003.

Korea remained a popular sending country for international adoptees to the United States in the 1970s and 1980s. During both decades, although the number of international adoptess to the U.S. grew overall, Korea continued to dominate the scene, sending more than half of the total number of inter-country adoptees to the United States in each decade—53 per cent in the 1970s and 57 per cent in the 1980s.

As Russia and China became major sending countries of adoptees to the United States during the 1990s, the percentage of Korean adoptees entering American families declined to less than 20 per cent (17.6%) of the total of inter-country adoptees during that decade. The percentage of Korean adoptees to the United States decreased further during the early years of the 21st century. Table 6.1 presents data on the numbers, gender, and ages of Korean adoptees to the United States between 1986 and 2003. Focusing on numbers, note the steady decline in numbers of adoptees from Korea to the United States between 1986 and 1995. Between 1996 and 2003, the yearly totals fluctuated but in none of these years did they reach two thousand adoptees.

2. *China*

As with Korea, officially, the emigration of Chinese orphans to the United States for the purpose of adoption also dates back to the late 1950s. However, the INS statistics indicate that the designation used for "China" changed over time. Between 1957 and 1981, counts of adoptees to the United States from China also included children born in Formosa/Taiwan. Between 1982 and 1994, the INS began to report totals separately for "mainland China" and, beginning in 1995, for the *People's Republic of China.*

In the earliest years, the Office of Immigration Statistics reported that the numbers of adoptees from China and Formosa to the United States were small. For example, between 1957 and 1963, Americans adopted a total of only 407 children from China

Table 6.1: Korean Adoptees to the United States by Sex and Age, 1986-2003

Year		*Sex*[a]		*Age*[c]		
	Total	*% Male*	*% Female*	*%<1 Year*	*%1 to 4 Years*	*% 5+ Years*
1986	6188	41.00%	59.00%	71.00%	19.00%	10.00%
1987	5910	42.00%	58.00%	73.00%	19.00%	8.00%
1988	4942	45.00%	55.00%	78.00%	14.00%	8.00%
1989	3552	47.00%	53.00%	78.00%	14.00%	8.00%
1990	2603	49.00%	51.00%	81.00%	12.00%	7.00%
1991	1817	49.00%	51.00%	86.00%	10.00%	4.00%
1992	1787	47.00%	53.00%	90.00%	7.00%	3.00%
1993	1765	50.00%	50.00%	91.00%	7.00%	2.00%
1994	1757	49.00%	51.00%	94.00%	5.00%	1.00%
1995	1570	53.00%	47.00%	92.00%	7.00%	1.00%
1996	1580	56.00%	44.00%	93.00%	6.00%	1.00%
1997	1506	53.00%	47.00%	93.00%	6.00%	1.00%
1998	1705	55.00%	45.00%	94.00%	6.00%	b.
1999	1956	52.00%	48.00%	93.00%	6.00%	1.00%
2000	1711	57.00%	43.00%	92.00%	8.00%	b.
2001	1863	55.00%	45.00%	93.00%	6.00%	1.00%
2002	1713	58.00%	42.00%	93.00%	7.00%	1.00%
2003	1793	57.00%	43.00%	94.00%	5.00%	1.00%
Total	45718					
Average %		48.00%	52.00%	84.00%	11.00%	5.00%
N =		22159	23557	38251	5256	2205

Notes: (a) Sex of two adoptees unknown.
(b) less than .5%.
(c) Ages of 6 adoptees unknown.

Source: U.S. C.I.S., Immigrants Admitted as Orphans by Sex, Age and Region and Selected Country of Birth (Table 14, 1986-1991 & Table 15, 1992-2002 & Table 10, 2003).

and Formosa. This number represented four per cent of all international adoptees to the United States during this time period. Between 1964 and 1969, the percentage of the total inter-country adoptees to the United States accounted for by China and Taiwan grew to only six per cent.

Small numbers of "Chinese" adoptees continued to join American families in the 1970s (N = 598 from China and Taiwan) and 1980s (N = 253). In 1990 and 1991, the total number of Chinese children adopted by Americans was less than 100 (N = 90). However, between 1992 and 1994, although still relatively small, these numbers began to show systematic increases.

In 1995, the number of Chinese orphans Americans adopted jumped dramatically by almost three fold over the 1994 number (from 748 to 2,049). As Table 6.2 shows, thereafter, the total number of Chinese adoptees to the United States continued to rise in almost every consecutive year, peaking at 6,638 adoptions to the United States in 2003. *Between 1995 and 2003, Americans adopted a total of 38,854 children from China.* This number accounts for 26.5 per cent of the international adoptees to the United States during that nine-year period.

Table 6.2: Chinese Adoptees to the United States by Sex and Age, 1995-2003.

Year		*Sex*		*Age*[a]		
	Total	*% Male*	*% Female*	*% <1 Year*	*% 1-4 Years*	*% 5+ Years*
1995	2049	2.00%	98.00%	82.00%	17.00%	1.00%
1996	3318	2.00%	98.00%	77.00%	21.00%	2.00%
1997	3295	2.00%	98.00%	60.00%	38.00%	2.00%
1998	3988	2.00%	98.00%	38.00%	60.00%	2.00%
1999	4009	2.00%	98.00%	49.00%	49.00%	2.50%
2000	4943	3.00%	97.00%	57.00%	41.00%	2.00%
2001	4629	4.00%	96.00%	47.00%	51.00%	2.00%
2002	6062	4.00%	96.00%	43.00%	54.50%	2.50%
2003	6638	5.00%	95.00%	49.00%	48.00%	3.00%
Total	38931					
Average %		3.00%	97.00%	53.00%	45.00%	2.00%
N =		1198	38931	20553	17527	840

Note: (a) Ages of 11 orphans unknown.

Source: U.S. C.I.S., Immigrants Admitted as Orphans by Sex, Age and Region and Selected Country of Birth (Table 15, 1995-2003 & Table 10, 2003).

(c) South America

Between 1957 and 1972, less than 200 (N = 198) South American adoptees joined families in the United States. Beginning in 1973, increases in the annual totals for South American adoptees to the

United States began to exceed 100 and, thereafter, to rise dramatically for a while. The peak year for South American adoptees to the United States during the 1970s was 1979 (N = 892). Yearly totals for adoptees from this part of the world began to exceed 1,000 in 1985 (N = 1,172) and continued to rise during the remainder of the 1980s, peaking at 1,757 adoptees to the United States from South America in 1989. As Table 6.3 shows, yearly totals of South American adoptees fluctuated during the 1990s but began to drop *below 1,000* in 1996 (N = 805). Yearly totals dropped *below 500* in 1998 (N = 497) and remained below 500 through 2003.

Table 6.3: South American Adoptees to the United States by Sex and Age, 1986-2003

Year	*Total*	*Sex*		*Age*[a]		
		% Male	*% Female*	*%<1 Year*	*%1 to 4 Years*	*% 5+ Years*
1986	1235	52.00%	48.00%	67.00%	17.00%	16.00%
1987	1363	50.00%	50.00%	63.00%	19.00%	18.00%
1988	1650	50.00%	50.00%	67.00%	18.00%	14.00%
1989	1757	50.00%	50.00%	69.00%	19.00%	12.00%
1990	1957	50.00%	50.00%	69.00%	19.00%	12.00%
1991	1949	48.00%	52.00%	73.00%	16.00%	11.00%
1992	1418	48.00%	52.00%	67.00%	23.00%	10.00%
1993	1471	48.00%	52.00%	69.00%	24.00%	7.00%
1994	1205	48.00%	52.00%	66.00%	23.00%	11.00%
1995	1004	50.00%	50.00%	64.00%	23.00%	13.00%
1996	805	51.00%	49.00%	53.00%	33.00%	14.00%
1997	501	52.00%	48.00%	45.00%	40.00%	15.00%
1998	497	46.00%	54.00%	50.00%	29.00%	21.00%
1999	459	48.00%	52.00%	52.00%	28.00%	20.00%
2000	452	47.00%	53.00%	59.00%	22.00%	19.00%
2001	429	48.00%	52.00%	56.00%	23.00%	21.00%
2002	466	47.00%	53.00%	58.00%	22.00%	20.00%
2003	406	47.00%	53.00%	57.00%	20.00%	23.00%
Total	19024					
Average %		49.00%	51.00%	65.00%	21.00%	14.00%
N =		9410	9664	12332	4075	2612

Note: (a) Sex of five adoptees unknown.

Source: U.S. C.I.S., Immigrants Admitted as Orphans by Sex, Age and Region and Selected Country of Birth (Table 14, 1986-1991 & Table 15, 1992-2002 & Table 10, 2003).

Columbia was the major contributor of South American adoptees to the United States between 1970 and 2003. This country alone sent almost half (49.4%) of all the South American children adopted by U.S. families.

(d) Central America

According to U.S. government statistics, adoptees from Central American countries began to arrive in the United States in 1976. Between 1976 and 2003, more than twenty thousand (N = 23,047) Central American adoptees joined American families. Annual numbers of Central American adoptees did *not* begin to exceed

Table 6.4: Central American Adoptees to the United States by Sex and Age, 1986-2003

Year		Sex[a]		Age[b]		
	Total	*% Male*	*% Female*	*%<1 Year*	*%1 to 4 Years*	*5+ Years*
1986	626	50.00%	50.00%	51.00%	30.00%	19.00 %
1987	654	50.00%	50.00%	51.00%	30.00%	19.00%
1988	568	50.00%	50.00%	48.00%	32.00%	20.00%
1989	595	49.00%	51.00%	49.00%	32.00%	19.00%
1990	700	51.00%	49.00%	49.00%	32.00%	20.00%
1991	770	46.00%	54.00%	56.00%	29.00%	15.00%
1992	892	51.00%	49.00%	56.00%	30.00%	14.00%
1993	878	52.00%	48.00%	54.00%	36.00%	10.00%
1994	621	50.00%	50.00%	61.00%	29.00%	10.00%
1995	555	46.00%	54.00%	60.00%	28.00%	12.00%
1996	521	55.00%	45.00%	66.00%	24.00%	10.00%
1997	808	48.00%	52.00%	70.00%	25.00%	6.00%
1998	1004	47.00%	53.00%	69.00%	24.00%	7.00%
1999	1061	46.00%	54.00%	69.00%	24.00%	7.00%
2000	1570	46.00%	54.00%	71.00%	23.00%	6.00%
2001	1642	46.00%	54.00%	76.00%	19.00%	6.00%
2002	2404	48.00%	52.00%	76.00%	18.00%	6.00%
2003	2381	50.00%	50.00%	75.00%	21.00%	4.00%
Total	18250					
Average %		49.00%	51.00%	66.00%	25.00%	9.00%
N =		8868	9380	11967	4537	1738

Notes: (a) Gender of two adoptees unknown (2000, 2001).
(b) Age of eight adoptees unknown.

Source: U.S. C.I.S., Immigrants Admitted as Orphans by Sex, Age and Region and Selected Country of Birth (Table 14, 1986-1991 & Table 15, 1992-2002 & Table 10, 2003).

500 annually until 1983 (N = 557). As Table 6.4 shows, these numbers did not begin to exceed 1000 adoptees annually until 1998 (N = 1,004). However, in both 2000 and 2001, annual totals of adoptees from Central America surpassed 1,500. In 2002 and 2003, the Central American totals surpassed 2,000 each year.

Of the seven Central American countries that sent adoptees to the United States between 1976 and 2003, *Guatemala contributed almost two-thirds* (65.4%, N = 15,074). About three in 10 (30.2%) Central American adoptees to the United States came from El Salvador (13.3%, N = 3,064), Honduras (10%, N = 2, 287), and Costa Rica (6.9%, N = 1,588) combined. The remaining less than 5 per cent of Central American adoptees came from Panama (N = 496), Nicaragua (N = 344) and Belise (N = 158).

(e) Eastern Europe

Beginning in its earliest tables, the INS included in the "Europe" category, countries we would now consider part of either Central or Eastern Europe. These countries include, for example, Greece, Turkey, Czechoslovakia, Yugoslavia, Hungary, Lithuania, Poland, and the U.S.S.R. Thus, Eastern Europe is a rather amorphous entity and some may disagree with which countries should be included. For purposes of discussing trends in Eastern European sending countries, I will begin where the official U.S. records do.

Between 1957 and 1964, *Greece* was a major sending country of international adoptees to the United States. During those years, 1,268 Greek children were adopted into families in the United States. Adoptees from Greece continued to join American families annually between 1964 and 1986 (N = 927). Beginning in 1990, however, Greek adoptees to the United States arrived only intermittently and in very small numbers. Totals for 1990 (N = 16), 1994-96 (N = 25), 1998-2000 (N = 12) and 2003 (N = 3) reflect this trend.

Data indicate that *Poland* also began sending children for adoption to the United States as early as 1957. Between 1957 and 1969, 319 Polish children were adopted by Americans. Adoptions of Polish children to the United States have continued at a steady pace since then. During the 1970s, they totalled 156 children. In the years between 1980-89, Americans adopted 344 Polish children. The total then doubled to 766 adoptees in the 1990s.

In the four years between 2000 and 2003, the total number of inter-country adoptees from Poland to the U.S. reached 364 children. Although Poland has been a consistent sending country, to date, having sent fewer then 2,000 children to the U.S. for adoption since 1957, Poland does not fall into the category of a major sending country. Although building up momentum more recently, the principal Eastern European sending countries of adoptees to the United States include Russia, Romania, the Ukraine, Kazakhstan and Bulgaria. Because most of the Eastern European adoptees to the U.S. came from these five countries, and most came from Russia alone, in this section, I divide the analysis into Russia, four other major European sending countries, and the remaining smaller Eastern European sending countries combined.

1. *Russia*

According to U.S. government records, between 1957 and 1963, only two children from the U.S.S.R. joined American families as adoptees. These records also show a marked absence of adoptees to the United States from the Soviet Union until 1991. In 1991 and 1992 combined, Americans reportedly adopted 444 orphans from the Soviet Union. Subsequently, the numbers of Russian adoptees to the United States began to rise dramatically. According to Table 6.5, between 1993 and 2003, almost 37 thousand (N = 36,685) Russian children entered American families through adoption.

A look at data for 1990-1999 from an independent but reputable data source, the International Social Science Resource Centre for the Protection of Children in Adoption (ISS/IRC), indicated that Americans first adopted Russian orphans in 1992 (N = 145). In the next year, the number of Russian adoptees more than quadrupled (to N = 695). The numbers of Russian adoptees to the United States began to grow dramatically throughout the rest of the 1990s, peaking at 4,491 adoptees in 1998. By 1999, the ISS/IRC reported that Americans had adopted a decade total of 17,991 Russian orphans. The discrepancy between the INS and the ISS/IRC data sources are that the latter were obtained from sending countries. Still, the ISS/IRC data only *underestimates* the 1990s decade count by 236 children.

Table 6.5: Russian Adoptees to the United States by Sex and Age, 1993-2003

Year		*Sex*		*Age*[a]		
	Total	% *Male*	% *Female*	%<1 *Year*	%1-4 *Years*	% 5+ *Years*
1993	695	45.00%	55.00%	21.00%	57.00%	22.00%
1994	1324	49.00%	51.00%	22.00%	56.00%	22.00%
1995	1684	49.00%	51.00%	26.00%	53.00%	21.00%
1996	2328	52.00%	48.00%	20.00%	61.00%	19.00%
1997	3626	49.00%	51.00%	28.00%	51.00%	21.00%
1998	4320	52.00%	48.00%	36.00%	47.00%	17.00%
1999	4250	50.00%	50.00%	39.00%	44.00%	17.00%
2000	4210	49.00%	51.00%	30.00%	51.00%	19.00%
2001	4210	48.00%	52.00%	23.00%	57.00%	20.00%
2002	4904	49.00%	51.00%	27.00%	53.00%	20.00%
2003	5134	49.00%	51.00%	30.00%	50.00%	20.00%
Total	36685					
Average %		49.00%	51.00%	29.00%	52.00%	19.00%
N =		18082	18598	10654	18925	7097

Note: (a) Age of nine adoptees unknown.

Source: U.S. C.I.S., Immigrants Admitted as Orphans by Sex, Age and Region and Selected Country of Birth (Table 14, 1986-1991 & Table 15, 1992-2002 & Table 10, 2003).

2. *Other Major Eastern European Sending Countries*

Between 1990 and 2003, Americans also adopted over twenty-three thousand (N = 23,264) children from other Eastern European countries. Three-quarters of these adoptees came from four sending countries: *Romania,* the *Ukraine, Kazakhstan* and *Bulgaria.* As Table 6.6 shows, almost eight thousand of these adoptees came to the United States from Romania.

The data in Table 6.7 point out that over 4,600 adoptees came from the Ukraine.

According to Table 6.8, nearly three thousand adoptees came to the United States from Kazakhstan between 1998 and 2003.

Table 6.6: Romanian Adoptees to the United States by Sex and Age, 1993-2003

Year		*Sex*		*Age*		
	Total	*% Male*	*% Female*	*% <1 Year*	*% 1-4 Years*	*% 5+ Years*
1990	90	37.00%	63.00%	50.00%	41.00%	9.00%
1991	2552	46.00%	54.00%	56.00%	39.00%	5.00%
1992	145	51.00%	49.00%	32.00%	54.00%	14.00%
1993	88	50.00%	50.00%	9.00%	63.00%	27.00%
1994	197	39.00%	61.00%	13.00%	57.00%	30.00%
1995	260	45.00%	55.00%	12.00%	70.00%	18.00%
1996	554	49.00%	51.00%	8.00%	84.00%	8.00%
1997	558	47.00%	53.00%	3.00%	85.00%	12.00%
1998	388	45.00%	55.00%	10.00%	76.00%	15.00%
1999	887	52.00%	48.00%	19.00%	67.00%	14.00%
2000	1103	50.00%	50.00%	21.00%	64.00%	15.00%
2001	781	53.00%	47.00%	26.00%	55.00%	19.00%
2002	169	42.00%	58.00%	1.00%	60.00%	39.00%
2003	197	45.00%	55.00%	5.00%	66.00%	19.00%
Total	4985					
Average %		49.00%	51.00%	16.00%	67.00%	16.00%
N=		2448	2537	819	3350	816

Source: U.S. C.I.S., Immigrants Admitted as Orphans by Sex, Age and Region and Selected Country of Birth (Table 14, 1986-1991 & Table 15, 1992-2002 & Table 10, 2003).

Table 6.7: Ukranian Adoptees to the United States by Sex and Age, 1993-2003

Year		*Sex*		*Age*[a]		
	Total	*% Male*	*% Female*	*% <1 Year*	*% 1-4 Years*	*5+ Years*
1993	248	48.00%	52.00%	30.00%	56.00%	14.00%
1994	163	51.00%	49.00%	35.00%	45.00%	20.00%
1995	5	40.00%	60.00%	20.00%	40.00%	40.00%
1996	10	40.00%	60.00%	0.00%	40.00%	60.00%
1997	65	51.00%	49.00%	15.00%	68.00%	17.00%
1998	168	42.00%	58.00%	18.00%	66.00%	16.00%
1999	307	46.00%	54.00%	14.00%	69.00%	17.00%
2000	645	51.00%	49.00%	20.00%	67.00%	13.00%
2001	1227	55.00%	45.00%	19.00%	63.00%	18.00%
2002	1093	54.00%	46.00%	8.00%	60.00%	32.00%
2003	691	49.00%	51.00%	1.00%	69.00%	30.00%
Total	4622					
Average %		51.00%	49.00%	15.00%	63.00%	22.00%
N =		2377	2245	674	2927	1017

Note: (a) Ages of four adoptees unknown.

Source: U.S. C.I.S., Immigrants Admitted as Orphans by Sex, Age and Region and Selected Country of Birth (Table 15, 1993-2002 & Table 10, 2003).

Table 6.8: Kazak Adoptees to the United States by Sex and Age, 1998-2003

Year		*Sex*		*Age*		
	Total	*% Male*	*% Female*	*% <1 Year*	*% 1-4 Years*	*5+ Years*
1998	54	33.00%	67.00%	59.00%	26.00%	15.00%
1999	108	42.00%	58.00%	57.00%	35.00%	7.00%
2000	392	39.00%	61.00%	44.00%	48.00%	8.00%
2001	664	43.00%	57.00%	38.00%	48.00%	14.00%
2002	801	44.00%	56.00%	34.00%	43.00%	23.00%
2003	819	48.00%	52.00%	33.00%	41.00%	24.00%
Total	2838					
Average %		44.00%	56.00%	38.00%	44.00%	18.00%
N =		1244	1594	1061	1257	520

Source: U.S. C.I.S., Immigrants Admitted as Orphans by Sex, Age and Region and Selected Country of Birth (Table 15, 1998-2002 & Table 10, 2003).

Table 6.9 shows that just over two thousand adoptees came from Bulgaria.

Table 6.9: Bulgarian Adoptees to the United States by Sex and Age, 1992-2003

Year		*Sex*		*Age*		
	Total	*% Male*	*% Female*	*% <1 Year*	*% 1-4 Years*	*% 5+ Years*
1992	90	47.00%	53.00%	16.00%	65.00%	19.00%
1993	126	43.00%	57.00%	1.00%	57.00%	42.00%
1994	101	44.00%	56.00%	0.00%	48.00%	52.00%
1995	108	44.00%	56.00%	1.00%	60.00%	39.00%
1996	157	46.00%	54.00%	0.00%	76.00%	24.00%
1997	137	54.00%	46.00%	0.00%	75.00%	25.00%
1998	147	45.00%	55.00%	1.00%	75.00%	24.00%
1999	213	43.00%	57.00%	1.00%	67.00%	32.00%
2000	207	42.00%	58.00%	2.00%	52.00%	26.00%
2001	288	49.00%	51.00%	1.00%	71.00%	28.00%
2002	261	47.00%	53.00%	2.00%	74.00%	25.00%
2003	196	44.00%	56.00%	1.00%	79.00%	20.00%
Total	2031					
Average %		46.00%	54.00%	2.00%	70.00%	28.00%
N =		928	1103	35	1418	578

Source: U.S. C.I.S. Immigrants Admitted as Orphans by Sex, Age and Region and Selected Country of Birth (Table 15, 1992-2002 & Table 10, 2003).

As Table 6.10 shows, the remaining 5,804 adoptees came to the United States from a variety of other Eastern European countries.[21]

Table 6.10: Other Eastern European Adoptees to the United States by Sex and Age, 1990-2003

Year	*Total*	*Sex*		*Age*[a]		
		% Male	*% Female*	*% <1 Year*	*% 1-4 Years*	*% 5+ Years*
1990	78	53.00%	47.00%	45.00%	41.00%	14.00%
1991	151	42.00%	58.00%	34.00%	42.00%	25.00%
1992	606	48.00%	52.00%	28.00%	52.00%	20.00%
1993	328	44.00%	56.00%	28.00%	48.00%	24.00%
1994	540	44.00%	57.00%	20.00%	52.00%	28.00%
1995	586	47.00%	53.00%	26.00%	49.00%	25.00%
1996	489	48.00%	52.00%	29.00%	45.00%	26.00%
1997	495	48.00%	52.00%	15.00%	56.00%	29.00%
1998	340	50.00%	50.00%	21.00%	54.00%	25.00%
1999	364	52.00%	48.00%	14.00%	63.00%	23.00%
2000	325	46.00%	54.00%	15.00%	55.00%	19.00%
2001	420	47.00%	53.00%	21.00%	57.00%	22.00%
2002	519	48.00%	52.00%	29.00%	52.00%	19.00%
2003	584	45.00%	54.00%	36.00%	41.00%	20.00%
Total	5825					
Average %		47.00%	53.00%	24.00%	52.00%	24.00%
N =		2744	3075	1447	2964	1395

Note: (a) Age of 19 adoptees unknown.

Source: U.S. C.I.S., Immigrants Admitted as Orphans by Sex, Age and Region and Selected Country of Birth (Table 14, 1990-1991 & Table 15, 1992-2002 & Table 10, 2003).

Between 1990 and 2003, almost sixty thousand (N = 59,949) adoptees from Russia and other Eastern European countries joined American families. This number reflects almost one-third (32.9%) of the inter-country adoptees entering the United States in those years.

3. *Inter-country Adoptions Completed in the United States or Abroad*

Countries vary in requirements for where the adoption of emigrant orphans *must* or *may* take place. Some sending countries require that adoption take place before the child leave his/her birth country.

Other countries may allow children to be escorted to the receiving country and adopted there. Sometimes, policies change. Information about where a child was first adopted matters because it points to whether the sending nation or the receiving one has primary control over the adoption process. This information also provides clues as to where adoption costs are being spent and to the potential for complications in the re-adoption process in the U. S. and for obtaining new birth certificates when errors occur in sending countries which require children to be adopted before they leave.

Between 1957 and 1985, the INS distinguished between immigrant-orphans admitted to the United States "to be adopted" and those "adopted abroad." A look at the changing policies of sending countries as to where the adoption must take place is interesting.

In regard to Korean adoptees, between 1957 and 1963, the large majority (94.5%) of these children were adopted in Korea. However, between 1964 and 1969, the majority (68%) of Korean orphans adopted by Americans left Korea *before* they were officially adopted.

In 1970, 41 per cent of all immigrant orphans were "adopted abroad." The percentage of Korean children adopted abroad continued to decline. That percentage dropped to a low of 11 per cent in 1983, and showed only slight increases in 1984 (13.2%) and in 1985 (14.4%).

In the early years of adoption of children from China and Formosa/Taiwan, Americans were more likely to adopt Chinese children in their birth countries (83% between 1957 and 1963, and 64% between 1964 and 1969) than in the United States (17% and 36% respectively). No information on country of official (original) adoption appears to be available for subsequent years. However, the trend has been in the direction of increased numbers of children "adopted abroad"—especially from the major sending countries of Russia and The People's Republic of China.

(a) Age and Gender Breakdown of Adoptees

Beginning in 1986, the INS/CIS began to report data on age and gender breakdowns of "immigrants admitted as orphans." Patterns and variations in the data are described for the countries discussed above.

1. *Korean Adoptees*

The data on gender, presented in Fig. 1(a), show that female adoptees from Korea outnumbered males between 1986 and 1992 and in 1994—but only slightly in some years (e.g., in 1990 and 1994). Beginning in 1995, male adoptees began to outnumber females, reaching the largest yearly male-female gap to date (16%) in 2002.

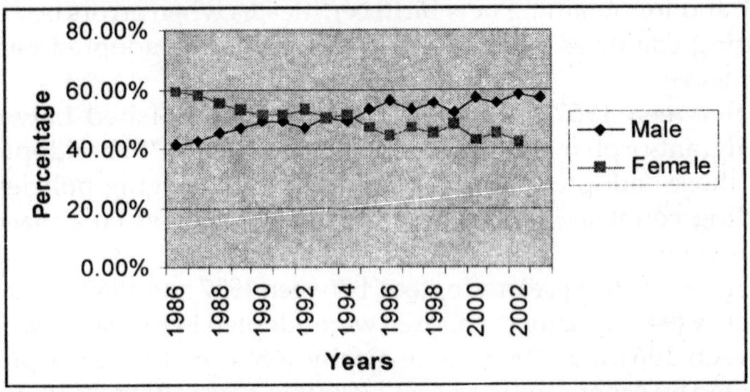

Fig. 1(a): Distribution of Korean Adoptees to the United States by Sex, 1986-2003

The statistics for *Korean adoptees* are most interesting in regard to *age*. Fig. 1(b) shows that, between 1986 and 1989, Korean "immigrants admitted as orphans" *under one year old averaged 75 per cent*. During the 1990s, the percentage of Korean adoptees under one year old increased to an average of *90 per cent*. This average percentage increased to about *93 per cent* between 2000 and 2003.

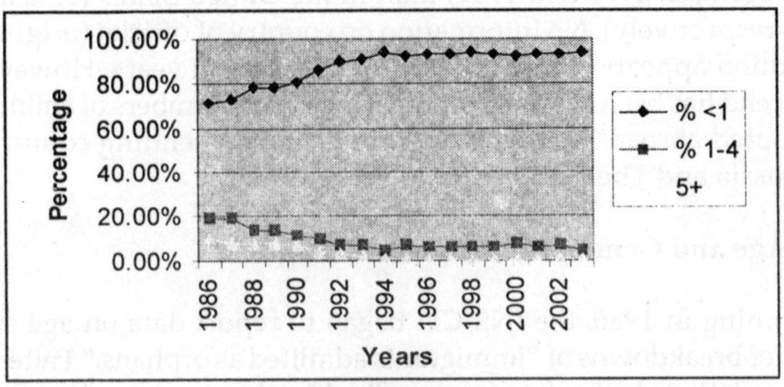

Fig. 1(b): Distribution of Korean Adoptees to the United States by Age, 1986-2003

2. *Chinese Adoptees*

Statistics on the gender and age breakdown of Chinese adoptees to the United States are interesting but not surprising. Fig. 2(a) shows that Chinese females have been much more likely than Chinese males to be available for inter-country adoption. However, although annual totals of adoptees to the U.S. from Mainland China between 1986 and 1991 (not shown here) were much smaller than they were in the 1990s, the data on gender during those years are less skewed in the direction of female adoptees than after 1991. At no time since the INS reported immigrant adoptee statistics by gender did the percentage of female adoptees to the United States from China drop below 52 per cent. More typically, since 1995, the percentage of Chinese girls adopted by American families ranged between 95 per cent (2003) and 98 per cent (1995 and 1996).

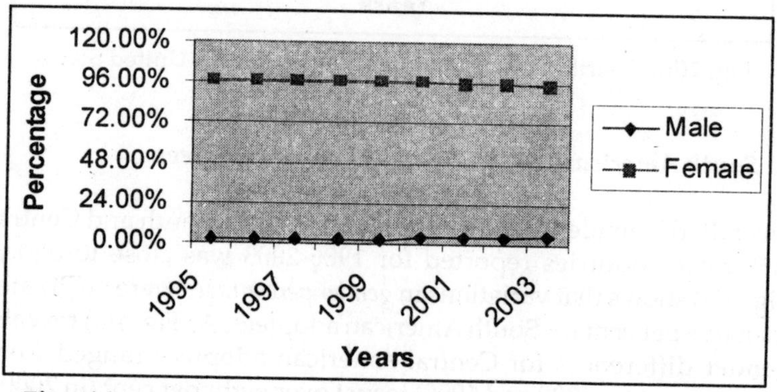

Fig. 2(a): Distribution of Chinese Adoptees to the United States by Sex, 1995-2003

As shown in Fig. 2(b), the percentage of Chinese adoptees that joined their American families as infants under one year old declined between 1995 and 1998, increased to 57 per cent in 2000, and has since remained in the 40 percentage range. Although earlier data show fluctuations from the mid-1980s to the early 1990s, the statistics also indicate that, *on average*, 53 per cent of Chinese adoptees to the United States between 1986 and 2003 arrived in their new families as infants.

The percentage of adoptees aged one through four years old

varied from a low of 17 per cent (in 1995) to a high of 60 per cent (in 1998). On average, 45 per cent of the Chinese adoptees entering the United States between 1995 and 2003 were between one and four years. Only two per cent of Chinese adoptees were age five or older.

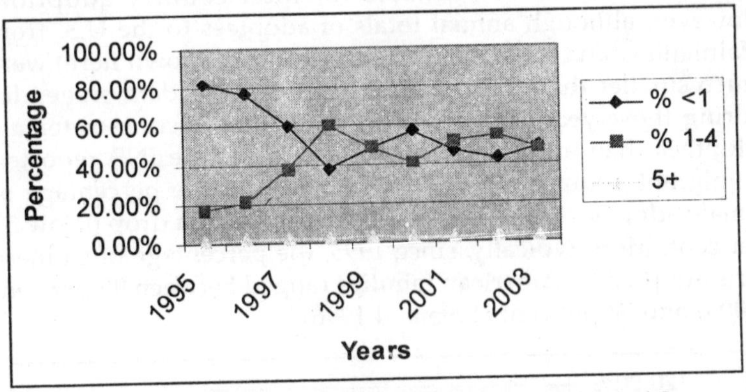

Fig. 2(b): Distribution of Chinese Adoptees to the United States by Age, 1995-2003

3. *South American and Central American Adoptees*

Overall, the gender ratio of adoptees from both South and Central American countries reported for 1986-2003 was close to equal. Fig. 3(a) shows that variations in *gender percentages* were no greater than five per cent for South American adoptees. As Fig. 4(a) reveals, gender differences for Central American adoptees ranged from two per cent (in 1989 and 1990) to just over eight per cent (in 2000), the latter in the direction of more females than males.

After Korean adoptees, those from South and Central America are most likely to enter their North American families as infants. Figs. 3(b) and 4(b) show that, on average, 65 per cent of South American and 66 per cent of Central American children were less than 12 months old at their adoption. For South American adoptees, the percentage of children in that age category varied from a high of 73 per cent (1991) to a low of 45 per cent (1997). For Central American adoptees, the percentages of children adopted as infants ranged from a high of 76 per cent (2001 and 2002) to a low of 48 per cent (in 1988).

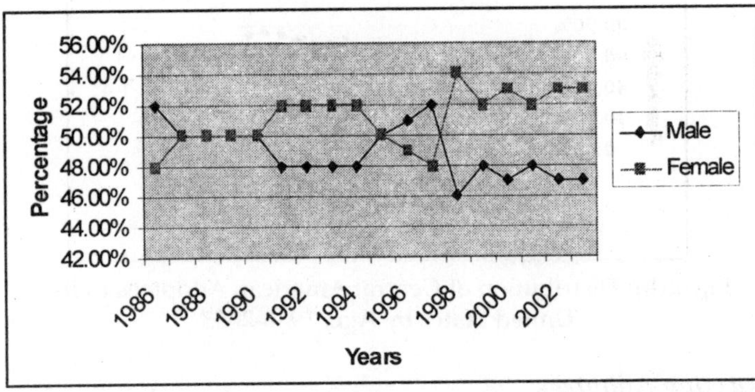

Fig. 3(a): Distribution of South American Adoptees to the United States by Sex, 1986-2003

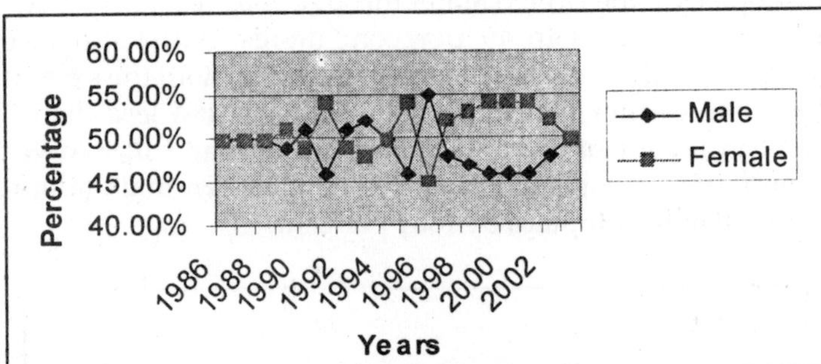

Fig. 4(a): Distribution of Central American Adoptees to the United States by Sex, 1986-2003

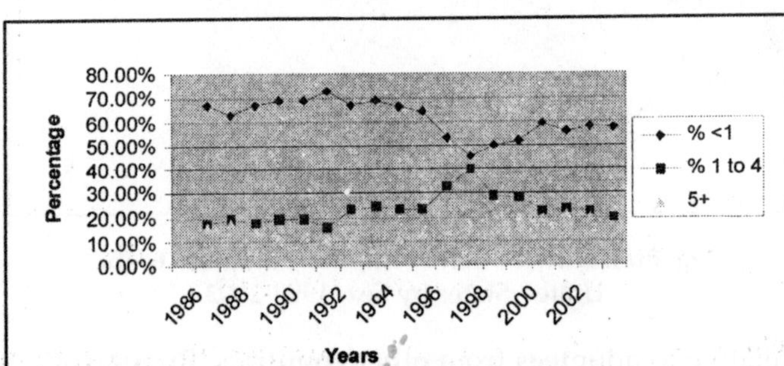

Fig. 3(b): Distribution of South American Adoptees to the United States by Age, 1986-2003

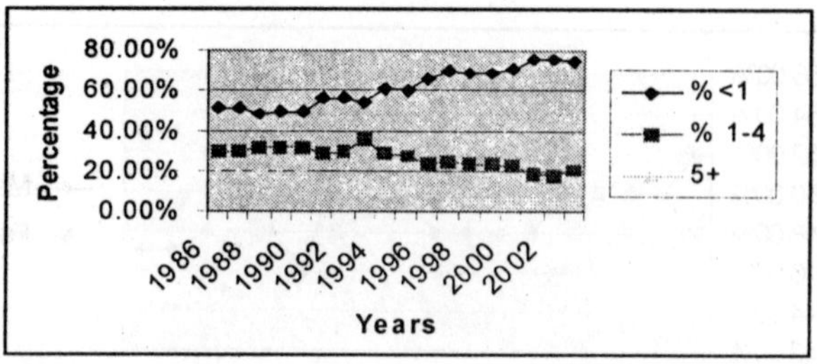

Fig. 4(b): Distribution of Central American Adoptees to the United States by Age, 1986-2003

4. *Russian Adoptees*

As Fig. 5(a) shows, on average, the gender breakdown for Russian-born adoptees to the United States through 2003 was close to equal: 51 per cent females to 49 per cent males. Although yearly breakdowns show some gender discrepancies, with the exception of 1993, the gender distribution typically varied less than five per cent in favour of females in any single year.[22] In two years, 1996 and 1998, the percentages of Russian-born male adoptees exceeded female adoptees by four per cent.

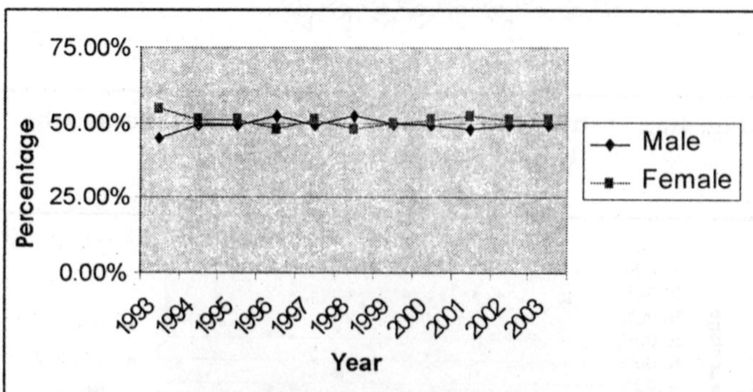

Fig. 5(a): Distribution of Russian Adoptees to the United States by Sex, 1993-2003

Relative to adoptees from other countries, Russian adoptees to the United States were far more likely than those from Asia, South and Central America to arrive in their new families beyond infancy. Fig. 5(b) shows that between 21 per cent (1993) and 39 per cent (1999) Russian adoptees were infants when they joined their American families. The modal age range for Russian adoptees was between one and four years old (52% of adoptees). Between 1993 and 2003, approximately one in five Russian adoptees to the United States was at least five years old. Thus, in regard to age at adoption, Russia stands in marked contrast to China and especially to Korea. Infants under one year old were the majority of adoptees from both Asian countries.

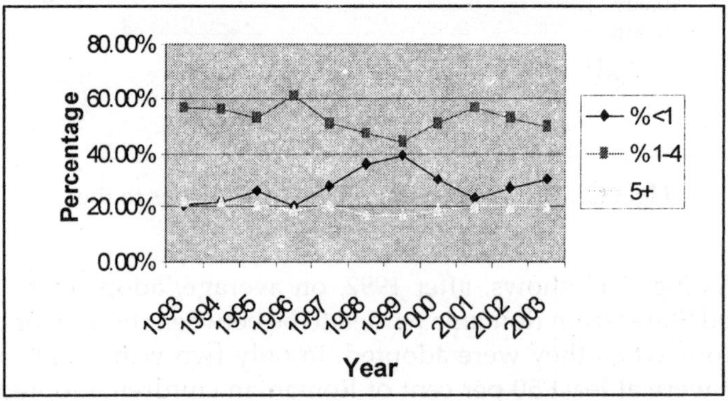

Fig. 5(b): Distribution of Russian Adoptees to the United States by Age, 1993-2003

(b) Gender and Age Distributions of Adoptees from Romania, Ukraine, Kazakhstan, Bulgaria and Minor Eastern European Sending Countries

In the other Eastern European countries, the pattern of female to male preponderance is clear. This pattern varies *in average percentage,* however, from three per cent for Romanian adoptees, to six per cent for adoptees from the minor sending countries, included in aggregate fashion, to eight per cent for Bulgarian adoptees, and 12 per cent for Kazak adoptees.

1. *Romania*

In 1990, a Romanian female was 1.7 times as likely as a Romanian male to be adopted to the U.S. The *gender gap* favouring female Romanian adoptees varied from 26 percentage points (in 1990) to gender balance (in 1993 and 2000). In nine of the 14 years between 1990 and 2003, female adoptees outnumbered males. (see Fig. 6(a)).

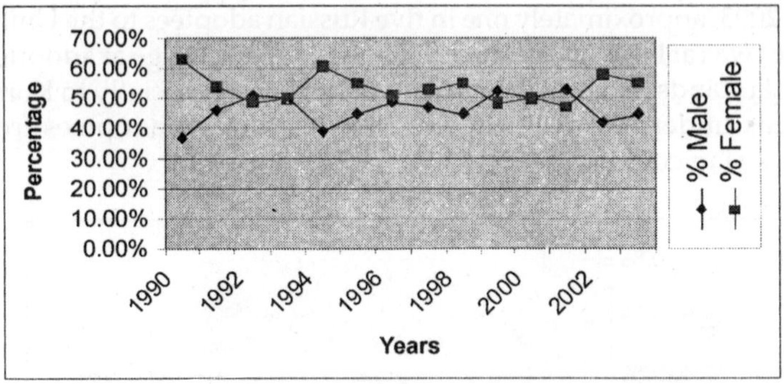

Fig. 6(a): Distribution of Romanian Adoptees to the United States by Sex, 1993-2003

As Fig. 6(b) shows, after 1992, on average, adoptees to the United States from Romania tended to be between the ages of one and four when they were adopted. In only two years (1990 and 1991) were at least 50 per cent of Romanian children adopted to the United States infants.

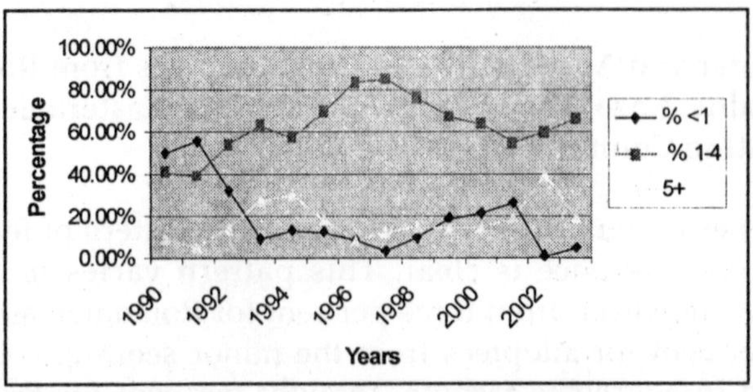

Fig. 6(b): Distribution of Romanian Adoptees to the United States by Age, 1993-2003.

2. ***Ukraine***

The Ukraine was the only major Eastern European sending country that showed an *aggregated average* that slightly favoured males. As Fig. 7(a) shows, however, the gender gap for six of these 11 years

(1993, 1995, 1996, 1998, 1999 and 2003) favoured females. Percentages in favour of female adoptees from the Ukraine varied from 20 per cent in 1995 and 1996, to two per cent in 2003.

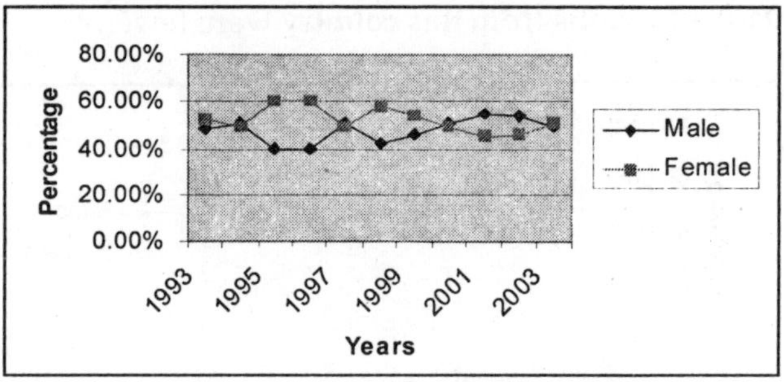

Fig. 7(a): Distribution of Ukranian Adoptees to the United States by Sex, 1993-2003

As Fig. 7(b) shows, the clearest trend in ages of Ukranian adoptees to the U.S. was one to four years old. After first being observed in 1993, this trend persisted between 1997 and 2003. The likelihood of an infant born in the Ukraine being adopted by an American family peaked in 1994 (35%), and declined thereafter.

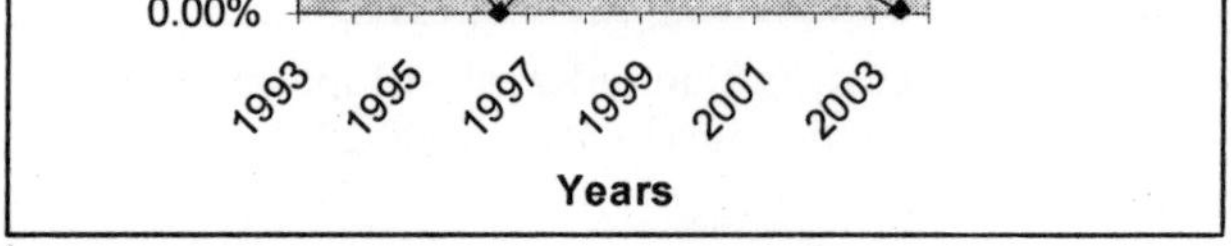

Fig. 7(b): Distribution of Ukranian Adoptees to the United States by Sex, 1993-2003

3. ***Kazakhstan***

As Fig. 8(a) shows female adoptees from Kazakhstan outnumbered males in all years. The *gender gap* was largest in 1998 (34% in favour of females), but showed a *decline* over time to four per cent in favour of females in 2003. Fig. 8(b) shows that in Kazak adoptees to the United States were most likely to enter their new families as infants only in 1998 and 1999. In subsequent years, the percentages of older adoptees, especially those aged one to four years, increased and infant adoptions from this country were fewer.

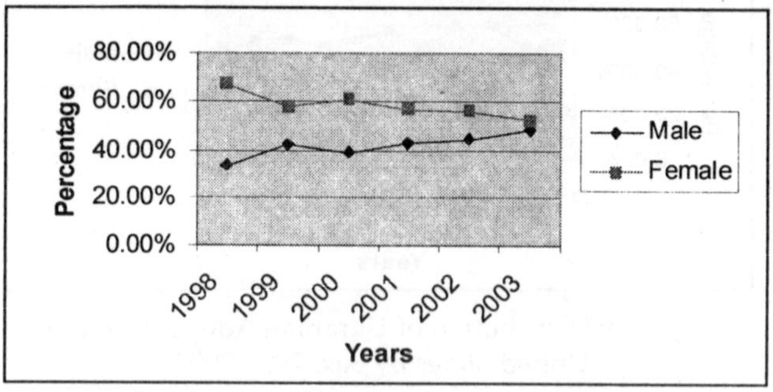

Fig. 8(a): Distribution of Kazak Adoptees to the United States by Sex, 1998-2003

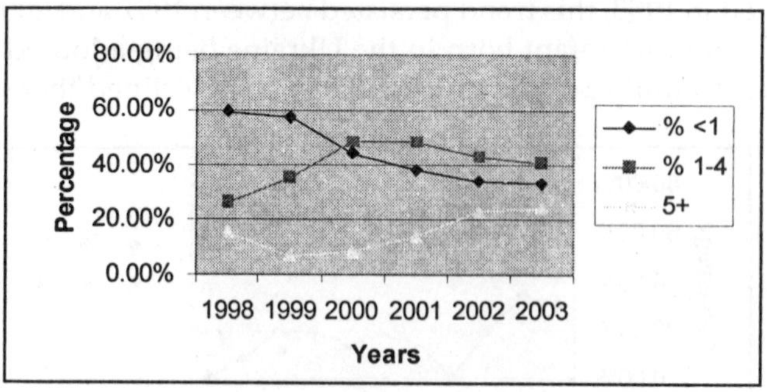

Fig. 8(b): Distribution of Kazak Adoptees to the United States by Age, 1998-2003

4. *Bulgaria*

In every year between 1992 and 2003, except for 1997, adoptees from Bulgaria to the U.S. were more likely to be female than male. The *gender gap* for adoptees from this country varied from a high of 16 percentage points in favour of females (in 2000) to a low of two percentage points (in 2001). [See Fig. 9(a)]

In regard to age distribution, as Fig. 9(b) shows, Bulgarian adoptees to the United States most likely joined their new families generally when they were past infancy. The child's age at adoption generally fell into the one to four years old category. However, between 1994 and 1996, a notable percentage of Bulgarian adoptees were five years old or older when they entered their American families.

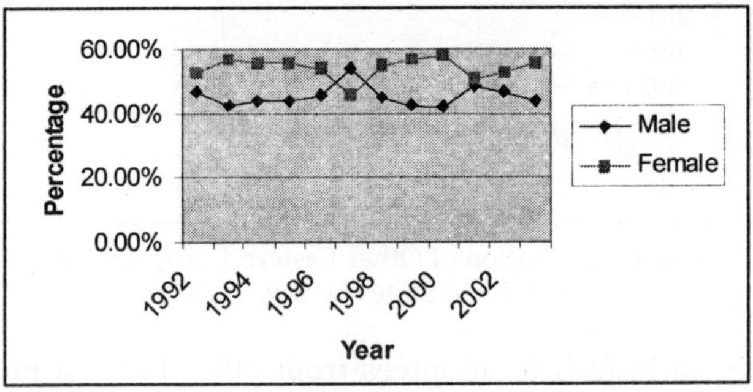

Fig. 9(a): Distribution of Bulgarian Adoptees to the United States by Sex, 1992-2003

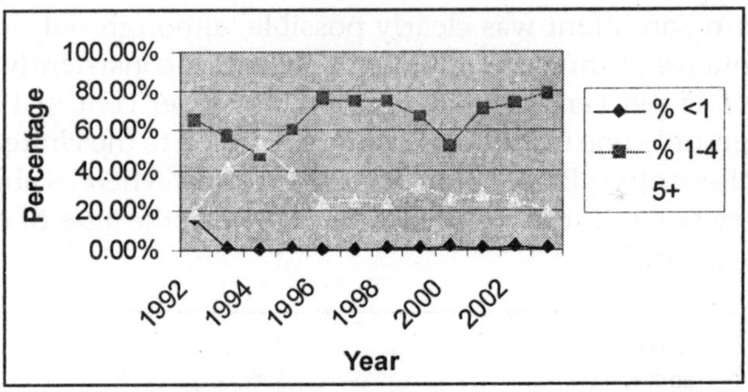

Fig. 9(b): Distribution of Bulgarian Adoptees to the United States by Age, 1992-2003

5. *Other Eastern European Countries*

The data in Fig. 10(a) indicate that, between 1990 and 2003, on average, females from other Eastern European sending countries outnumbered males in all but three years—1990, 1998 and 1999. The *gender gap* varied from a high of 16 per cent in 1991, to parity in 1998. With the exception of 1999, when male adoptees exceeded female adoptees by four per cent, the trend in gender *disparity* was in the direction of more female than male adoptees.

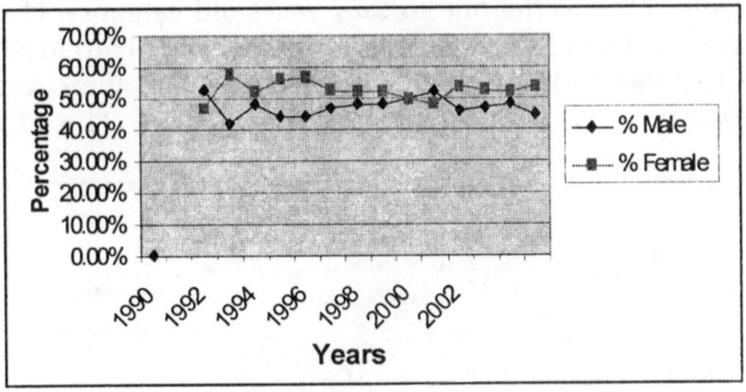

Fig. 10(a): Distribution of Other Eastern European Adoptees to the United States by Sex, 1990-2003

Age variations in adoptees from other Eastern European countries to the United States are similar to those reported for Russia. As Fig. 10(b) shows, children from these sending countries were typically between one and four years old at adoption. Adopting an infant was clearly possible, although not probable. Percentages of infant adoptions fluctuated inconsistently from a high of 45 per cent in 1990, to a low of 14 per cent in 1999. On average, only one in four infant adoptees came to the United States from these other Eastern European countries, whereas about one in every two of these adoptees came between the ages of one and four years old.

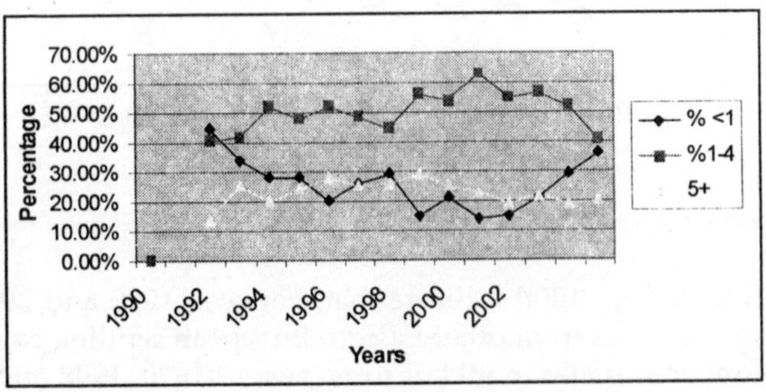

Fig. 10(b): Distribution of Other Eastern European Adoptees to the United States by Age, 1990-2003

Trends in Inter-country Adoptions of Children *Worldwide*

Using data for 1980-89 reported by Kane[23] and, for 1990-1999, collected and made available to me by the International Social Science Resource Centre for the Protection of Children in Adoption (ISS/IRC), I offer a perspective on international adoptions by Americans relative to the global numbers of inter-country adoptions during that same time period. A look at the numbers of inter-country adoptees since 1980 reveals that this type of adoption has become a worldwide phenomenon.

During the 1980s, inter-country adoptees came predominantly from Asia, South America, Central America, and the Caribbean. Korea, India, Sri Lanka, and the Philippines were the important Asian sending countries of children adopted worldwide in those years. Kane reports that "international adoption increased by 62 per cent during this period; and that 90 per cent of the children came from only 10 sending countries."[24]

Although the number of children adopted from Korea declined during the later part of the 1980s, Korea still ranked *first overall* as a sending country *worldwide* during that time, sending 61,235 Korean children to other countries for adoption. The number of children "sent" by this one country represents the largest contingent (44.2%) of children exported for inter-country adoption world-wide during the decade of the 1980s. In that decade, India ranked as the number two sending country of adoptees worldwide (N = 15,325). Columbia (N = 14,837) followed close behind. Brazil (N = 7,527) and Sri Lanka (N = 6,815) ranked 4th and 5th respectively as important sending countries of adoptees internationally. During the 1980s, these *five* sending countries *together* contributed more than one hundred thousand (N = 105,739) of the inter-country adoptees worldwide. The remaining 44 sending countries[25] for which data are available accounted for 32,806 adoptees.

During the 1980s, people in 14 receiving countries adopted a total of 162,661 children born outside those receiving countries.[26] Where did the United States rank in terms of inter-country adoptions during the 1980s? The data indicate that the United States ranked as the *number one* "receiving" country: Americans adopted nearly half (N = 77,606) of the inter-country adoptees "sent" worldwide during the 1980s. No other country came even close to adopting the numbers of children born in other countries that joined American families between 1980 and 1989. In adopting 11.4 per cent (N = 18,501) of these children, France ranked a distant 2nd place. Sweden held 3rd place, adopting about one in 10 (N = 15,788) of all inter-country adoptees. Holland, with 7.1 per cent (N = 11,525) ranked 4th, and Italy, with 6.2 per cent (N = 10,055) ranked 5th during the 1980s.The numbers of children adopted by the remaining nine of the top 14 receiving countries ranged from a high of 3.8 per cent (N = 6,157) children adopted to Switzerland to a low of 0.1 per cent (N = 187) inter-country adoptees to Spain.[27]

During the 1990s, the decade total for inter-country adoptions worldwide increased, although not dramatically so. According to ISS/IRC data, between 1990 and 1999, 175,013 children were adopted worldwide by people living outside their adopted child's/children's birth countries. In 1990, these data show only five countries "receiving" inter-country adoptees: The United States, France, the Netherlands, Denmark, and Iceland. In 1991, the number of receiving countries for inter-country adoptees increased to eight. Except for a drop to seven in 1992, the number of receiving countries for inter-country adoptions worldwide varied from 11 to 14 during the remainder of that decade. In contrast, the number of "sending" countries of inter-country adoptees varied during this time period from a low of 57 countries in 1990, to a high of 147 countries in 1998.

Clearly, the United States was again the number one "receiving" country for inter-country adoptees during the 1990s. The numbers of inter-country adoptees rose by about 12 per cent over the 1980s decade total. The increase was also reflected in the numbers of adoptees who came to the United States between 1990 and 1999: Couples and individuals living in the United States adopted 60 per cent (N = 104,644) of these children. In contrast, France again held a distant second place to the United States, with children adopted from other countries by French families comprising 18.1 per cent of the total inter-country adoptees worldwide.

Inter-country adoptions have been evident in the countries of the Netherlands and Denmark for many years. However, according to the ISS/IRC data, the numbers of adoptees to both countries remained relatively small throughout the 1990s. These numbers ranged from a low of 249 children adopted to the Netherlands toward the end of the decade (in 1997) to a high of 830 children adopted to this country at the beginning of the decade (in 1990). For Denmark, the numbers reported by the ISS/IRC varied from a low of 433 children early in the decade (in 1992) to a high of 696 adoptees at the end of the decade (in 1999).[28] The numbers for Iceland varied between four children (in 1992) to 23 children (in 1999). Between 1996 and 1999 (years for which the ISS/IRC data were available), inter-country adoptees to Italy varied in number from a low of 2,019 children (in 1997) to a high of 2,649 children (in 1996).

Adoptions to the United States from Russia and Eastern Europe in Global Perspective

With the *worldwide 1990s* decade total for Russian children adopted outside their birth country standing at 22,756 the ISS/IRC data reveal that Americans adopted 83 per cent of the Russian adoptees (N = 18,831) sent worldwide for adoption. During that decade, Americans also adopted:

- 87 per cent of the children sent from the Poland (N = 694) for adoption worldwide;
- 77 per cent of the Ukranian adoptees (N = 1,036) worldwide;
- 44 per cent of the Romanian adoptees (N = 5,808) sent worldwide; and
- 33 per cent of the Bulgarian (N = 1,056) adoptees worldwide.

Summary

This article introduces the discussion of three major threads that impact on adoption, both within and across national boundaries: Attitudes towards adoption in the socio-cultural context in which family formation occurs or expands; the availability of potential adoptees in country; and the *ease* or *difficulty* of adopting available children. Clearly, the United States is a society where attitudes toward adoption vary by ethnic and racial categories as well as over time. In the United States, "informal" adoptions among relatives, close friends, or neighbours have been replaced by a myriad of laws that require the involvement of judges, social workers, and others who have a vested interest in regulating adoption—the process, the likelihood, and the outcome.

Although practiced on a limited basis in the early decades of the 20th century, domestic adoptions of non-relative children increased in popularity in the United States after World War II. Out-of-wedlock motherhood continued to be stigmatized well into the 1960s. Domestic adoptions in the United States reportedly peaked in 1970. Thus, as Melosh states, adoption became the "legitimate" social response to the problem of illegitimacy. Adoption was moving from the personal to the public realm.

However, between 1973 and 1995, domestic adoptions declined. The availability of legalized abortion, beginning in 1973, took its toll. Along with a decline in the number of infants and young children available for domestic adoption, a variety of forces also worked against the opportunity for some Americans to adopt domestically.

External forces entered the adoption picture in the form of humanitarian concerns. Wars expanded the pool of potential adoptees who included children born from relationships between American GIs fighting in foreign wars and native women as well as children who lost their families in conflicts in South Korea, Viet Nam, and Cambodia.

Poverty in Mexico, South and Central America also created an opportunity for adoptees from this part of the world to join American families. Adoptees came to the United States from South America in the 1970s and 1980s, and from Central America beginning in the 1980s. In the 1990s, the plight of large numbers of children living in orphanages in Eastern European countries captured America's attention. The media brought home some of the social problems and issues that forced these "beautiful" children into often bleak, institutional settings and the care of non-relatives hired to provide for their basic needs.

Note: The author gratefuily acknowledges Transaction Publishers for permission to use previously published material.

Notes

1. Roman Espejo, (Ed.) (2002), *Adoption: Opposing Viewpoints*. San Diego: Greenhaven Press, Inc.

2. Mary Kathleen Benet (1976), *The Politics of Adoption*. New York: The Free Press.
3. Conversation with Inuit specialist, Janet M. Billson, Ph.D., on 11/10/2003.
4. E. Wayne Carp (1998), *Family Matters: Secrecy and Disclosure in the History of Adoption*. Cambridge, Mass: Harvard University Press.
5. David Schneider (1968), *American Kinship: A Cultural Account*. London: Tavistock.
6. Benet, *ibid*.
7. Adam Pertman (2000), *Adoption Nation*. New York: Basic Books.
8. Jason Fields, Living Arrangements of Children, at p. 9, Current Population Reports, pp. 70-74, Census Bureau (April 2001). Includes children 18 years old and younger and about 500,000 children living with one biological parent and a step parent who adopted them Melosh, *ibid*., p. 106. Cited in p. 1 of the Overview of Adoption in the United States, http://www.adoptioninstitute.org/FactOverview.html retrieved electronically on 5/23/2003.
9. Barbara Melosh (2002), Strangers and Kin: The American Way of Adoption. Cambridge, MA: Harvard University Press.
10. Melosh, *ibid*., p. 106.
11. *Ibid*.
12. Penny Maza, Adoption trends: 1944-1975, at Table 1, Child Welfare Research Notes, No. 9 (August, 1994) cited in Overview of Adoption in the United States, *ibid*., p. 2.
13. The estimate refers to formerly married women, ages 44-54. A. Chandra, A. Joyce, P. Maza, and C. Bachrach, *Adoption, Adoption Seeking and Relinquishment Adoption in the United States*, p. 5, Advance Data, No. 306. National Center for Health Statistics. Cited in Overview of Adoption in the United States, *ibid*., p. 1.
14. National Center for Health Statistics, U.S. Department of Health and Human Services, *Fertility, Family Planning, and Women's Health: New Data from the 1995 National Survey of Family Growth*, page 8, Vital Statistics 23, No. 19 (May, 1997). Cited in Overview of Adoption in the United States, *ibid*., p. 1.
15. Victor Flango and Carol Flango. *How Many Children Were Adopted in 1992? Child Welfare* Vol. LXXIV, No. 5 (Sept./Oct. 1995), p. 1022, cited in Overview of Adoption in the United States, *ibid*., p. 2.
16. Flango and Flango, *ibid*.
17. In families that adopt domestically, an inter-racial and/or cross-cultural dimension may also be part of their adoption experience.
18. Data obtained from selected tables compiled by the federal government.
19. *Ibid*.
20. *Ibid*.

21. The countries in this category include Albania, Armenia, Belarus, Estonia, Hungary, Latvia, Lithuania, Moldova, Poland, the Republic of Georgia, Uzbekistan, other republics, and unknown republics.
22. The one exception was in 1993, when female adoptees outnumbered male adoptees by 10 per cent.
23. Saralee Kane, The Movement of Children for International Adoption: An Epidemiologic Perspective, *The Social Science Journal*, Vol. 30, No. 4 (1993), pp. 323-339. See pp. 324-325 for a discussion of materials and methods Used to collect data from receiving countries and from two sending countries, Korea and Columbia, for selected years.
24. Kane, *ibid.*, p. 323.
25. The 44 sending countries are Chile, Philippines, Guatemala, Peru, El Salvador, Mexico, Haiti, Poland, Honduras, Thailand, Madagascar, Romania, Costa Rica, Paraguay, Taiwan, Japan, Bolivia, Dominican Republic, Indonesia, Mauritius, Ecuador, Ethiopia, Jamaica, Hong Kong, Lebanon, Panama, Yugoslavia, Turkey, Rwanda, Canada (Quebec only), Portugal, Djibouti, China, Greece, Bangladesh, Vietnam, Pakistan, Austria, Belize, Nicaragua, Ghana, Fiji, Iran, and the United States.
26. Kane, *ibid.*
27. Kane, *ibid.*
28. No numbers were reported.

7

Negotiating Identity
Post-colonial Reflections on Transnational Adoption

PAL AHLUWALIA

I guess you don't get it. The whole point is, there is nothing you can do to make shit better. You're white in a white supremacist society, and that's all there is to it. You purchased a coloured kid (sometimes two or three) as a white person. You can never take that back. There is little you can do to repair the damage. No amount of cultural lessons, no amount of anti-racist work you do, no amount of money that you give, no amount of slang or phrases that you learn, can change the structure that you are a part of. —*Kil Ja Kim*

Exile is predicated on the existence of, love for, and bond with one's native place; what is true of all exile is not that home and love of home are lost, but that loss is inherent in the very existence of both.

—*Edward Said*

In 2000, I had the opportunity to visit the West African nation Senegal. During that visit, I went to Goree Island which is located off the coast of Senegal, only a few kilometres from Dakar. The island, I learnt, had been rejuvenated and made tourist friendly with several restaurants and hotels built recently. At one level, it seemed like any other coastal haven with beautiful beaches and thousands of people basking in the sun. However, what Goree Island is renowned for is its position as a centre of the trans-atlantic slave trade with an estimated 20 million Africans passing through the island between the mid-1500s and mid-1800s. As I walked around the island, now transformed into a kind of a museum, I visited slave houses where the remnants of the slave trade were all too evident. It seemed that from the very walls of the houses one could sense the intense suffering that millions of Africans endured and I was profoundly moved and found it difficult to comprehend the scale, magnitude and horror of the slave trade.

Goree Island has become a site where many African-Americans visit, to try and come to terms with slavery and to establish some sort of connection with Africa. For most, it is difficult to establish their origins and in some way Goree Island represents an over-determined site through which they can come to terms with the past. As the African-American novelist Alice Walker wrote, "I do not know from what part my African ancestors came, and so I claim the continent" (as cited in Kanneh, 1998: 114). As I walked around, I could see many African-Americans who had simply broken down and were being consoled, as guides walked them through the intricacies of what life on the island was like for captured slaves who were being prepared to be shipped to the new world. It was clear to me that for many of the African-Americans this visit was a kind of return, an opportunity to come to terms with the past, a search for an Africa and an identity that only existed in the imagination. But more importantly, it was a deeply moving experience, one that entailed coming to terms with the suffering of their ancestors, and a time when some sort of closure, if that was at all possible, could be affected.

I have dwelt on this experience precisely because of the profound similarities that I want to suggest transnationally adopted children endure. For both, there is an overwhelming desire to establish a connection with their origins in order to come to terms with the past and to gain some understanding of their identity. In both cases, we are looking at the commoditisation of human bodies and the need for some understanding of why their 'own people' were complicit in their relocation. It is these return narratives that have become an important means in the attempt to move on, to be able to function in the two worlds in which they live.

Origins and Displacement

Jacques Derrida points out that there are no ontological origins. He argues that, "a meditation upon the trace should undoubtedly teach us that there is no origin, that is to say, simple origin; that the questions of origin carry with them a metaphysics of presence" (1976: 74). The corollary of the anxiety of origin in Derrida's work is the predominance of displacement, a concept which is usually associated with Freud's interpretation of dreams, but which has expanded from a technical psychoanalytic term to a process encompassing a wide range of deconstructive strategies in poststructuralist theory. As Krupnick points out, Derrida does not theoretically articulate displacement, but deconstruction itself proceeds by way of displacement, first reversing a binary opposition and then displacing it (1983: 1). For Derrida, it is not simply the case that the binary oppositions of metaphysics should be neutralised. Rather, deconstruction entails a reversal and displacement because within familiar philosophical binaries there is always a violent hierarchy. One term of the binary is always superior to the other. It is the task of deconstruction to disrupt that hierarchy, to place the superior term under erasure. As Spivak points out, the task for deconstruction is:

> *To locate the promising marginal text, to disclose the undecidable moment, to pry it loose with the positive lever of the signifier, to reverse the resident hierarchy, only to displace it; to dismantle in order to reconstitute what is always already inscribed (Derrida 1976: lxxvi).*

A crucial part of Derrida's hermeneutic is to usurp origin. This erasure of location, of the place of 'origin,' is linked in Derrida to the deconstruction of history, the narrative of the past. The end of history for Derrida is a deconstruction of origin, which is the beginning of indeterminacy.

The trope of displacement in deconstruction continually rehearses the refrain of loss and displacement. "Older forms of thinking and feeling *must* change with such a displacement. Displacement itself takes on a new sense. It refers not to an essentially conservative 'reformulation' that has the effect of keeping the best of the old while adapting to new circumstances. Instead, displacement now refers to a violent intervention intended to shake and demoralize the old order" (Krupnik, 1983: 12). For

Derrida, origin itself is the condition of displacement. It ceases to be a point of incarnation and becomes the energising condition of his discourse.

This is why there can be no beginning. We begin where we are. The "source" is transformed into an energising presence. In *Of Grammatology* Derrida, explaining why Rousseau should be taken as a beginning, a "decisive articulation of the logocentric epoch" (162) says, "We must begin *wherever we are* and the thought of the trace, which cannot take the scent into account, has already taught us that it was impossible to justify a point of departure absolutely. *Wherever we are:* in a text where we already believe ourselves to be" (162). Or, speaking of *différance,* he says, "there is nowhere to *begin* to trace the sheaf or the graphics of *différance.* For what is put into question is precisely the quest for a rightful beginning, an absolute point of departure, a principal of responsibility" (1982: 6). It is this sense of the trace that makes it vital to realise that for post-colonial subjects there is no escape from colonialism. It is in the aftermath of colonialism that the post-colonial subject deals with the present and confronts the future.

It is this idea of displacement that I want to suggest is most helpful in approaching the questions of transnational adoption. It is precisely in this way that we can look at transnational adoption, as a "beginning," that *disappears* into the present moment, becoming the constitutive reality of Derrida's concern with displacement, rather than its origin. For, what does the quest for a return to the point of origin entail? Transnational adoptees, when they embark on the journey of reclaiming the past, of coming to terms with their sense of loss, realise that there is no simple comfort in returning – that they are inevitably caught in the two worlds in which they co-exist – it is through this recognition of the traces that are contained in them, through this displacement, that they are able to negotiate identity.

Modernity and Transnational Adoption

Adoption is an ancient institution, that is, at its core, about constructing a family. By the middle of the twentieth century, adoption was viewed as an ideal solution for heterosexual couples who were unable to have children of their own. By the 1990s, transnational adoption had become a viable option not only for heterosexual couples but also for homosexual and single parents who sought "to (re)consolidate and (re)occupy conventional structures of family and kinship" (Eng, 2003: 1). At the same time, the very practice was seen as a mechanism that, "offered birth mothers and their babies second chances for normal lives, without the shame of being unwed and illegitimate" (Herman 2002: 340). It was also in the twentieth century that adoption was modernised and became a way of transforming those who were not related to each other into kin, "through systematic 'matching' techniques that replaced, rather then supplemented, natal families" (339). Matching, however, reinforced the centrality of blood relationships undermining the very institution of adoption as an inferior mode to the normal way of making a family. It is this obsession with what constitutes a 'normal' family that continues to cause a great deal of anxiety about the capacity of homosexual couples and singles to be effective parents and role models.

The story of modernising adoption practices and processes is as much a story about modernity itself, where these very practices and processes were rationalised, professionalised, bureaucratised and given scientific substantiation. As Ellen Herman points out, "making adoption modern entailed establishing a new paradigm, *kinship by design*, and then radically distancing that paradigm from modes of family formation that relied on commerce, sentiment, intuition, accident, or simply common sense" (Herman, 2002: 339). The modernisation of adoption created a new professional class of brokers in the adoption market who were charged with determining the suitability of both the children and the adoptive parents. However, this did not eradicate the moral questions at the heart of adoption – namely, what is a family; where did one come from; and where does one belong?

Since the Second World War, as working class children became difficult to obtain for domestic adoption, transnational adoption became an attractive option. The desire for infertile couples to have children was, and remains, part of the general social pressure that deems a family incomplete without children. As David Eng points out, "the possession of a child, whether biological or adopted, has today become the sign of guarantee not only for family but also for full and robust citizenship – for being a fully realized political economic and social subject" (Eng, 2003: 7-8).

The history of transnational adoption is relatively recent. It began in the wake of the aftermath of the Second World War and the ensuing humanitarian crisis in which transnational adoption to the U.S. first began with emigration of European orphans from Germany and Poland. After the Korean War and amidst the Cold War, an intense movement of transnational adoption took place. Since that time, over 200,000 South Korean children have been involved with nearly 150,000 residing in the U.S. and the rest in Europe, Canada and Australia. The history of transnational adoption particularly in the United States is linked inextricably with the history of U.S. military occupation and involvement overseas (Gailey 1999: 3).

Transnational adoption involving the movement of predominately non-white children to the West began most intensively after the Korean War. While transnational adoption in the twentieth century involved mostly non-white children, after the collapse of communism, large numbers of children from Eastern Europe were also adopted. For example, in the last decade in the United States alone, nearly 139,000 children have been adopted internationally. Of these, nearly 50,000 have been from China and Russia (Volkman 2003: 1). When the total number of children being adopted throughout the West is taken into account, we can see that there is a colossal movement of children from predominately poor nations.

Transnational adoption, portrayed as the saving of non-white children from poor countries, was legitimised as being highly progressive and anti-racist. However, as Erika Kleiman argues, the "primary reason people adopt from abroad is that they cannot find the children they want in the United States" (as cited in Shiu, 2001). Following the collapse of communism, came the opportunity to adopt from former Soviet bloc countries and this witnessed a significant drop in adoptions from Asian countries. As a consequence, adoptions from Romania and Russia became more prevalent. It is abundantly clear, "that as soon as white children were available, prospective international adopters opted for race over all other considerations" (Gailey, 1999: 5).

Transnational adoption involves an exchange between countries. It entails a transaction where the birth mother and sending country are often represented as being morally deficient whilst the adopting parents and country are portrayed as saviours.

The exchange for children normally involving a payment, a fee, or a donation "is a transaction [that] creates an orderly relation of states to one another through the movement of valued resources (children) in adoption" (Yngvesson, 2002: 237; Kim, 2004). Transnational adoption inevitably raises questions about race, culture and nation. As Pauline Strong notes:

> *Adoption across political and cultural borders may simultaneously be an act of violence and an act of love, an excruciating rupture and a generous incorporation, an appropriation of valued resources and a constitution of personal ties* (as cited in Volkman: 4).

In transnational adoption, the child is often separated from his or her state of origin, which in some cases involves sealing the record and the alteration of the child's birth records with the names of the adoptive parents inscribed whilst the birth parent's identity is erased. As Toby Volkman points out, "the prevailing 'clean break' model of domestic adoption was transposed, in inter-country adoption, in a 'clean break' from biological progenitors and from the national or cultural origins of the child" (Volkman, 2003: 32). This is done, so that "it can be connected to a new family, a new name, a new nation. The child is given a new identity. It now *belongs* in a new place" (Yngvesson, 2003: 7). The severing of the past means that an older identity is ruptured and the child "can be reembedded in a new place, almost as though he or she never moved at all" (7). In the 1950s, this practice was implemented with little attention paid to how these children would fit into societies where the norm was homogeneity.

Displacement and Dislocation amongst Transnational Adoptees

Frantz Fanon who was deeply influenced by Jean-Paul Sartre and his book, *Anti-Semite and Jew* (1965) in *Black Skin, White Masks* extends the notions of recognition and non-recognition through the trope of racial identity. However, what is significant about the two, is that Sartre was not writing as a Jew whereas Fanon was writing from the lived experience of being black. The major lesson that Fanon learned from European existentialism was the "basic concept of non-being that he used to describe the conditions of aridity and paralysis that often follow ego collapse" (Henry, 1996: 234). For Fanon, this book is not simply an account of white "negrophobia" but the desire "to explore the lived-experience and moral possibilities open to a black living in a negrophobic world" (Kruks, 1996: 128). It is in this context that Homi Bhabha's work is important in terms of understanding the dilemmas of the adoptee who is constantly faced with living in two worlds, the world of the adopted parents, where she or he is faced with the reality that they are not the same as everyone else, that they are so eager to be a part of, and a place that exists in their imagination – an origin that they do not know. Toby Volkman reports that Korean adoptees who grew up thinking that they were like their white Scandinavian parents had by adolescence shifted their perception of their own identity. "Only 28 per cent of the respondents considered themselves Korean-American or Korean-European as they were growing up; by contrast, 64 per cent of the respondents as adults, viewed themselves as Korean-American or Korean-European" (2003: 37).

In his essay, "Of Mimicry and Man", Homi Bhabha illustrates the manner in which mimicry became an important strategy of colonial power and knowledge. But for Bhabha, mimicry is not a simple aping of the imperial master. Rather, it characterises the ambivalent relationship between both the colonizer and the colonized. This is necessarily so, because when the imperial master encourages its colonial subject to "mimic", the resultant product is never exactly the same. As Bhabha points out, "mimicry represents an *ironic* compromise" which entails that "colonial mimicry is the desire for a reformed other, *as a subject of a difference that is almost the same, but not quite*" (1994: 86). Mimicry for the colonized is about becoming like the colonizer whilst remaining different. But mimicry has a menacing side—it has the potential to become mockery and parody. As Bhabha notes, "mimicry is at once resemblance and menace" (86).

The idea of menace and mimicry coexist, where the "*menace* of mimicry is its *double* vision which in disclosing the ambivalence of colonial discourse also disrupts its authority" (88). It is Thomas Macaulay's 1835 "Minute on Indian Education" which Bhabha cites as the colonial process of mimicry that gives rise to the "mimic man":

> *We must at present do our best to form a class who may be interpreters between us and the millions whom we govern; a class of persons, Indian*

> *in blood and colour, but English in taste, in opinions, in morals, in intellect* (87).

It is this sense of the double – mimicry and menace – which is created by Macaulay's vision. The mediating Indian who mimics the imperial master no longer remains the model colonial subject because the product of mimicry is ultimately beyond the control of the colonial master. The "mimic man" has the potential to become an insurgent subject. As Bhabha notes, "the ambivalence of colonial authority repeatedly turns from mimicry—a difference that is almost nothing but not quite—to menace—a difference that is almost total but not quite" (Bhabha 1994: 91).

In the case of adoption, the idea of mimicry is all too evident. Transnational adoptees grow up in cultures and societies that problematise their very difference – these children grow up thinking and trying to be the same as everyone else only to be confronted by racism which challenges their conception of the self. As "mimic children", these adoptees are the same but not quite. One of the most significant consequences of inter-racial transnational adoption of is that it makes adoptive parents aware of the shocking racism that their children have to endure. The effect of this racism and racial alterity is that these issues are brought into the "privatized space of the white American nuclear family, even as our national borders continue to be sealed in unprecedented ways" (Eng 2003: 32).

We are all too aware that race and racism are social constructions with poignant effects in different historical contexts. It is within such a configuration that we need to consider how it is that current transnational adoption practices themselves have a powerful capacity to reproduce tropes of race and racism in new, complex and often unintended ways. The effect of the modes of prejudice that adoptees face needs to be conceptualised within the broader forms of racism that migrants, refugees, diasporic peoples and post-colonial subjects continually endure. Transnational adoptees, especially those who come from the Third World, from Asia, Africa and South America, are often elided with immigrants and refugees from those very geographical locations. As Ann Anagnost points out:

> *There is also a recognition, born from the necessity of dealing with the Immigration and Naturalisation Service, that adoption* is *a form of*

> *immigration and that this might potentially align the child alongside lesser-valued bodies, such as illegal aliens or persons of nationalities with historically restricted quotas... (2000: 398).*

The effect of this racism is that adoptive parents are increasingly confronted with cultural difference and multiculturalism at a deeply personal, family level. Transnational adoption poses real difficulties, destabilising the quagmire of contemporary race politics by introducing subjects who do not fit neatly into the web of representations prevalent within race discourses. For David Eng, "Mail-order brides" and "domestic servants" are obvious examples of the exploitation of Third World women whose labour is vital to the maintenance of First-World middle class families. The figure of the international adoptee is fraught with difficulty within this configuration of power and he questions on "which side – capital or labour – does the trans-national adoptee fall?" (Eng, 2003: 5).

The movement of human bodies from sending country to adopting nation, from abject poverty and abandonment, to affluence and 'family', means that imperialist histories and practices are confronted within the very private space of the family. However, the commoditisation of human bodies is mitigated through the belief that adoption is about rescuing children from their desperate circumstances and the rhetoric of the gift. For example, in her discussion of Chinese adoptees, Ann Anagnost points out that this "language of the gift implies a personal relationship with a donor, here identified as China as a nation or the Chinese people as a whole. This identification of China as a benefactor puts the adoptive parent in a somewhat ambivalent relationship to the Chinese state" (2000: 399).

It is in this way that the official narrative of the nation, the representation of Chinese subjects and the Chinese nation and politics are brought into an acute juxtaposition with the desire that the adopted child belongs to an ancient culture, a great civilisation that needs to be recognised and celebrated. This is a narrative which is often in conflict with a narrative of a society that mistreats it citizens and abuses human rights, that imposes harsh penalties on those who transgress the one child policy, that forces mothers to abandon their daughters. The roots of this ambivalent relationship is necessitated by the need to somehow differentiate the adopted child from the "other" migrants who are so suspiciously encountered often in ghettoes and who occupy an altogether different world. This world is one that Homi Bhabha so accurately captures in the following description:

> *I have lived that moment of the scattering of the people that in other times and other places, in the nations of other, becomes a time of gathering. Gathering of exiles and émigrés and refugees, gathering on the edge of 'foreign' cultures; gathering at the frontiers; gatherings in the ghettos or cafes of city centres; gathering in the half-life, half-light of foreign tongues, or in the uncanny fluency of another's language; gathering the signs of approval and acceptance, degrees, discourses, disciplines; gathering the memories of under-development, of other worlds lived retroactively; gathering the past in a ritual of revival; gathering the present. Also the gathering of the people in the diaspora: indentured, migrant, interned; gathering of incriminatory statistics, educational performance, legal statutes, immigration status...*(Bhabha 1990: 291).

How does a transnational adopted child who has no knowledge of this world deal with it as they face the powerful forces that racialize them when they emerge "from the womb of domestic affect into the larger social world" (Anagnost, 2000: 414). It is because of this dilemma that there has been a perceptible shift in the way in which adoption is being handled. From a regime of secrecy and keeping adoptees in the dark, we have moved to a new culture where adoptees are increasingly being encouraged to "explore their multiple identities: to retain a name, to imagine their birth families, to learn about 'birth cultures', perhaps to visit the birth country" (Volkman, 2003: 2).

Celebrating Culture and Return Narratives

The change in adoption practices with an emphasis on openness and an awareness of the importance for the adoptee to know something about their culture, heritage and origins has meant that a plethora of organisations have been set up in the West where adoptive parents gather to impart something of the birth culture to their adopted children. The easiest way to achieve this goal is to learn about the civilisations from which they originate, through food, art, and history with national holidays and observances looming large in the cultural imaginary that Ann Anagnost has so aptly described as "culture bites" (2000: 413). These ventures are seen as a vital part in instilling pride in adopted children who are encouraged to participate in some form of readily available cultural activity that will connect them with the culture of their birth. It is these cultural vignettes that have come under attack on the grounds that providing these "appealing little packages of culture is in itself a form of racism and 'worse than nothing', eliding more painful histories of oppression, colonialism, and Asian American immigration" (Chang in Volkman: 39). The fetishization of the birth culture is a way to satiate the longings for origins and the mother's body. As Volkman puts it, "the genetic linkage of the child is unknown, but the cultural heritage can be studied, celebrated, performed and embodied" (Volkman, 2003: 42).

In the world of transnational adoption, two stories predominate – one of abandonment and the other concerning roots. In the former, the child's past is a burden and once freed from that, he or she can be assimilated fully into the new family and culture. In the latter, the child is seen as part of the birth culture and nation and there is a strong pull that involves a connection often established through returning there (Yngvesson, 2003: 8). However, it is not clear that these stories are mutually exclusive.

The meaning of a trip back to the country of origin is an attempt to come to terms with the experience of abandonment. This entails also realising that there is no such thing as a motherless child. The question of roots that appears to pervade most adoption stories is based on the assumption that there is a past that can be reclaimed. The search usually is predicated on the belief that if one can simply locate the right papers, the right person, some one who was involved in brokering the adoption, it will be possible to come to terms with the past. This quest for origins is part of that story where "an alienated self must be reconnected to a ground (an author, a nation, a parent) that constitutes its identity" (Yngvesson, 2003: 13). The idea of returning to a homeland that is simply waiting there is, Stuart Hall argues, one fraught with difficulty. Rather it is something that:

> *...is narrated. It is grasped through reconstruction. It is not just a fact that has been waiting to ground our identities. What emerges from this is nothing like an uncomplicated, dehistoricized, undynamic, uncontradictory past. Nothing like that is the image which is caught in that moment of return* (1997: 38).

Barbara Yngvesson tells of a couple who went to Chile with

their ten-year old son and the manner in which the adoptive parents were bonding with the country often while their son had no obvious interest in the events that preoccupied his parents. She describes how the parents collected in a small plastic bag earth from outside the hospital where their son was born.

> *...their son's past was made present in the plastic bag that they took back with them to Sweden. It contained fragments of a place and was powerfully associated with the memory of their son's birth – and would become part of the story of their return* (2003: 16).

The search for origins, the trip back to the birth nation is as much about the desire of the adoptive parents to connect with, what is after all, an alien culture.

It is amongst Korean adoptees that we can glean perhaps some of the most profound insights regarding the struggles of straddling the two cultures in which they find themselves. Following the 1988 Seoul Olympics, South Korea came under considerable attack for the way its children, in particular those with a bi-racial identity, were being treated as commodities in transnational adoption. Adoption as a business and a cost effective way of dealing with social welfare problems was highly criticised. There has been an attempt since, to link these adoptees to the global Korean family. In 1998, President Kim Dae Jung went so far as to apologise for the mistreatment and the sending away of Korean children. Although Korean adoptees are now recognised as "overseas Koreans" and have certain entitlements such as the right to work, medical and pension rights as well as the freedom to buy real estate, this recognition "disregards the difficulties of negotiating the 'cultural citizenship' of Korean adoptees in South Korea and elsewhere" (Kim, 2003: 59).

For many Korean adoptees, the return visit has not been easy. The discourses of return "underwrite a personal narrative of self-realisation, completion, and closure that ... is not only an impossible task to accomplish but also creates fragmentation and further displacement rather than wholeness" (Eng, 2003: 28-9). This is further complicated because in many cases the return visit has been a managed affair with the state actively involved in indoctrinating them with essentialised notions of Korean identity and culture that they are encouraged to embrace. It is these essentialised notions of identity that adoptees often reject leading to a certain tension between "opposing notions of identity as either biologically given or culturally achieved" (Kim, 2003: 61).

Adoptees not only have had to come to terms with their abandonment but also have faced discrimination, prejudice and alienation from a culture with which they have had little contact. They might well have ethnic and biological connections but the practice of everyday life for them is significantly different having been raised within white cultures. As Elena Kim argues, the return to " 'Korea', for many of them becomes demystified as a place of nostalgia, or 'home', as they come to accept that they are, as one American adoptee put it, 'genetically Korean, but culturally American'" (2003: 68).

Negotiating Identity

Edward Said sees similarities between exile and banishment, as conditions which make one a permanent outcast (Said, 1994). To this, we can well add the condition of the transnational adoptee. As Barbara Yngvesson and Maureen Mahoney point out, "broken stories – such as those of refugees, immigrants, adoptees and other diasporic populations – confront us all with the anxiety of lack of certitude" (2000: 78). Exile does not mean the total separation from your place of origin but is rather a condition where one never abandons the old nor completely accepts the new. It is not a state in which one can become complacent, comfortable and secure. Rather, it is a state that hones your skills for survival.

A key problem with adoption narratives is the strong pull of being forced to accept a constructed identity that is geographically based in a certain place that perhaps only exists in the imagination. Adopted children who grow up straddling different cultures (often born out of vicious racism) always retain a trace of the very origins that they so desperately seek. However, it is clear that they cannot be encapsulated by adoption narratives that are cast in binaries such as establishing a clean break and being 'reborn' in a new family, new culture or new nation or by the overwhelming desire of a return to an originary place that accepts them unproblematically. The reality of the lived experience of an adoptee is that they are never fully located in either culture – they constantly negotiate their identities in the practice of every day life. Adoptees are located in that space between their place of origin and the adoptive nation – a space where they constantly have to invent and reinvent identity so that they can transcend borders that are erected to contain them.

In order to combat this binary, it is useful to examine Derrida's (2000) notion of hospitality. He argues that:

> *...hospitality ... is part of being at home; there is no home, no cultural home, no family home without some door, some opening and some ways of welcoming guests. But in that case the hospitality is conditional, in that the other is welcome to the extent that he adjusts to the* chez soi, *to the home, that he speaks the language, that he respects the order of the house, the order of the nation state and so forth.*
>
> *That's conditional hospitality....but in contrast to which I try to think pure and unconditional hospitality, the idea of a pure welcoming of the unexpected guest, the unexpected arriving one* (Derrida 2002: 6).

The pure and unconditional hospitality for the adopted child is not to be forced to reinscribe their identity into the narrative of the new family, the new culture and nation whilst erasing the identity and culture of the birth parents. Rather, pure hospitality is a realisation that none of the actors involved in the process – the adoptees, the birth parents and the adoptive parents – are freestanding *vis-à-vis* the others, but that there is a pull toward the other parent, the other nation (Yngvesson, 2003: 8). The complexities of place are inextricably linked to the question of origins and belonging. It is only through this recognition and acceptance that the adoptee can construct an autonomous identity that has the trace of origin in the present that allows them to live in a world of their choosing.

References

Anagnost, Ann (2000) "Scenes of Misrecognition: Maternal Citizenship in the Age of Transnational Adoption", *Positions*, Vol. 8, No. 2, pp. 389-421.

Bhabha, Homi (1990), "DissemiNation: time, narrative, and the margins of the modern nation", in Homi Bhabha, (ed.), *Nation and Narration,* London: Routledge.

Bhabha, Homi (1994), *The Location of Culture,* London: Routledge.

Derrida, Jacques (1976), *Of Grammatology,* trans. Gayatri Spivak, Baltimore: Johns Hopkins University Press.

Derrida, Jacques (1982), *Margins of Philosophy*, Brighton: Harvester.

Derrida, Jacques (2000), *Of Hospitality*, Stanford: Stanford University Press. Trans. Rachel Bowlby.

Derrida, Jacques (2002), "What is owed to the Stranger?", *Arena Magazine*, 60, September, pp. 5-7.

Eng, David L., (2003), "Transnational Adoption and Queer Diasporas", *Social Text*, Vol. 21, No. 3, Fall, pp. 1-37.

Fanon, Frantz (1986), *Black Skin, White Masks*, London: Pluto Press. With an introduction by Homi Bhabha.

Gailey, Christine Ward (1999), "Seeking 'Baby Right': Race, Class, and Gender in US International Adoption", in Monica Dalen and Barbara Saetersdal (eds.), Oslo: University of Oslo.

Hall, Stuart (1997), "The Local and the Global: Globalisation and Ethnicity", in A.D. King, (ed.), *Culture, Globalisation and the World-System*, Minneapolis: University of Minnesota Press.

Henry, P. (1996), 'Fanon, African and Afro-Caribbean Philosophy', in L.R. Gordon, D.T. Sharpley-Whiting and R.T. White (eds.), *Fanon: A Critical Reader*, Oxford: Blackwells.

Herman, Ellen (2002), "The Paradoxical Rationalisation of Modern Adoption", *Journal of Social History*, Vol. 36, No. 2, pp. 339-385.

Hubinette, Tobias (2003), "Adopted Koreans and the Development of Identity in the 'third space', "*Adoption and Fostering*, Vol. 27, No. 4, pp. 1-9.

Kanneh, Kadiatu (1998), *African Identities: Race, Nation and Culture in Ethnography, Pan-Africanism and Black Literatures*, London: Routledge.

Kim, Eleana (2003), "Wedding Citizenship and Culture: Korean Adoptees and the Global Family of Korea", *Social Text*, Vol. 21, No. 1, Spring, pp. 57-81.

Kim, Hosu (2004), "Un/seen Bodies of American Dream: Birth Mothers and Adoptees in Inter-country Adoptions from Korea to the U.S." in Kathlen Bergquist and Dong Soo Kim, (eds.), *Transplanted Children: 50 years of International Korean Adoptions*, Forthcoming.

Kruks, S. (1996), 'Fanon, Sartre, and Identity Politics', in L.R. Gordon, D.T. Sharpley-Whiting and R.T. White (eds.), *Fanon: A Critical Reader*, Oxford: Blackwells.

Krupnick, Mark (ed.) (1983), *Displacement: Derrida and After*, Bloomington: Indiana University Press.

Said, Edward (1994), *Representation of the Intellectual*, London: Vintage.

Shiu, Anthony (2001), "Felxible Production: International Adoption, Race, Whiteness", http://social.chass.ncsu.edu/jouvert/v6il-2/shiu.htm.

Volkman, Toby Alice (2003), "Embodying Chinese Culture: Transnational Adoption in North America", *Social Text*, Vol. 21, No. 1, Spring, pp. 29-55.

Volkman, Toby Alice (2003), "Introduction", *Social Text,* Vol. 21, No. 1, Spring, pp. 1-5.

Yngvesson, Barbara (2002), "Placing the 'gift child' in transnational adoption", *Law and Society Review,* Vol. 36, No. 2, pp. 227-256.

Yngvesson, Barbara (2003), "Going 'Home': Adoption, Loss of Bearings, and the Mythology of Roots", *Social Text,* Vol. 21, No. 1, Spring, pp. 7-27.

Yngvesson, Barbara and Maureen A. Mahoney (2000), "'As one Should, Ought and Wants to Be': Belonging and Authenticity in Identity Narratives", *Theory, Culture and Society,* Vol. 17, No. 6, pp. 77-110.

Part III
ETHICAL ISSUES

8

Forgotten Ethics and Values in Modern Procreation

RENÉ A.C. HOKSBERGEN and JAN J.F. TER LAAK

Introduction

This article discusses a controversial topic: the application of modern reproductive technology. It is possible that the moral and ethical rules are more or less established and will lead to similar conclusions over the controversial and complex ethical problems accompanying the application of modern reproductive technology. From research it is known that a large number of adoptive parents first try several modern reproductive techniques (Hoksbergen *et al.*, 1999). It is an important issue for adoptive parents to consider ethical consequences of the use of modern reproductive technology.

An Example of Reproductive Technology

Her name is Annecy and she was flown from the United States to the Netherlands as an embryo and implanted in a surrogate mother. There were high expectations that Annecy would possess exceptional genetic qualities. She would be the cream of the crop, the hi-tech of modern reproductive technology. This required a careful search for a suitable partner. Highly potent Sunny Boy was found and Annecy was artificially inseminated. Since Sunny Boy was highly fertile his semen was drawn each day to ensure that his offspring was numerous and geographically spread. This effort succeeded. When Sunny Boy passed away in 1999 he had half a million daughters spread all over the world and 300,000 remained in the Netherlands (Zomeren, 1996). It is primarily the daughters, who are of interest; male offspring mainly serves as semen and meat supplier.

We referred above not to people, but to cows and steers. Modern reproductive technology is the standard procedure of ensuring qualitatively high-level animal offspring. These special cows produce about 16,000 litres milk per year or some forty to fifty litres per day; that is about 4,200 gallons per year or some twelve gallons per day. These are cows with a prominent udder, always full to the brim. They are glossy in colour and big and lean, suggesting production of lots of milk. Big, lean and full uddered cows have become prized.

There is perhaps a drawback. These cows look almost identical since they have the same genetic base. This tinkering may lead to unpleasant surprises in the future as human beings begin to control the existence of these animals, because for survival variance in animal characteristics is vital. The 'cowmakers' are ready for the next decades and their cows fit perfectly into the world of microwave, airbags, megabytes, and Europeans' ski vacations in Colorado. At the level of human procreation the issue is more complex. Nevertheless the gynaecologists seem also well on their way. Despite these seemingly positive achievements in the management of reproduction of both animals and men, questions regarding human ethics emerge.

Consequential and Deontological Norms in Human Procreation

Human reproduction, a traditional, and a modern type of freedom hold: first, the personal freedom to decide the number of children in the family, and second the manner of conception as a consequence of modern reproductive technologies. Normative considerations are associated with both freedoms. It can be asked if the freedom to reproduce any number of children represents an absolute and timeless norm. Until the end of the eighteenth century, reproduction had no consequences for the socio-economic conditions. In case of overusing agricultural land or hunting grounds, it was possible to move elsewhere. This was practiced in the United States and Canada during the nineteenth, and the first half of the twentieth century. While local overpopulation could be a concern, globally no such a problem existed. At that time, socio-economic circumstances did not call for highlighting the issue of overpopulation. This implied that the right to unrestricted reproduction was not challenged. The British economist Thomas Robert Malthus (1766-1834) was the first scholar who pointed out the economic consequences of the increasing population. In his *Essay on the Principles of Population* he assessed that the population doubled every twenty-five years. In addition, he predicted that the rate of increase of food production could never match this exponential trend. He himself did not call for birth control. This was left to the New Malthusian Union established in 1881. Ideas of representatives of the Union were heavily contested, and it took nearly another century before their initiatives for birth control became government policy in some countries.

Despite the apparent fact that the norm of unimpeded reproduction is a product of its time, it is declared a human right. According to the United Nations Universal Declaration of Human Rights:

> *Men and women of full age without any limitation due to race, nationality or religion have the right to marry and to found a family... the family is the natural and fundamental group unit of society* (Declaration, 1948).

Westerners are not inclined to examine the consequences of such human rights carefully. It is still asserted that people can reproduce without limit and no statement is added about the responsibilities associated with this reproductive behaviour. It is possible that this statement is not challenged because the declarations of the United Nations are a product of Western thinking. It is also possible that it is a luxury of morality in our democracies. The dominant morality holds that the individual fulfillment of needs and individual exertion of autonomy are central.

Richard Hull (1990), however, critically examined our fundamental right to found a family and to reproduce ourselves. Hull described six conditions in which the moral duty is to renounce reproduction: transmission of disease to offspring; unwillingness to provide prenatal care; inability to rear children; psychological harm to offspring; over-population and unmarried, single persons or homosexual couples.

Although we may declare that all our needs are met, these needs are, however, partly elicited and guided by market mechanisms. Limitless needs require craving for possessions and possibly the greed of others. It is very likely that a political party, which called for reductions in purchasing power in the interest of future generations, would be stillborn. Their political program would suggest that there is scarcely a need to think about future generations. Yet, we are depleting our fossil fuels at a rapid rate and we fly from Europe to snow covered areas of the United States for sports. It is obvious that the Western consumption pattern cannot be conveyed to people in the whole world. Continued environmental pollution would be catastrophic and unbridled consumption would be reduced to no consumption at all.

A consequentialist requires that whenever a person undertakes an action, all possible consequences should be taken into consideration. Our basic intuition in moral acts forces us to think about the consequences and results of our intended actions, and consider alternative actions.

From ontological ethics, norms should play a role in all our actions and decisions. Deontological norms force the examination of the character, and the underlying motives of actions and decisions. In satisfying needs, both the nature and reasons for these needs and their consequences must be examined. By this manner the act and decision to reproduce are amenable to consequential and deontological norms.

Unimpeded Reproduction and the Homo Manipulans

The human species is recently developed into a *Homo manipulans,* a manipulator of nature (Emson, 1992). Human beings believe they have the right to exploit all natural sources, and contrary to other living beings, they are partly independent of the ecosystem. This independency is a recent achievement for a small privileged part of the world population. It is, for example, impossible for the Australian Aborigines and the Inuit to live independent of their ecosystem.

However, the notion of interdependency of man and his ecosystem is now beginning to penetrate human consciousness. Modern medical scientists generally reflect the limited normative consequentialist approach and undervalue the importance of the interdependency of people and their ecosystem. Of course, we feel relieved when successfully cured by physicians. Generally, physicians are successful. Consider the facts that the average age of the Westerner has significantly increased and child mortality has decreased. In Western countries the average death rate in the first five years of life is sixteen per 1,000 live births, but 104, in developing countries (Galjaard, 1994). Yet, the paradox is that the enduring of the earth is endangered by these same medical interventions. This success has a dark side, and there is a lack of political measures, which would limit the negative consequences of unimpeded reproduction for specific large groups and for future generations.

Adriaan de Groot (1995) argues that the United Nations should consider adding to their agenda the issues of threatened quality of life of future generations, and of long-term strategies to face this threat. This could result in broadening the scope of thinking of the *Homo manipulans* and lead to embracing the principle that *Communis salus singulis constat.*

The benefit of all depends on each individual. The contemporary emphasis on the here and now would shift towards an emphasis on the consequences for the future. This principle is essential for reproduction. In a moral sense, it is mandatory for each individual to reflect on the consequences of unimpeded reproduction at the micro level of his own nuclear and extended family, and at the macro level of the world population. The argument is not new. The so-called Rome Report 'Limits to Growth' already underscored this (Meadows, 1972).

The contributions of medical science to the population growth are complex. Medical interventions lead to an explosion in population across the planet. It took nearly 100,000 years before three billion people populated the world by 1960. It took, however, only forty years more to double to six billion people (Galjaard, 1994). In the Third World the contribution of medical science has a dark side, and leads to humanly degrading situations in Calcutta, Bombay, and Manila. In particular children and old people are the victims.

Physicians consider it as their first task to cure, and seem less concerned about the consequences of their interventions for population growth. It would have been useful if a similarly successful demographic program of birth planning paralleled the medical progress. In addition, medical-biological research could have given priority to research into fertility. This could have resulted in the availability of the birth control pill at an earlier period, for example in 1900 instead of 1955. At this time, we are still waiting for an appropriate pill for men as alternative to condoms, vasectomy, and sterilisation.

Besides efficient interventions promoting population growth, physicians invented means for birth control, which were only partly successful because of the strong influence of religion. This influence decreased in the Western countries after World War II, and consequently birth-reducing measures became possible. It is evident that the adoption of birth control measures in specific groups, in Moslim countries, and in the Third World will take more time than in the Western countries.

The Chinese government is an exceptional example. It introduced a one child per family policy. This affected the population growth, but had side effects. It caused a dramatic rise of adoption of Chinese girls in Western countries. For example, in the Netherlands there were 567 and 800 adoptions from China in 2003 and 2004, respectively (Ministerie van Justitie, 2005). In addition, children of undesired gender, primarily female, are killed or not cared for properly, sometimes resulting in a slow death. These excrescences occur in China and India, although caregivers and social workers do their utmost to alleviate the life of abandoned or relinquished children.

Less drastically than in China, birth control and family planning have been promoted in recent years in almost every country. To take the Netherlands as an example: the population has taken steps decades earlier, and between 1970 and 1975 the birth rate declined with thirty per cent. Despite the opposition of the Catholic Church, the use of the pill as well as other preventive measures became common after 1961. Sex education for young children was also organized in the 1960s and is now a part of the school curriculum. This 'cognitive pill' is perhaps more effective than the contraceptive pill. In the Netherlands the number of teenage pregnancies and abortions is lowest in the world. Relinquishing a child for adoption is a rare occurrence: no more than two to four children are relinquished per million inhabitants per year. The same number is found in the Scandinavian countries. In the United States adoption by non-relatives is about thirty children per million inhabitants (Flango & Flango, 1995). China, India, and other countries might take the Northern European experience to heart and at least institute sex education for young children at school.

In the Western world, a balance has been achieved in population growth. This part of the world, however, wrestles with serious environmental problems, caused by the rate of consumption. There is no complete balance. In the Western world there is no balance with respect to the second type of freedom, the manner in which we conceive our descendants.

Modern Types of Conception

Until recently, it was impossible to intervene to correct most causes of infertility and consequently manipulate the quality of the offspring. We had to wait and see whether a child was a healthy boy or girl, or showed obvious specific life-limiting or as yet invisible handicaps. Because humanity strives to maximize the satisfaction of needs, means were sought to ensure that a desired child could be provided, and that it would be as healthy as possible. Before this time, surrogate mothers were used and on occasion foundling children were taken into families as biological children.

Recently this picture changed drastically. The techniques of artificial insemination via a donor, AID, and in-vitro fertilisation, IVF, were discovered (Hoksbergen, 1995). There are two important indications for AID: the sperm of the spouse is infertile and the genetic history of the spouse or the genetic combination contains a serious risk for the child. The discovery of in-vitro fertilisation is even more recent. On July 25th, 1978, the first child conceived in this way was born in an English hospital. The critical discovery was that gametes could be frozen and thereafter successfully used was of critical importance. This also opened the way to study gametes for undesirable qualities.

Artificial Procreation, Norms and Values

Since 1970 AID has been extensively utilized in the Netherlands, and in most other countries. Physicians used this technique for infertile couples. In general, the parents were told not to reveal the manner of conception to their child and were restricted from information about the donor. He remained anonymous and information about the donor was frequently destroyed. Physicians scarcely considered the psychological consequences of this type of conception for the offspring. They told parents about the presumably positive results, and protected the privacy of the donor. Initially, a similar approach was followed for ovum donation.

However, changes in ovum donation are currently underway in the Netherlands. Following the Swedish law of 1985, in 1993 Dutch legislation was introduced which would permit an AID-child to meet the donor if this served its interest. This bill has been accepted in the beginning of 2004 after a lot of resistance by gynaecologists. The anonymity of donors is past. However, only for children born since 2004.

In the meantime, the policy of various sperm banks is now to advise parents to be open about the conception of their children. In addition, for all donors a so-called donor passport is developed which includes data about the donors.

Let us critically examine the ethical consequences of the practice of gynaecologists not to inform the child that the social father or mother is not the biological parent. The first question to answer is: Does having a child have such an all-embracing value that considerations of deontological and consequentialist norms become irrelevant? We do not think such values exist. It is well known that both the press and society paint unwanted childlessness negatively. Terms such as unfeminine, desperation, anguish, suffering, victims, and hopelessness are used repeatedly to describe the women (Franklin, 1990; Woollett, 1991). Such negative judgements of the childless couples compared with descriptions of the hope, joy, and happiness of the thrilled new parents help to explain why many women, couples will go to great lengths to have a child. We do not want to deny or discount the great sadness associated with an inability to have children. It is clear that people want to know from whom they are descended (Lifton, 1979; Hoksbergen & Walenkamp, 1991; Storsbergen, 1995). Such knowledge promotes the development of a sense of identity (Van Kampen, Koops, Meerum Terwogt, Reijnders, 1990). In addition, such information is sometimes needed for medical reasons, and it is an inherent responsibility of the parents to provide this information to their child. Much research revealed that children who discover that their parents are not their biological parents, suffer from psychological pain that can be traumatic. The child-parent relationship can be disrupted for a longer period or even definitively (Baran & Panor, 1989). One effect of the discovery that the parent is not the biological parent, can be a fixation on searching for the unknown parent. Usually this search is successful and the lie will come to light. Children sense when something is not quite right and parents inadvertently release information. Usually the information is revealed during divorce proceedings. Many psychological problems can be reduced through communication with fellow-suffers. For infertile parents, it is therefore important that the grief caused by infertility can be discussed (Mazor, 1992). This prevents the negative effects of denial, excessive reserve and perhaps even depression. Research has shown that an open attitude on the part of the parents concerning the background of the child can strengthen the child-parent relationship (Kirk, 1981; Hoksbergen, Juffer & Waardenburg, 1987; Van Kampen et al, 1990). Such an attitude of openness is essential to the loving approach to the wanted child.

A second question to answer is; should secrecy be recommended to parents because an anonymous donor was used? The general objections to secrecy have already been set forth. There are the severest concerns about the use of anonymous donors: How is the interest of the child served by withholding his genetic background? Children act differently when they do not grow up with their biological parents. We cannot know at conception if our child will later suffer psychological damage. As parents, we have the obligation to take into account the essential needs of our child. Knowledge about the child's background promotes stable development of the sense of identity (Brodzinsky & Schechter, 1990; Reijnders & Meerum Terwogt, 1994). At every step, which leads to donor reproduction, we must recognize the consequences of this type reproduction. The donor is to a certain extent responsible for the consequences of all those involved. This seems a generally accepted norm. Giving semen or ova is not the same as giving blood. The results are different and the donor should realize this. Should a donor or a relinquishing mother or father have the right to remain unknown to his or her offspring? Do privacy rights apply to adults who freely consent to the creation of a biological related child? (Speirs,1998). It is expected that people are responsible for their actions. Has the child asked to be given life? Both the deontological norm, respect, the helpless child, and the consequentialist norm that the offspring can suffer from an unknown background, are applicable here. Children born as a result of donor-assisted conception who are denied knowledge of their family history are at a medical disadvantage compared with children brought up by their biological parents (Simson, 1998). Open records will simply resolve this medical disadvantage. Again the consequentialist norm is of relevance here.

In addition to AID, recently also embryos can be donated. Procreation can now occur with the semen or ova or an embryo, which have existed for a long period outside the owners. The technique of freezing has made it possible to initiate conception some time before or, in some case many years prior to the implantation in the womb of the potential mother. In this way, the genetic base of mankind has become a product with a many related uncertainties, which can lead to unclear practices with significant consequences for the children conceived in this way. We will give two examples.

First, in an article by Michael Taylor in the San Francisco Chronicle of 17 November, 1995 we read that three doctors have been accused of taking the eggs and embryos from women without their consent and transferring them to other women, who were also not aware that the eggs or embryos were taken without the donor's (women) consent. Two of the doctors involved fled the country.

Second, in the Netherlands, a twin was born in 1994 who had two fathers. The couple used IVF and due to an error of the clinic, one boy was from the (white) spouse of the mother and the other child from a black father also being treated at the clinic. These parents located the biological father as concern was raised about the identity development of their son. The social father remains, the legal father of the child.

The preservation of gametes presents new problems with consequences for all parties concerned, the producer, the offspring, and the end users. One question is whether the producer of gametes may decide how long these should be kept. Another is, how long a user may wait before using the product, for instance, in cases where career does not permit childbearing at a given moment. These possibilities have consequences primarily for the offspring.

They can develop psychological and identity problems if they realize that they have been preserved as a product for a while, or that their conception was organized artificially. Furthermore, can we be completely convinced that there are no negative physical consequences due to freezing and preserving of gametes over longer periods of time? Again, the consequentialist norm should be considered.

Professional Norms

It appears that we have accepted the reproductive techniques, without asking questions about the consequences both for the offspring and the users, usually women. It is worth asking whether we have been aware of the relevant professional norms involved in using these techniques. Have gynaecologists not been too ready to conform to views about the value of the traditional family in society? Perhaps this is the reason that there was so much sympathy for the desperation and anguish of infertile couples and not for the developmental and psychological consequences for both parents and offspring? This attitude also makes it clear why reproductive technology has been seen as an exclusively medical practice. In this medical area, the principle *in dubiis abstine* (when in doubt, abstain) should be applied.

Conclusion: the Reorientation of Modern Reproduction

Our foregoing arguments have made clear that Emson's (1992) conclusion that "the language of dominance and exploitation is seldom balanced by that of duty and responsibility to the exploited system" must be endorsed. Emson argues as well for the 'reimposition of the controls from which evolution freed us'. Must we not add here that a critical review of the increase in freedoms is also required? The evolutionary development with regard to reproduction has resulted in partial restrictions to freedom. This is so with regard to the freedoms of children conceived in an unconventional manner. To formulate this thesis positively, we conclude that our consciousness can help us to attain equilibrium in the disharmonious consequences of the maximizing nature of evolution. Natural selection is a part of evolution. This ensures that qualities, which are good for the species, are developed to the maximum. This is the reason that our brains have developed to such an advanced stage. There is no reason to think that this process will stop. Evolution in and of itself gives us no norms, and evolution knows no morality. Norms must come from the human species. We ask for reflection, therefore, on the part of concerned parents but also on the part of gynaecologists and politicians, with regard to the ethical principle that people have a right to respect for their own choices, as long as those choices do not harm others (the autonomy principle).

This rethinking of the autonomy principle is essential in the practice of modern reproduction. It is too one-sided for professionals to emphasize the autonomy of parents and donors (Boer, 1992), because it leaves the autonomy of the non-conventionally conceived child unattended. The child has no choice in the matter. It is conceived this way and the parents decide for the child whether he will receive information about his genetic background. Should we not offer the child the option of deciding what he will do with the information about his conception?

Comparatively, the autonomy of adoptive parents and the adopted child seems reasonably in balance in most European Countries. Organisations and other information sources recommend strongly that parents inform their child about his adopted status and provide it with the material and psychological support to let him learn about his background. This is the practice of most parents. In the Netherlands, relinquished children have the right to obtain information about their biological parents. In addition, so-called roots trips, these are travels to the country of origin, are encouraged for foreign adoptees. With regard to this group of parents, the rethinking has already taken place. Consequentialist norms are intensely considered by adoptive parents and adoptive professionals. Therefore, negative consequences of being relinquished for adoption are taken seriously and they are kept as limited as possible.

We hope valid arguments contribute to a critical use of reproductive technologies. For the medical professionals, the parents and the donors, the relevance of norms and the autonomy principle should be better understood. These norms and principles should be translated into a practice in which complete openness to the helpless child comes first.

References

Baran, Annette & Panor, Reuben (1989), *Lethal Secrets: Parents, Children, Donors, and Experts Speak Out.* New York: Warner Books.

Boer, Theodore A. (1992), Opheffing van anonimiteit van donors bij kunstmatige inseminatie; een morele beoordeling van tegenargumenten. (Abolition of the anonymity of donors in artificial *insemination: a moral evaluation of counterarguments).* Nederlands Tijdschrift voor Geneeskunde, 136, 28, pp. 1332-1335.

Brodzinsky, M. and Schechter, D. (1990), *The psychology of Adoption.* New York: Oxford University Press.

Declaration of Human Rights (1948), 16, I and III.

Emson, H.H. (1992), A Right to Reproduce? *The Lancet,* Vol. 340: 31-10, p. 1083.

Flango, Victor E. & Flango, Carol R. (1995), How many children were adopted in 1992? *Child Welfare,* 74, 5, 1018-1031.

Franklin, S. (1990), Deconstructing Desperateness: the social construction of infertility in popular representations of new reproductive technologies. In: M. McNeil, I. Varcoe & S. Yearley. *The New Reproductive Technologies.* London: McMillan, pp. 200-224.

Galjaard, Hans (1994), *Alle mensen zijn ongelijk. De verschillen en overeenkomsten tussen mensen: hun erfelijke aanleg, gezondheid, gedrag en prestaties* (All people are unequal: The differences and similarities between people: Their hereditary aptitudes, health, behaviour and accomplishments). Amsterdam: Uitgeverij Balans.

Groot de, Adriaan D. (21-7-1995), Het recht op voortplanting bedreigt de aarde (The right to reproduction threatens the earth). In: *NRC-Handelsblad.*

Hoksbergen, René A.C., Juffer, Femmie & Waardenburg, Berte C. (1987), *Adoptive Children at Home and at School.* Lisse/New York: Swets and Zeitlinger.

Hoksbergen, René A.C. & Walenkamp, Hans (1991, eds.), *Kind van andere ouders. Theorie en praktijk van adoptie* (Child of other parents. theory and practice of adoption). Houten/Antwerpen: Bohn Stafleu van Loghum.

Hoksbergen, René (1995), *Hoe ver gaan we? Moderne voortplanting in feitelijk en ethisch perspectief* (How far shall we go? Modern Reproduction in Factual and Ethical Perspective). Baarn: Uitgeverij Ambo.

Hoksbergen, R.A.C. and co-workers of the Rumanian project (1999), Adoptie van Roemeense kinderen: ervaringen van ouders, die tussen 1990 en medio 1997 een kind uit Roemenië adopteerden. Utrecht: Universiteit Utrecht Afdeling Adoptie. (Adoption of Romanian Children: experiences of parents, who adopted a child from Romania between 1990 and medio 1997).

Hoksbergen, R.A.C. (2001), *Vijftig jaar adoptie in Nederland, een historisch-statistische beschouwing.* (Fifty years adoption practice in the Netherlands, a historical-statistical view). Utrecht: Utrecht University, Adoption Department.

Hull, Richard T. (1990), *Ethical Issues, the new Reproductive Technologies.* Belmont: Wadsworth Publishing Company.

Kampen van, Lex, Koops, Wim, Meerum Terwogt, Mark, and Reijnders, Carolien (1990), Onbekendheid met de biologische vader als een belemmerende factor in de identiteitsontwikkeling: een empirische exploratie (The unknown father as an impediment to the development of identity: an empirical exploration). *Nederlands Tijdschrift voor de Psychologie,* 45, pp. 283-288.

Kirk, David (1981), *Adoptive Kinship. A modern institution in need of reform.* Port Angeles: Ben Simon.

Ligtenberg, Leo (30-9-1995), Nederlander en Amerikaan kunnen het goed met elkaar vinden (The Dutch and the Americans get along well). *Nrc Handelsblad.*

Lifton, Betty Jean (1979), *Lost and Found. The Adoption Experience.* New York: The Dial Express.

Mazor, Miriam D. (1992), Emotional Reactions to Infertility. In: Kenneth D. Alpern. *The Ethics of Reproductive Technology.* New York/Oxford: Oxford University Press, pp. 32-38.

Meadows, Dennis (1972), *The limits to growth. A report for the Club of Rome Project on the predicament of mankind* (MIT-report). Massachusetts Institute of Technology. De Meern: Het Spectrum.

Ministerie van Justitie (2005), Statistische gegevens betreffende de opneming in gezinnen in Nederland van buitenlandse adoptiekinderen in de jaren 2000-2004 (Statistical data concerning the adoption of foreign children in the Netherlands in the years 2000-2004). Den Haag: Ministerie van Justitie Directie Justitieel Jeugdbeleid.

Reijnders, Carolien & Meerum Terwogt, Mark (1994), Achtergronden en behandeling van afstammingsproblemen (Backgrounds and treatment of problems of descendancy). *Psychotherapie,* Vol. 20(3), pp. 148-162.

Roskam, Edward (29-9-1996), De evolutie geeft ons geen normen (Evolution gives us no norms). *NRC-Handelsblad.*

Speirs, Jennifer (1998), Children's Rights or Adults' Rights? In: Eric Blyth, Marilyn Crawshaw & Jennifer Speirs. *Truth and the child 10 years on: Information exchange in donor assisted conception.* Birmingham: The British Association of Social Workers, 15-18.

Simson, Sheila A. (1998), Truth and the child: a Genetic Perspective. In: Eric Blyth, Marilyn Crawshaw & Jennifer Speirs. *Truth and the child 10 years on: Information exchange in donor assisted conception.* Birmingham: The British Association of Social Workers, 19-22.

Storsbergen, Hester (1995), Geadopteerd zijn is... (To be adopted is). In: René Hoksbergen, Hester Storsbergen & Cock Brouwer-van Dalen. *Het begon in Griekenland. Een verkenning van de achtergrond van in Griekenland geboren, geadopteerde jongvolwassenen en de betekenis van de adoptiestatus* (It began in Greece: An exploration of the backgrounds of Greek-born, adopted young adults and the meaning of their adoption status). Utrecht: Isor, pp. 47-213.

Zomeren van, Koos (9-3-1996), De onbereikbare koe (The unattainable cow). *NRC-Handelsblad*.

9

Ethical Dilemmas in Adoption Counselling

NILIMA MEHTA

Introduction

Ethics is a philosophical science with a set of moral standards, values and guiding principles that govern professional practice. The field of ethics involves systematising, defending and recommending concepts of right and wrong behaviour. As professionals working in the field of Adoption, we need to ensure that we are guided by the principle of "Best Interest of the Child".

As per the United Nations Convention on the Rights of the Child (UNCRC), a child's most basic right is to be brought in a nurturing family environment in his family of birth. The next option is a family in his own country of origin so that the child continues to live within his own socio-cultural milieu and then is Inter-country/Inter-racial adoption that is adoption by foreigners. Long-term institutional care is the last option in the process of rehabilitation for a child without a home. The Hague Convention also emphasizes this priority and hence all the countries that have ratified the UNCRC and the Hague Convention have to harmonise their policies, procedures and laws accordingly.

There are many ethical issues and dilemmas that confront the professionals in the process of adoption counselling. The responsibility of the social workers is to the vulnerable child, to the birth parents and the adoptive parents.

The justifications to many ethical dilemmas are,

"It is in the Best interest of the Child"

"But it does not harm anyone"

"It is for everyone's good"

"It is like a white lie, that only helps and does not hurt"

But the important question is—"Is it an ethical decision?"

Counselling Birth Parents

The major issue in counselling birth parents is related to their decision for relinquishment.

- Have the birth mother/birth parents been counselled adequately to prevent abandonment?
- Are alternative support services like Sponsorship, Foster Care, Day Care, and Counselling offered to the birth mother/birth parents in order to keep the child?
- Has she been made completely aware of the implications of relinquishment and surrender document?
- Has she been explained properly of the two months reconsideration period, during which she can claim the child back?
- Has she been told of the confidentiality of the identity of adoptive parents and not having any access to any information of her child, after the adoption?
- That her right to confidentiality about her own identity may in future conflict with the child's Right to information about his won identity?
- Offering any kind of money to the birth mother to influence the decision to surrender the child would not be "helping" the mother, but is linked to the child and is completely unethical.
- When the Birth Mother comes for counselling in the early stages of pregnancy what should the social worker recommend—Abortion? Keep the child? Surrender the child? The ethically correct practice is that all the options are offered to the birth mother and then she is helped to make an informed decision.

Counselling Adoptive Parents

While counselling the adoptive parents, one encounters several situations that are difficult for the social workers and counsellors.

Following are some of the circumstances that create ethical dilemmas.

- When adoptive parents want to have a "secret adoption", i.e. "pretend" their adopted child as their own biological child. The argument and justification by the parents is that if it is in the interest of the child and for its acceptance into the family, then what is wrong?
- The adoptive parents have already "located" a child and want to just "take" the child directly from the birth mother, with an exchange of money and according to them it harms no one!
- Some prospective adoptive parents do not want to go through the legal process of adoption but want to take the seemingly easier option of preparing a false birth certificate in their own name. From their point of view, what is wrong?
- Prospective adoptive parents are extremely particular about the child they want to adopt—like the "Blue Eyed Blonde Baby—or the Perfect Baby Syndrome" and often "reject" several children based on their likes and dislikes. Is this in the Best Interest of the Child? What is the priority, finding "parents for a child" or "child for parents?"
- At the same time is it right for adoption agencies to "reject" parents because of inappropriate attitudes, instead of counselling them for modification of their attitudes and preparing them positively for adoption? Of course, "Non-Acceptance" of adoptive parents, is an acceptable decision if it is not in the interest of the child to be placed with them.
- In the context of socio-cultural realities in India, especially in rural India and smaller towns where adoption is not socially accepted, can the parents be blamed for a conservative attitude to adoption?
- How much information should be shared with prospective adoptive parents about the social, religious, cultural background of the birth mother and the child? For example, what if a child is born out of wedlock or as a result of a rape situation or to a sex worker, as a result of incest or from a birth mother who is mentally ill? Medical information should be shared because it can directly

impact the child, but what about other information? Sharing the information could result in the child not getting adopted, but is withholding the information, ethically correct? This is a serious ethical dilemma in adoption placement.

Counselling the Adoptee

Counselling the adopted child at different stages of growth and development also presents a challenge to counsellors.

- Withholding the fact of adoption, from the child for fear of sharing and the insecurity about the impact on the child is a serious ethical issue. Can you keep such personal and vital information about a child's life a secret from the child himself?
- Telling the child an "untruth" or "half truth" is also morally wrong—but is often justified on the grounds that it is "for her own good". When the information could disturb the child emotionally, why should it be shared is often the dilemma faced by parents and counsellors.
- In the child's "Search for Roots", whose right prevails?—The child's right to information or the birth mother's right to confidentiality?
- Should counselling the adoptee take into consideration the socio-cultural relations of a particular country and constitute laws, policies and programming accordingly? What if they are in conflict with UN instruments or International legislations?

Besides these there are also ethical considerations and dilemmas before International Adoption Referring Agencies, Adoption Placement Agencies, the Government Authorities, Scrutiny Agencies and the Voluntary Co-ordinating Agencies.

- Children are sometimes not released for adoptions by residential institutions, because their grants depend on the number of children and their own convictions that institutions are good for the children. Is this in the Best Interest of the Children?

- Sometimes children may be denied to domestic/in-country adoptive parents and foreign parents are preferred because of the money involved in the process. Linking funds to the number of children given in adoption is definitely unethical. The Adoption Coordinating Agencies (ACAs) are sometimes faced with this dilemma with adoptive placement agencies.
- The Scrutiny Agencies also face the challenge of ensuring that the child has been voluntarily relinquished, that there has been no force, coercion and no exchange of money during the surrender process and that the birth mother has been explained the implication of relinquishment.
- CARA is also faced with the challenge of ensuring that the Enlisted Foreign Agencies and Recognised Adoption Placement Agencies are all engaged in ethical adoption placements.
- Because of some instances of malpractices in adoption, the entire adoption programme gets a bad name and the governments of various sending countries get more vigilant and strict. In order to ensure that there are no malpractices, to protect the rights of children and ensure their safety, more and more safeguards and rules are imposed—all these are in the "Best Interest of the Child", but at the same time they delay the whole process of the child being with his adoptive parents and can that be in the "Best Interest of the Child"?

The dilemmas that are faced in the process of Adoption are dilemmas because of a certain kind of conflict between the rightness or wrongness of the actions and the goodness or badness of the consequences of the actions. If doing what is right, produces something bad, or if doing what is wrong produces good—then what is morally correct?

And of course, as in all ethical dilemmas in life, there are no easy answers!!

10

Escorting Children in Inter-country Adoptions

VICTOR GROZA and CURTIS PROCTOR

The term "best interests of the child" is imprecise. While the principles of "best interests" are set out in the United Nations *Convention on the Rights of the Child,* the actual practices are not explicit. It includes virtually any practice affecting the welfare of the child as well as the family and child welfare policies undergirding specific practices. In this article, we question whether escorting the child from his or her birth country to the adoptive parents fully protects the welfare of the adoptee. Escorting is the practice of an adult not adopting the children retrieving the child from his or her birth country and physically accompanying the child to his or her adoptive family in another country. The escort takes legal and physical custody of the child, and is responsible for their care until they are delivered into the hands of their adoptive parents. Barbara Irving (a retired American social worker who ran an international adoption agency), suggests that "(an) escort is in essence a 'transportation assistant' arranged via either the placing agency in the adoptive parents' country or the sending agency abroad. Escorts are screened, but that process varies by location." Dean Hale (a U.S. social worker in international adoption and adoptive parent) of Holt International Children's Services remarked about this definition, "From a functional point of view, the definition is correct. Yet it does seem to frame escorting ... in a negative way. I hope that it can be expanded to include the escort as more than a mechanical transfer agent. We work hard to transition (a) child to escort and from escort to parents." As Dean's comments indicate, escorting is a complicated issue with significant psychosocial implications.

There are no data on how many children are escorted from their birth country to their adoptive country each year but the practice is not the norm. Some countries (for example, South Korea) permit a child to be escorted from their birth country to their adoptive parents; other countries (for example, Russia) prohibit the practice. Yet, each country purportedly embraces the notion of the best interest of the child. Beth Brindo (an American social worker and adoptive parent) commented, "I do not think there is a perfect answer to the question because there are at times competing interests regarding the question (of whether) to escort or not to escort". To further explore this issue, we examined it from several perspectives: the adoptive child, the adoptive parents, and the adoption agency.

After a search of several data bases (PsychLit; ERIC, MedLine) for any research or social science literature on escorting, and finding none, we solicited comments from adoptive parents, social workers in sending countries, social workers in receiving countries, and social science researchers in several countries. Throughout this chapter, when we used comments from any of these sources, we cite them and have a record of their comments. Added to their comments are our own reflections based on social work practice experience in child welfare.

The Adoptive Child

Children only differentiate between what is familiar and unfamiliar, not what is good for bad for them. Unlike the child welfare system in the United States where children enter adoptive families from foster family care, the majority of children adopted internationally enter their adoptive families from institutions (Groze & Ileana, 1996). Institutionalisation often offers inadequate sanitation, nutrition, medical care and an ineffective nurturing environment; children are at high-risk for impaired health, development difficulties, behavioural aberrations and attachment problems (Rutter, 1995; Miller & Hendrie, 2000) and have fewer opportunities to develop selective attachments (Smyke, Dumitrescu & Zeanah, 2002). There is no doubt that institutions hurt children and the sooner we can get them permanently out of an institution, the better for children. However, change is traumatizing, even when the change is in the child's best interest. Some children show their trauma by shutting down and becoming numb. They appear quite, passive or even unaffected by the change. A family can interpret this behaviour as "good nature" when in actuality it is shock and numbing. Other children immediately protest when separated from the familiar setting. So, there is a range of responses when the familiar environment is changed for children.

If children are traumatized by change, and they all are, who should be the person comforting them? Rather than a stranger, no matter how kind the stranger may be, the best situation would be for the adoptive parent to become the source of comfort right from the beginning of change.

From an attachment perspective, one event that activates the attachment system is real or perceived danger (see Crittenden & Clausen, 1993; Crittenden, Patridege & Cassidy, 1991). Anxiety, fear, fatigue and illness all increase children's vulnerability, providing a natural opportunity for parent-child attachment. Moving a child from a familiar situation is fear-inducing for some but anxiety-producing for all. For long trips, both the escort and child become fatigued. It is not unusual for children to suffer from minor ailments as they make the long journey and the food, water, sights, smells and taste are so different from what is normative for them. When children are escorted, the multiple, naturally occurring opportunities for building parent-child attachment are lost. In fact, the child attaches to the escort, only to have that connection broken when they arrive to the country of adoption. This is yet another loss that an adoptee must suffer, a point echoed by Maina Shetty and Roxana Kalyanvala (social workers in domestic and international adoptions in India).

Karen Kaye (a single adoptive mom) talked about the bonding promoted by the experience. She wrote, "Seeing the confusion and hurt that my daughter was experiencing immediately upon separation from the orphanage personnel created a very quick bond on my part. I wanted to ease her anxiety in any way I could. In the process I pulled out every maternal instinct I had. It was rough and I was more than a little cranky, but as in other such traumatic experiences in life, it creates a closeness with others that would take much longer to gain without the immediacy of the child's needs. I will always remember my daughter crying when I took a shower and having to keep the curtain open in the hotel so she could see me. I will also recall how far she leaned over her high chair the first time I left the breakfast table in the hotel so she could keep an eye on me. That set up the strongest connection as quickly as could be. This child wanted and needed me—especially in this chaotic time of multiple hotels, eateries and crowds."

Barbara Irving provides more contexts to the issue of attachment and escorts. She offers that "While there is a definite risk to the child's emotional development when having an escort/stranger transport and 'deliver' him/her to the new parents (i.e. another transition when the child is very vulnerable), many children are already enduring these changes in caretakers just prior to placement. Some children are brought from foster care into institutions prior to the arrival of the adoptive parents, and some children are moved for either 'convenience' or other paperwork issues (i.e., travelling to a major city for the child's visa) to expedite the placement." In essence, some children will suffer multiple attachment and losses before they enter their adoptive family, even if the family travels to the child's country of origin.

Felicia Demchuk (an American special educator and adoptive parent) offers additional comments about the experience of children adopted from other countries that has implications for escorting. She writes, "The child, whether an infant, toddler, or school-aged, has likely been exposed to very limited experiences, related both to human interactions and sensory input. Their world likely consists of ' ... a very structured routine. They have probably had a minimum of nurturing verbal and physical interactions with caretakers, and in some cases their basic human needs for food, water, and comfort have not been met consistently... [All] children have had to develop coping mechanisms in order to deal with an environment of deprivation...'

It is probable that the child is accustomed to very limited sensory input as well. Most of us have had experiences where a smell reminds us graphically of either pleasurable or traumatic events. The olfactory sense can produce powerful emotions and feelings for us. For a child who has been exposed to the limited environment of an orphanage, the strong smells of that environment create a boundary for their world. This is especially true for children who have had limited visual, auditory, and tactile input. Although children who have been institutionalized frequently have few toys, visual stimulation, and verbal interaction, they cannot be cut off from the smells of their current home... . Another potential result of a lack of sensory input is an inability to habituate. When they are bombarded with a large amount of input via multiple sensory pathways, it is difficult for them to integrate and manage this amount of stimulation. Reactions to this neurologically 'traumatic' event may range from withdrawal and self-protective self-stimulation, to externalizing, aggressive behaviours or emotional melt-downs.

As a parent who spent three months in Russia waiting for a drawn-out adoption to conclude, I can empathize with a parent who is eager to complete the adoption process quickly in order to return to the comfort of their own home... It is difficult and traumatic for us to be removed from our typical ecology, and we need to recognize that it is even more difficult for this child to be removed from his ecology... What I learned to recognize during my extended stay, was that this extended amount of time spent bonding with my child was therapeutic and necessary for her emotional well-being. As we had daily visits in her environment, she gradually got used to progressively more intensive human interaction on her 'own turf'. Later, when she was able to do home (apartment) visits with us, she was able to slowly get used to our smells, the textures of our materials (sheets, blankets, toys), the textures and tastes of different foods, and the sounds of our voices. Although she continued to be overwhelmed by sensory input after three months, that period of time allowed her to experience her new environments without being immediately assaulted by change, and it allowed a less stressful attachment process to ensue. Further, by the time she was required to travel, in a car, train, and airplane, she was with adults with whom she was familiar. This caretaker wasn't changed during those stressful experiences, and it was part of the process of developing attachments with a consistent adult (one adoptive parent)."

Eileen McHenry (the Executive Director of a humanitarian agency and adoptive parent) offers additional insight. "Most importantly, I think (our daughter) feels very special when we tell her the story of her Dad going back to Romania twice—and her Mom staying 7 weeks in order to bring her home. While we sadly don't have a 'birth story' for her, we do have one heck of a good 'adoption story.' She loves to hear us tell that story."

From the perspective of an adopted child, it is widely recognized that the fewer moves a child encounters, the less additional trauma children experience. It is not the physical act of moving but the connecting to others and the subsequent losses when the connections are broken that negatively affect children. The evidence from professionals and parents indicate clearly that it is usually in the child's best interest for the parent to travel to the birth country and take them home. There is little evidence for children that escorting is good for them.

The Adoptive Parent(s)

As Alison Pentland (an adoptive parent in Canada and adoption advocate) wrote, "There are so many real factors that might prevent an adoptive parent from escorting their child—emotions, work commitments, financial hardships, an unstable country. However, I believe that adoptive parents should always escort their children, unless this personal 'factor' is weighted above the specific child considerations—and I don't believe in most cases it would be... Our first child was an infant and escorted... by the same person who had fostered him since being placed (for) adoption by his birth mother. The country was politically unstable and the host said they had no time or staff to support us in the country. Those two factors seemed reasonable in making our decision to have him escorted. Our second adoption, we knew a stranger would be escorting our daughter— that, coupled with our experience as parents, a slightly older (more aware) infant, and the political stabilisation of the country, encouraged us to go. My husband went and brought back our daughter with pictures and stories of his stay there. Those memories... are priceless (gave us) the opportunity for my daughter to start bonding with our family and not be re-traumatized by yet another stranger on a long plane ride to Canada."

For adoptive parents, they loose the multicultural experience of travel which can cue them into the life, value, culture and other experiences of being in-country that they can share with the child as the child gets older. There is so much to be gained from experiencing what the child experiences, albeit as an adult. The opportunity to take photos of every thing, every where helps document the specific place and time. You never know what will be meaningful to either the parents or the adoptee in years to come, as the adoptive parent can then be an "authority" of what the country was like "when you were adopted." As such, adoptive parents can fill in, albeit with their own perceptions, history for the child and their life prior to adoption. By not going, there is no substitute. It is a time and place that cannot be replaced by a subsequent trip. So, a once-in-a-lifetime experience is missed. Barb Irving wrote that "...in an ideal world, we should require parents to escort their child *and* regularly return to visit their child's birth country, in order to maintain the kind strong ties most professionals in the field advocate! That initial visit at time of placement does not enable the true 'connection' we want families to maintain, and much is lost/fades away if that is the only trip the parents ever make to their child's homeland."

Dean Hale (an adoption worker and adoptive parent at Holt International Children's Services) outlined the many benefits of parents traveling to the child's country. He wrote,

- It enables the adopting parents to see child in a familiar environment.
- It provides the opportunity for easing transition trauma, and going at child's pace.
- Adopting parent can often gain information or insight about child, history or cultural background that often is not recorded in official reports... the information that parents gain is more of the nature of nuances rather than substantive.
- Adopting parent can learn of child's patterns, significant relationships, how the child is calmed (this varies by family and there are cultural differences), dietary preferences, daily routine, temperament, etc.
- There is extraordinary symbolism attached with parent going to child to receive child. It connotes respect for country and culture, and a willingness to adjust to child's needs. In simple terms, the parent cares enough to travel to receive the child.
- Adopting parents can obtain items of symbolism, e.g. original clothes and purchased items, that can represent/symbolize country of origin.

- It eliminates the extra separation/attachment cycle associated with using a stranger to escort the child.
- Parents can take photos of significant people, places etc. Given the growth rates in some developing countries, child care facilities may be replaced with new structures. Skylines can change in a matter of a few years. So photos can capture this historical information. Carole Stiles (an American social worker with Holt International) and Nuria Fuentes Palaez (an adoption research at the University of Barcelona) both commented about that parents going to the child's country of birth for their adoptive child deepens their understanding and respect for the child's origins.

One task of an adoptive family is to claim the child. Claiming is both a legal and psychological/family system process. The legal process of claiming involves appearing in court to complete the adoption. Psychological/family system claiming is the process of when the family feels and acts that the child in "theirs". Claiming is delayed when a legal event occurs without the adoptive family being present. That is not to say that it permanently, negatively affects it. It just delays claiming. Every delay places more risk on the developing family system.

The staff of International Social Services also weighed in on the issue. While they supported the notion of parents going to the child's country of origin, they also suggest that "...not all adoptive parents would be able to emotionally cope with the conditions in some of the third world countries or those in Eastern Europe, and should not be asked to do so... this would not reflect their ability to parent; some people are simply more sensitive than others."

Anna Belle Illien (an International Adoption Agency Director) provided a rationale for escorting. She suggests that... "it is absolutely not ideal for someone who has never parented before to receive their child for the first time in a foreign country where they do not speak the language. They do not know anything about babies and what is normal and OK and what is not. The trip is rough for everyone. There is no routine on a trip. The new parent arrives home exhausted and usually needs help the first few days. When the child is escorted, the parents are rested and in a familiar environment. It really makes a difference when they can start their routines immediately with the child where they have access to their support system and their pediatrician. I have nothing but good things to say about the advantages of escorting..."

For parents, there are both positive and negative aspects to escorting. Most opinions from adoptive parents, professional and researchers indicate that escorting is not in the child or family's best interest. However, there are at least some compelling rationale for times when it might be in the family's best interest and, indirectly, in the child's best interest to allow escorting.

The Adoption Agency

There are tremendous costs in international adoption. Fees for inter-country adoption range from $7,000 to $25,000, including agency fees, dossier and immigration processing fees, and court costs. However, there may be additional costs for the following that are usually not included in the fees such as foster care for the child (usually in South and Central American adoptions), children's medical care and treatment, and parents' travel and in-country stay to process the adoption abroad (length of stay or number of required trips varies). So, there are additional fees running from $1000 to $10000 or more. Understandably, most families would like to control costs. Dean Hale of Holt International suggests that there is no economic incentive for parent to ask for an escort. The Department of Labour usually requires agencies to pay overtime to staff who escort if they are a non-exempt employee. This can be a significant additional cost to the adoption.

Also, the process may take longer time if parents want an escort. According to Dean Hale, in India, the U.S. CIS office approves the I-600 "orphan visa petition" the same day. By contrast, if adopting parents file the I-600 with their stateside US CIS office, processing can take a month. Then government to government communications (CIS to State) to the proper U.S. Consulate in India can take another two weeks. (These government-to-government messages frequently get misdirected which leads to additional delays.) So it is less expensive and faster for adopting parent to travel.

An agency might promote escorting if a business plan suggests such a practice would increase their market share of international adoptions and the agency is either in a growth strategy or operating as a for-profit business although all are supposedly non-profit. The only rationale that would promote escorting as a fundamental part of agency services is if agencies are following business principles rather than good practices in adoption.

Convention on Rights of the Child Related to Escorting

The United Nations General Assembly in 1990 adopted the Convention on the Rights of the Child as international law (and ratified by 192 countries, excluding the United States) which can provide basic principles that escorting may violate. For instance, Part I, Article 3 insists that all decisions made about children must be in their best interest (Office of the United Nations High Commissioner for Human Rights, 2006). Although the "best interests" are relative to each case, universally, any practice that delays or prevents attachment as quickly as possible is suspect for "best interests".

Part I, Article 18, states the primary responsibility for the upbringing and development of the children lies with their parents or legal guardian (Office of the United Nations High Commissioner for Human Rights, 2006). As previously discussed, when a child can be traumatized by the travelling for adoption, the best person to provide comfort would be the adoptive parent and not a stranger. The adoptive parent can begin to establish a consistent response to the child's emotional needs, whereas the escorting adult cannot.

Finally, Part I, Article 33 states that children should be protected from economic exploitation (Office of the United Nations High Commissioner for Human Rights, 2006). Further, the agencies that promote escorting or hire such escorts are not subject to overview. With very little international regulation of private agencies to begin with, some agencies that find the employing of escorts as a "cost-cutting" sales pitch to adoptive parents are rewarded yet again for possibly unethical practices.

Conclusion

The summation of the discourse we have presented is rudimentary. However, the issues raised cannot be dismissed and point towards the allegation that escorting is not in the best interest of children.

Albeit, controlled-studies do not exist that support or refute the positive outcomes of escorting. However, without theoretical guidance, accountability of the agencies for escorting, or empirical evidence, escorting should not be supported. Even with limited evidence, we must begin to explore avenues for investigating how the adopted children and their families have faired subsequently after using an escort. Even without data, escorting does not seem consistent with a best practices approach to adoption.

If escorting has to happen, as it may in rare occasions, Dean Hale of Holt International works in partnership with the social worker staff at the overseas organisation to prepare child for the transition and to structure pre-departure visits with the sending country. He offers the following protocol that we amended slightly:

- A 1 to 1 child/escort ratio.
- Escort is limited to select people who are well known to (the agency). Usually we limit escorts to employees. This provides us a greater opportunity to supervise.
- If a child has a significant medical problem that may need attention during travel, we may send a medically trained person.
- The escort is screened. In addition to internal protocols, we do a criminal history and child abuse check on potential escorts. Escorting is demanding and requires a person with good health and the stamina, to do what is right for the child. They will likely need to go for 50+ hours without sleep and be able to make wise judgements in a state of sleep deprivation. We screen out escorts who have inadequate sensitivity/understanding to the separation trauma that the children experience.
- The escort is trained. We have an escort manual. Escorts are required to attend a formal two hour training. This training covers a wide spectrum of topics including: separation, stages of grief and loss, basic health care, blood pathogen training, information for how to care for child, how to manage transitions, psycho-social issues, as well as logistics information. We also encourage the escort to have first aid training.
- The escort must always remain with the child. The escort goes straight-through and personally affects the transfer

of child to adopting parents, and stays overnight at the destination. No extra intermediaries are permitted....

- On return to the U.S. the escort is debriefed.
- The escort keeps records of ins and outs, behaviour's and significant events.
- The escort spends time in the child's care center to build relationship and trust before departure. Often this takes several days. This is not a scoop and run.

As a final conclusion, we recognize that our assertion will be met with concern and criticism by some practitioners in international adoption. We hope that this chapter will serve as a catalyst for a more comprehensive dialog about the practice of escorting, as well as stimulate research on this adoption practice. Until evidence suggest otherwise, we conclude that a best practice in international adoption is for parents to travel to the child's country of origin for adoption.

References

Groze, V. & Ileana, D. (1996), A follow-up study of adopted children from Romania. *Child and Adolescent Social Work Journal,* 13(6), 541-565.

Miller, L. Hendrie, N. (2000), Health of Children Adopted from China. *Paediatrics,* 105(6): E76.

Office of the United Nations High Commissioner for Human Rights (2006), Convention on rights of the child. Retrieved on May 21, 2006, from http://www.ohchr.org/english/law/crc.htm#part1

Rutter, M. (1995), Clinical implications of attachment concepts: retrospect and prospect. *Journal of Child Psychology & Psychiatry,* 36(4): 549-71.

Smyke, A.T., Dumitrescu, A. & Zeanah, C.H. (2002), Attachment disturbances in young children. I: The continuum of caretaking casualty. *Journal of the American Academy of Child and Adolescent Psychiatry,* 41, 972-982.

11

Heritage Camps and Heritage Tours

CHRISTINE FUTIA

Introduction

The Heritage Tours of India conducted by different agencies and individuals in receiving countries are an effort to familiarize the adopted children from India with the cultural tradition of their country of origin and with the rich Indian legacy. The essence of the Heritage Camp and Heritage Tour movement, which touches all western countries that have had adoptions from India, can be attributed to the following antecedents:

(1) A person cannot grow up with a solid self-image if s/he does not understand his cultural roots. "My children identify as Americans, yet the world perceives them as Indian-Americans (or as Indians) because they carry their identity in their face, their skin colour, etc."

(2) One cannot be proud of something of which one has no concept—or even worse, of which one has a cartoon-like concept. Until recently, the only character on American television that came from India was a comical fellow who worked in a convenience store on the cartoon program "The Simpsons". This is *Not* the way we want our children to see themselves.

Now as the Indian-American community increases in size and influence, there are a few wonderful role models in films and on TV. The young woman who played the lead in "Bend it Like Beckham" (a favourite film of the Futia children) is now a lead on the E.R. (Emergency Room) series playing a very capable doctor. As Mrs. Futia says, "You cannot imagine how much that means to my children."

(3) More importantly, the Indians who have come to live in America have certain values, which may not reflect the totality of the great, diverse nation from which they have come. Participants try to study all of the different communities in India during Indian Heritage Camps, but it is only when actually visiting India that an adoptee can experience the true nature of his motherland.

(4) Our children may be rebuffed by Indian-Americans here, who want their children to associate with high-born Indians—assuming that our "dark" adoptees must be low-born. There has been some heartache associated with this for some of our older children. Yet in India, we find our children welcomed with open arms, as long-lost relatives. People of all stations in life take the time to talk with them, explain customs, and share stories and experiences. Our children indeed feel embraced by their country.

As long as there is inter-country adoption from India, which I believe will always be the case, then it is essential that Heritage Tours and Heritage Camps continue to operate, to give our children a true sense of pride in being part of the Indian Diaspora. My children were very interested in the new dual 'citizenship' proposal, but when they learned that they could not receive Indian passports through this program, they were extremely disappointed. They would be very eager to become Indian passport-holders again if it were possible to do so.

"In 1973, at the age of 16, I was selected as a Rotary International Exchange Student. I opted to live with a family in a small village in coastal Karnataka. My parents, Ramesh and Shanti Pai, were traditional vegetarian small-town Konkani Brahmins. There were three other teenagers at home and lots of extended family to keep us busy. We had a tiny hut on the beach and occasionally enjoyed bathing in the Arabian Sea. Daddy was often out of station on business but Mummy ruled the home with an iron fist and kept all of us studying hard. There was much love and laughter in the house. More than 30 years later, I am still very close to my Indian family, and they consider me a daughter of their house. I was included in Daddy's death rites when he passed away in February 2005. I enjoy all the family weddings and other gatherings and travel to India as often as I can to visit the family that remain there, as well as the others who live in California and Dubai..."

In those days you could not call the USA from Manipal and letters to the US took two weeks. I was very homesick a lot of the time, I got pneumonia during the monsoon, and I also caught lice. My Indian family's "adoption" of me and care and concern for my mental and physical well-being laid the groundwork for my own adoption of three Indian children in 1987, 1991 and 1994.

All three children show some permanent effects of their very difficult starts in life. Leo Rajan has several learning disabilities, but through the help he has received since he was a baby we believe he will be able to live on his own, hold a job, get married, and become an independent adult. His greatest ambition is life is to work for an airline, either on the ground or as a flight attendant. We think this is in his grasp and are doing everything we can to support this ambition. He will soon start a 2-year program in Travel and Hospitality which will prepare him for careers in commercial aviation, cruise lines, travel agencies, and hotels. This should give him ample choices for the future.

Leo really values his Indian heritage, as do all three of the children. Bollywood music has really helped to connect them to their homeland, and we have been able to participate in quite a few cultural events here in the US as well as travelling to India or visiting or Indian family here in the US. Having permanently lost their first families, to be claimed as kin by the Pai family means the world to my children. I count my blessings every night that this family has joined together with ours in such a special way. To have my children included on the *mandap* (altar) at a family wedding and treated as equals by the *pundit* (priest) is no small thing—especially because they are (to quote my Indian friends) "quite dark".

My daughter Annie has some learning disabilities, but she works very hard in school and has a very sunny disposition. She probably does not have the intellectual capacity for an advanced degree, but she is hoping to find a para-medical profession such as laboratory technician where she will be able to flourish. Annie is currently "in love" with another boy from her same orphanage in Kolkata. Steven is a year older, and they have been "together" for almost 2 years now. They met at our annual Indian heritage camp called SPICE (more on that later). Because Steven lives about 1.5 hours away by plane, the two of them are always working hard to save their money so they can visit each other. These visits take place under the careful supervision of our family and Steven's, to ensure that everything is proper. They are both very young but they do plan to be married in about 5 years...so only time will tell. Steven hopes to go into some kind of a construction business.

My son Peter came to us with a small special need—slightly malformed feet. This proved to be a very minor affliction, but later in life we learned that he suffers from mental retardation and severe mental illness. We are able to get good help for him in terms of medication and schooling, but he will never be able to live on his own. Of course, this has brought us a lot of sadness, but we have accepted our fate and his, because there are never any guarantees in life, whether you adopt your children or give birth to them. When he is not in one of his periods of instability, Peter is one of the most loving and empathic children you have ever met. He is very precious to us and right now we are focusing on making the arrangements that will enable him to live independently in a group home when he is an adult, using government benefits plus some savings of ours. We are working hard to ensure he will not be a burden on his brother and sister.

In 1996, I took my daughter Annie (age 6) back to India where we visited Manipal and Kolkata. We had a great time together, but on my next trip in 1998, Leo and I travelled with another mother and son, and we learned how much more fun it was to explore India with friends by our side. I made one or two more trips with just one other family, but then my friends from SPICE heritage camp pleaded with me to lead a larger tour so more of them could avail of the experience of visiting their children's homeland. I am an executive with a large food company, so I have both the income and the vacation time to be able to offer such a tour (I do not charge my costs to the group, but cover them myself), so I have been able to make these trips affordable for my friends. So, this truly is a labour of love for me. I am very organized and I enjoy making sure each detail is perfect so that the children and parents get as much as possible from each day that they are in India.

Here is a little bit of information about SPICE heritage camp, the fount from which all of this started. We have been going for 16 years now, and I have been helping to run the camp for a long time. The SPICE Indian Heritage Camp has been in operation for over a decade.

SPICE Indian Heritage Camp

SPICE was formed more than 22 years ago by three American families who were adopting children from India. Although SPICE stands for *Supportive Parents and Indian Children Everywhere,* the group has also included families with children from other south Asian countries such as Nepal, Pakistan, Sri Lanka and Bangladesh.

Each year, SPICE families come together for a family reunion and heritage camp, held at a family-oriented conference or retreat center. The group has met in Maryland, Ohio, North Carolina, Michigan and Pennsylvania in past years. In 2005, SPICE was held at the Living Learning Center of the University of Pittsburgh at Johnstown, PA from July 10-14, 2004. 50 families with more than 90 children were in attendance.

In addition to children from south Asia, bio-siblings and children adopted from other countries are more than welcome at SPICE. Each child is assigned to an age-appropriate class to pursue a curriculum centering on life on the Indian subcontinent. The heritage camp themes rotate from year to year, focusing on "Everyday Life in South Asia," "A Trip to the City," "Celebrations," "The Arts of South Asia" and "Expedition: South Asia."

The children attend parent-run heritage classes from 9.00 to noon during the first three days of the reunion. Care is provided for infants and toddlers so that parents can be free for teaching and supervision of older children. Older teens and young adult adoptees provide hands-on assistance with heritage camp activities. The classes culminate in a very special program presented to parents and guests on the third afternoon.

Afternoon and evening activities often include yoga classes, storytelling for younger children, a talent show put on by SPICE children, group discussions for adults, Bollywood movies, and cultural programs presented by members of the local Indian community. Meals are cafeteria-style American food with the addition of a special Indian dish at each lunch and dinner. One afternoon, children and parents dress in ethnic costumes and group pictures are taken. A favourite activity is shopping at the SPICE store, where all kinds of items are available for sale including books, *bindis*, bangles, stationery, incense, dolls, clothing, and much more. The proceeds from the store are directed to several charities in India.

Although SPICE started out as an East Coast group, attendees at recent reunions have come from as far as away California and Switzerland, as well as from many eastern and mid-western states. All families with an interest in south Asian adoption are welcome to attend the reunion. The conference center is handicapped accessible, and children with special needs are assigned a one-on-one helper to ensure that they participate fully in all activities.

Children, teens and adults who have attended SPICE will attest that the fellowship they enjoy at each reunion is indescribably special. There is a very real sense that we are all part of one big family, bound together by our love for our children of South Asia. In 2006, SPICE will be held at the Johnstown location from June 25-29.

I could go on at great length about how wonderful the SPICE community is as a support group for families who have adopted from India, and how much it has taught us and our children about Indian culture over the years. Now that the Internet is part of all our lives, we have a mailing list where we can continue our SPICE discussions all year-round. We consider these families' extensions of our own family, and the children share a bond that can only be described as mystical—as if they were all related like cousins.

The first tour of SPICE was organized for a group of 14 in August 2002. One from the group was a young man in a wheelchair who suffers from cerebral palsy. We all pitched in to make sure that Alex enjoyed every activity, and found that there were always many helping hands to carry him or his chair. That time, we visited Jodhpur, Trivandrum, and then each family went to the city where their child had been born to visit their children's orphanage and learn more about the culture and history of the place. Then we rejoined at the end to travel home together.

The second tour was some time during August 2004 (a group of 16), beginning in Udaipur, continuing on to Mamallapuram, and then splitting up to visit the various places where the children had originally come from.

Each tour has been very special. We have managed to keep

the costs to the minimum per person for 17 days, including all airfare and every bit of ground expense including such incidentals as Internet time, tips, admissions, water bottles and laundry. We stay in decent, Indian-style 3-star hotels and travel by bus with a guide in each location. We have had children as young as 8 and as old as 20 in the group, and I find that a mix of ages works well because the older teens can act a little less "cool" when there are younger ones around.

After each tour, we create a digital movie of the experience, largely for the travellers but also for our other SPICE friends and for the public at large. Now I have tours coming up in 2006, 2007, 2008 and 2010. My groups are typically limited to 16, and I prefer to travel with people I already know from SPICE or the ICHILD lists. Since most of the adoptees are teenagers, we have to go in August, during the U.S. school holidays. This limits our options, but it's unavoidable. I choose one destination in the north, one destination in the south, and then each family travels to their own third destination, usually the place where the adoptee's orphanage is located. In Rajasthan, I've taken different groups to Jodhpur and to Udaipur. This gives the flavour of fortress, palace, camel and desert, and even during the rainy season it's quite dry. Moving on to the far south, I've taken different groups to Trivandrum and to Mahaballipuram. This gives the flavour of temple, elephant, rice paddy and beach. In Trivandrum, the monsoon is breaking up in August. In Mahaballipuram, it's very hot in August, but it doesn't rain much.

First and foremost, I want our kids to have fun. I want them to be warmly embraced by the Indian people they come into contact with. I want them to discover the depth and breadth of the Indian history and culture, and to gain respect for themselves as Indian people. I want them to begin to understand, without being told, why a woman in India might be compelled to relinquish a child for adoption. I want them to feel competent enough in India to stroll down the street on their own and stop at a shop to buy snacks. Most of all, I want them to feel sad when they leave India.

Any age is fine as long as the child is willing to go and the parent is excited about going. I find that the kids really pick up vibes from their parents. If their parent is comfortable, they will be comfortable too. I've had adoptees ranging from 8 to 19 on my tours, and I find that a mixed-age group typically works best. The teenagers—who relish giving their parents the cold shoulder whenever possible—enjoy "letting their hair down" with the younger kids. This gives them an outlet for their nervous energy, and of course the younger ones just soak it up.

I try to include one or two visits to orphanages or other child welfare projects, because this type of activity allows them to connect with their "India self", or the child they might have been if they had remained in India. They seem to have a lot of fun and often shrug off pool or internet time to play Ring Around the Rosie.

What the kids really enjoy are camel, elephant and horseback rides, visits to zoos and wildlife preserves, and shopping for handicrafts, clothes, jewellry and CDs.

When you're responsible for 16 souls, you can't leave anything to chance. You've got to know where you are going, how long it will take, what will happen there, where people will use the toilet, and where you will eat. In India, my two older children always play the role of junior tour guides, providing advice and support to the other adoptees and freeing me from spending all my time explaining everything.

The total cost is typically around $3300 complete. This includes flights, hotels, train tickets, meals, ground transportation, guides, special activities, admissions, water, snacks, internet, laundry and tips. We largely stay in 3-star Indian-style hotels, which are clean and comfortable but not luxurious. We travel in a small air-conditioned bus, and we have an English-speaking guide with us at all times. We eat mostly at multi-cuisine restaurants, which mean there are some western and Chinese dishes on the menu. When we're eating in a place where only Indian food is available, some of them will bring peanut butter to spread on their *roti* (Recipes for Indian daily breads are called *chapati, phulka* and *roti* and *paratha.* They are made of finely milled whole wheat flour and water), or will have some snack foods from their backpack to hold them over.

There is also an organisation called Ties that takes groups of adoptees and parents to India. Their program is very well-regarded and includes a social worker who works with the children as they "process" their experiences in their mother country. You can reach them at http://www.adoptivefamilytravel.com.

12

Ethical Practices and Safeguards in Adoption Placement

JAGANNATH PATI

The Convention on the Rights of the Child adopted by the General Assembly of the United Nations on 20 November, 1989 and ratified by India recognizes that each child should grow up in a family environment, in an atmosphere of happiness, love and understanding and a child, by reason of his physical and mental immaturity, needs special safeguards and care, including appropriate legal protection, before as well as after birth. It further states that in all actions concerning children, whether undertaken by public or private social welfare institutions, courts of law, administrative authorities or legislative bodies, the best interest of the child shall be a primary condition.

Article 21 of the Convention deals with safeguards pertaining to inter-country adoptions. It also emphasizes on priority to in country adoption, status of children in inter-country adoption to be equivalent to national adoptions, the placement of children should have no improper financial gain and the placement of child in inter-country adoption involves competent authorities of both the countries. The Government of India acceded to this Convention on 11th December, 1992.

India signed "Convention on Protection of Children and Cooperation in respect of Inter-country Adoption (1993)" on 9th January, 2003 and ratified the same on 6th June, 2003 with a view to strengthening international cooperation and protection of Indian Children placed in inter-country adoption. For the purpose of implementation of the Convention in the country, the Ministry of

Women and Child Development, Government of India, is functioning as the Administrative Ministry and Central Adoption Resource Agency as the Central Authority.

Among the non-institutional services, adoption is the most appropriate form of rehabilitation for the orphaned and destitute child since it ensures the child's right to family. It also meets the needs of persons who are considering parenthood through adoption. There is a growing recognition the world over that the main purpose behind placing a child in adoption is to serve Child's Best Interest.

A field like the rehabilitation of abandoned, orphaned and destitute children calls for total dedication to the highest standards of professionalism, competence, integrity and social vision. A code of ethics and professional conduct thus becomes imperative. The purpose of international adoption must be to provide children with a mother and a father in a way that respects their rights, not to enable foreign parents to satisfy their wish for a child at any price. The Hague Convention of 1993 calls for the establishment of a Contracting Authority in both receiving States and States of origin, which will accredit organisations working in the field of inter-country adoption. It creates a framework for cooperation between States and provides for safeguards and procedures to ensure that inter-country adoptions take place in the best interests of the child and with respect for his/her fundamental rights.

All children—regardless of race, ethnicity, gender, medical limitations or other conditions—deserve permanent, loving homes. If a child cannot remain with his or her birth family, or cannot be placed through domestic adoption, then international adoption offers a viable, positive solution. International adoption affects many people from all walks of life, cultures, countries, races, religions and means. It provides a home to a child in need of a permanent family, opens doors to another culture, and brings understanding and compassion between nations (http://www.jcics.org/2005Programs.htm).

As in other developing countries, some of the problems of non-institutional care system in India can be classified as under:

- Dearth of statistics and facts about total number of homeless children in the country, lack of research/data about human and social cost of children staying in orphanages;

- No data on total number of adoptable children in the country, total number of children legally free for adoption at a particular time and free for inter-country system (need for procedural changes);
- Children live excessively long in the orphanages;
- Families have to keep waiting for their children;
- Lack of transparency across the adoption process;
- Prolonged/uncertain adoption process adds additional barriers (domestic families back off due to the fear of the process while overseas families back off completely or choose other countries).

Teri Bell, who has remained in the field of adoption for over thirty years and worked with children in institutions in Romania, India, Korea ad several other countries, has a concern for older children languishing in orphanages. "Adoptive parents have a voice, adopted children have a voice, politicians, social workers and orphanage directors have a voice, but the children who lived through orphanage care do not, to my knowledge, have a voice. They are the experts; they are the young adults who can tell you how they have survived living outside of a family and without parental love. While some adopted persons are now able to questions their adoptive placements, how they came to be available for adoption and even if they ever should have been adopted, many children who never got the chance, have a great deal to say from a very different perspective. I have held these children in my arms, I have sat and listened to their issues, concerns and joys for hours at a time, but there are very few people out there listening to them. I would not attempt to speak for this group. They are as different with as many different responses to their upbringing as any other group of people. I know 'orphans' who are getting decent educations and further education or technical training following their high school experience. I have known 'orphans' who did not succeed in school, who are on the streets or incarcerated. I also know adult 'orphans' who have had a wonderful chance to 'make it' in their country of birth despite the obstacles placed in their way. These fortunate few still carry with them the burden of being orphans. Who will they marry, who will hire them, who will advocate for them, where do they go when they need support or help? I strongly feel that until academics listen and I mean really listen to the survivors of their systems we won't really know what we're attempting to fix."

Ethical Issues

Ethics is the branch of philosophy that concerns morality—questions of right and wrong. What a society considers ethical hinges on its beliefs about what is most important; thus ideas about ethics vary across times, cultures, and subcultures (International Adoption Consortium).

Ethics is a philosophical science with a set of moral standards, values and guiding principles that govern professional practice. The field of ethics involves systematising, defending and recommending concepts of right and wrong behaviour. As professionals working in the field of Adoption, we need to ensure that we are guided by the principle of "Best Interest of the Child" (Mehta N., 2003).

Research in developmental psychology tells us that children need stability and security and are harmed when they lose their ongoing intimate relationships with those few adults who provide their nurture and care. A large literature in psychology documents the importance of these relationships of attachment between caregiver and child, especially for young children. When these relationships are stable, they serve as a secure base from which the young child ventures forth into the world of other people, things, and events. Children who enjoy relationship of intimacy and security with their closest caregiver(s) in the first three years are more likely than those who do not to be curious and explore their environments. They are more likely to be friendly and successful relating to other children and new adult caregivers, better able to communicate, more able to play and learn independently, and more likely to grow up to have successful relationships in marriage and at work.

During its 37th Session from 13 September to 1 October, 2004, the UN Committee on the Rights of the Child adopted a decision that recognizes among other things "the frequency with which its Concluding Observations provided to States Parties following periodic consideration of their reports addressing serious difficulties regarding care provision for children in informal or formal fostering, including kinship care and adoption, or residential facilities, often recommending the strengthening and regular monitoring of alternative care measures". The Committee also recalled "the recommendation... that States Parties develop the use of alternative measures in order to avoid long-term placement of children in institutions that do not provide the type of setting children need, not only for survival, but also for development, including physical, mental, spiritual, moral and social development, in a manner compatible with human dignity and to prepare the child for individual live in a free society, in accordance with article 6.2 of the Convention" (ISS/IRC News Bulletin No. 72-73, Dec. 2004, http://www.iss-ssi.org).

In western standards, parents have a right to separate, divorce, and move including the right to exclude others from that function. They also have procedural rights to contest custody, visitation and adoption. But the assertion of any of these rights may conflict with the child's best interests. We must respect the child as a person and acknowledge that she is the most vulnerable party in the proceeding. Thus, regardless of the circumstances that lead the child' custody to be an issue, her best interest must be the central concern of the state. It is a moral wrong to decide issues of child placement based on adult conflicts and injustices that may have stemmed from adult behaviour without examining how these decisions may impact the child.

For the past 30 years, the number of families from wealthy countries wanting to adopt children from other countries has grown substantially. At the same time, lack of regulation and oversight, particularly in the state of origin, coupled with the potential for financial gain, has spurred the growth of an industry around adoption, where profit, rather than the best interests of children, takes center stage. Many countries around the world have recognized these risks, and have ratified Hague Convention on Inter-country Adoption. UNICEF strongly supports this international document, which is designed to put into action the principles regarding inter-country adoption which are contained in the Convention on the Rights of the Child. These include ensuring that adoption is authorized only by competent authorities, that inter-country adoption enjoys the same safeguards and standards, which apply in national adoptions, and that inter-country adoption does not result in improper financial gain for those involved in it. These provisions are meant first and foremost to protect children, but also have the positive effect of providing assurance to prospective adoptive parents that their child has not been the subject of illegal and detrimental practices. The case of children separated from their parents and communities during war or natural disasters merits special mention. It can not be a assumed that such children have any other living parents nor relatives. Even if both their parents are dead, the chances of finding living relatives, and a community or Home to return to after the conflict subsides, continues to exist. Thus, such children should not be considered for inter-country adoption, and family tracing should be the priority. This position is shared by UNICEF, UNHCR, the International Confederation of the Red Cross, and International NGOs such as the Save the Children Alliance (UNICEF).

Infants and young children with special needs are flooding the child welfare systems as never before, and disturbed teen's cycle in and out of placements, sometimes ending up on the streets. This crisis calls out for the creative and family solutions. All children, i.e. partially handicapped children, medical problem children, older children, children with Down's syndrome, are adoptable. Everyday, in every country of the world, countless numbers of children are separated from the families that give birth to them. The reasons are many-poverty, illness, death, lack of support, cultural stigmas and social barriers. Whatever the reason, the consequences in the lives of individual children can be devastating.

UNICEF and ISS launched a research and advocacy program in early 2004 calling for the development of specific international standards for improving the protection of such children. A joint working paper reviews the complex reality of care provision for these children and seeks to identify the main problems and an issue that needs to be broached in an internationally—accepted instrument. These include the unwarranted recourse to out-of-home care: inappropriate decisions regarding type of care; over burdened foster-care systems; lack of protection in informal care; undue recourse to residential care; inappropriate conditions in residential care; uncontrolled private residential facilities; inadequate permanency planning; children and parents with no voice; inadequate preparation of declare in emergencies, children affected by HIV/AIDS, cross-border care placements and care for separated children abroad care involving deprivation of liberty etc. The convention on the right of the child and other current international standards provide an overall framework in which to raise these problems but they do not set out comprehensive and detailed guidelines and rules that could clarify good practice, prevent abuses and establish responsibilities and accountability (ISS/IRC News Bulletin No. 72-73, Dec. 2004, http://www.iss-ssi.org).

All families have strengths and can make well-informed decisions about keeping their children safe when supported. Culturally responsive practices honour the family's customs, values and preferences.

International adoption is a worldwide phenomenon and by no means a minor one. Developing countries in Asia, South East Asia, Latin America and Africa can be termed as sending countries as far as inter-country adoption is concerned. Deprivation of parental care is perhaps the worst tragedy for a child who is innocent by all means. In most of the cases, it is subject to torture from mother's womb itself and therefore, all orphanages and adoption agencies must follow ethical standards while taking steps and measures before adoption procedure itself and while placing children in adoption also.

Reports of Unethical Practices

The Adoption Institute in USA has recommended to the State Department (http://www.adoptioninstitute.org/policy/hagueregs.html) that agencies be required to follow strict standards with respect to fees charged and information provided about children available for adoption and be prohibited from requiring adoptive families to carry cash abroad to pay fees unless there is no other alternative. It carried a survey and over 1,600 families responded about their experience on China and Russia.

- 13 per cent were not satisfied with the services they received from adoption agencies, with 16 per cent of parents who adopted from Russia reporting dissatisfaction compared with 6 per cent of those who adopted from China.
- 14 per cent would not recommend their agency to other families, with 19 per cent of parents who adopted from

Russia reporting they would not recommend their agency compared with 8 per cent of those who adopted from China.

- 14 per cent said their adoption cost more than the agency told them it would cost. Russian adoptions were more likely to exceed agencies' estimated costs (17%) than Chinese adoptions (9%).
- 15 per cent reported that their agency withheld information or told them inaccurate information about the child and the adoption process. 21 per cent of families adopting from Russia, and only 8 per cent from China, reported that their agency withheld information or told them inaccurate information about the child.
- Almost three-quarters of the families reported that agencies asked them to carry cash overseas to pay fees, with most carrying $3,000 or more.

Besides the above, there are several ugly stories in the net which speak about unethical practices above the adoption agencies which are involved in international adoptions in sending and receiving countries.

Adoption Cost

Any kind of donations must be voluntary. Expectation of donation as a precondition of matching is something criminal. Agreement of foreign agencies with adoption agencies of sending countries with regard to donations against commitment of certain number of children is certainly unethical. Total transparency should be maintained as far as adoption fees are concerned. At no cost, adoption should lead to profiteering. For all adoption related expenses, receipts should be issued to the concerned.

Article 10 of the Hague Convention says that an accredited body shall pursue only non-profit objectives. Article 32 of the Hague Convention state that no one shall derive improper financial or other gain from activity related to an inter-country adoption. Adoptive parents should not be emotionally blackmailed while taking custody of the children from the institution. This is highly unethical to expect donations from parents at this time. The Convention on Protection of Children and Cooperation in respect of Inter-country Adoption establishes standards to curb abuses in international adoption practice by,

- Requiring a central point of contact or central authority in each country to coordinate inter-country adoption policy and practice;
- Providing for a system of accreditation for inter-country adoption practitioners;
- Requiring that consent to adopt be informed and freely given;
- Prohibiting improper financial or other gain and requiring that only costs and expenses, including reasonable professional fees, be charged; and
- Requiring preservation of medical and other records.

In order to safeguard the child's biological link with his or her parents, the Convention stipulates that the parents must freely consent to the adoption. It also prohibits any contact between the prospective adoptive parents and the natural parents before the latter have taken the initial steps in the adoption process. Absolute transparency is required in all such matters so also accountability at each level failing which the program may be affected adversely.

Information concerning the costs and expenses and fees charged for the provision of inter-country adoption services by different agencies should be made available to the public. *Donations by prospective adopters to bodies concerned in the adoption process must not be sought, offered or made* (Second Special Commission on Practical Operation of the Hague Convention of 29 May, 1993 on Protection of Children and Cooperation in respect of Inter-country Adoption, 17-23 September, 2005).

Counselling

Adoption agencies should recognize the lifelong effects of adoption on all the parties to an adoption and provide counselling and support services. There is need of adequate counselling for bio-parent/s to take an informed decision. The social worker should acquaint himself or herself with the code and should follow the ethics very strictly. It is also possible that there is greater interference by the management in discharge of their duties, which make them helpless. Counselling is required at three stages, i.e. for bio-parents, for prospective adoptive parents and at post-adoption stage. It is essential that counselling should include information on effects of adoption. Consent of biological mother, wherever required, and only should be taken after the birth of the child and the agency has to ensure that the consent has not been induced by payment or compensation of any kind.

In case of proposing any older child for adoption, it has to be seen that the child has been counselled properly. If the child remembers her bio-parents/original family, all efforts must be made to trace her origin. The report of the counsellor should be enclosed with the CSR when it is forwarded to adoptive parents for consent or central authority for approval. It has been observed that such children who are able to remember their background information are more likely to be frustrated and in such cases chance of disruption seems to be high too. Surrender on the ground of poverty or gender issues should always be discouraged as there are always alternate ways available to retain the child with biological parents.

Counselling involves discussion, which usually has got emotional content. It is much more desired in case of biological parent/s while surrendering the child to get rid of stressful situation. Effective adoption counselling requires interpersonal skills, chiefly active listening and attending behaviour. Six activities that may be performed by counselling include advice, reassurance, communication, and release of emotional tension, clarified thinking and reorientation.

The need for counselling for the biological parents arises from the fact that the decision to surrender the child should be considered as the last alternative. The social worker should understand both *pros* and *cons* of relinquishment. The consequence should not mentally hurt to the biological parent/s any more. It has also been observed that in few cases, after effective counselling by the adoption agencies, the biological mothers have taken back their own children and that is what the effects of the counselling is. Professionally qualified candidates such as Master Degree-holders in Psychology and Social Work should be considered as eligible to discharge the duty of a social worker.

Article 21 of the Convention on the Rights of the Child (CRC) puts emphasis on counselling of biological parents as may be necessary. The Seventeenth Session of the Hague Conference on Private International Law, 1993 deals with safeguards to ensure that inter-country adoptions take place in the best interest of the child and also emphasizes respect for his or her fundamental rights as recognized in international law etc. Here it has been stated that before the child is surrendered, the persons, institutions and authorities whose consent is necessary for adoption, have to be counselled as may be necessary and duly informed about the effects of their consent, in particular whether or not an adoption will result in the termination of the legal relationship between the child and his or her family of origin. Such persons, institutions and authorities have to give their consent freely, in the required legal form.

In India, mostly women are often not very articulate in expressing and sharing their anguish over abandoning their child. Because of the social pressure on her, it is with a sense of relief that the birth mother agrees to let someone take over the responsibility of her child; her apprehensions are more related to keeping her identity secret. She experiences the reality of adoption and relinquishment only much later and it is then that she feels the loss of her baby. In some agencies, there are very high percentage of relinquished children, which is of course, not a good signal. In India, some of the adoption agencies processing inter-country adoption cases lost their recognition for various irregularities during 1999-2001 and it is interesting to note that all such agencies were involved in large number of surrendered cases of children.

Besides the above, counselling the prospective adoptive parents and post-adoption counselling are considered very relevant. The adoptive parents are already at pain without having a child of their own and they reach at an adoption center as a last resort. The approach to them should be very cordial and friendly. If they have any misconceptions, that should be cleared before making further query. They may have more than one hundred questions about the child to be adopted and the procedures involved etc. The professional social worker has to listen and reply them very patiently.

Pre-adoption Counselling

It is important to look into following aspects while attempting pre-adoption counselling:

- Emotional readiness and acceptance of adoption as an alternative way of achieving parenthood.
- Coping with childlessness and infertility issues without any residual sense of guilt, blame, inadequacy or deprivation.
- Stability of the marital relationship.
- Issues of "Bonding and Attachment" with a child who is not biologically related.
- Concerns about the child's social background.
- Heredity and Environment Issues.
- Process of selecting the child.
- Confidentiality in the adoption process.
- Acceptance of the child by family, friends and neighbours.
- Requests for "Secret" adoption.
- Anxieties about sharing the fact of adoption with the child in future.

Post-adoption Counselling

Post-adoption Counselling focuses on the following issues:

- Coping with parenthood and change of roles.
- Feelings of bonding and attachment.
- Acceptance of the child by relatives and friends.
- Sharing the fact of adoption with the child why, when, how.
- Disciplining issues in adoption.
- Issues related to the Child's Schooling and Academic performance.
- Child's needs to search for "Roots"—Social, Emotional and Legal Issues.
- Disruption in adoption placement.

Counselling the Biological Parent/s

No civilized society in the earth can permit killing of children under any pretext. In developing countries like India while a section of people have got access to amniocentesis and abortion at their own choice, others especially the poor are always in dilemma. The psychosocial status of biological parent/s or unwed mother can't be comprehended when they have to surrender a child in an institution. Whatever may be the reason, it is perhaps the most difficult decision in life. Such children might not have been planned.

Birth mothers after relinquishment of the child forfeit all rights over the child. In India, there is provision of a grace period of two months for reconsideration that means if after surrender of the child, the biological mother changes her decision within a period of two months; she can get back the child. But as per information received from Adoption Agencies from different parts of the country, hardly any biological mother approaches the agency to get back the child.

The need for counselling for the biological parents arises from the fact that the decision to surrender the child should be considered as the last alternative. She should understand both *pros* and *cons* of relinquishment. The consequence should not mentally hurt to the biological parent/s any more. It has also been observed that in few cases, after effective counselling by the adoption agencies, the biological mothers have taken back their own children and that is what the effects of the counselling is. In certain cases in India, it has been observed that some biological mothers have relinquished their children to the institutions for more than one time. It means some thing wrong with the counselling of the birth mother.

No single approach to counselling suits all situations or meets the requisite service demands. Effective counselling relies on interpersonal skills, chiefly active listening and attending behaviour. Active listening means acknowledging what the client has said; paraphrasing and summarizing her statements; reflecting back her feelings with summary statements or questions; encouraging her to speak and responding directly and honestly to her questions and to the information she provides about her personal situation. Attending behaviour means using non-verbal cues that show that the counsellor is playing close attention; leaning forward and facing the client, establishing the eye contact, smiling and sitting squarely, for example. Such non-verbal cues help establish rapport and trust between the counsellor and the woman.

In case of poor parents surrendering their biological child, the parents need to be counselled about the range of its repercussions. The Agency may arrange some kind of alternative arrangement like sponsorship for the child, so that the child should remain with their biological parents. In case the ground of relinquishment is poverty, the parents can be counselled as to how they can increase their source of income and improve their knowledge on family planning devices. In country like India, social stigma is the most important reason for relinquishing children. She experiences the reality of adoption and relinquishment only much later and it is then that she feels the loss of her baby. In some agencies, there are very high percentage of relinquished children, that is of course, not a good signal. There has been hardly any research in India about the pains of birth mothers that they do experience after losing the child. While such kind of studies are available in western societies, in case of India, such kind of study seems to be very difficult.

Counselling is an integral component of adoption services. Every biological parent/s or unwed mother needs and deserves effective and adequate counselling so that the decision by the biological mother is final. Good counselling is a discussion between provider and client that helps to work in the best interest of the child. A rare case of rethought while relinquishing the child can be considered as a major success from the point of view of the professional social worker.

The Seventeenth Session of the Hague Conference on Private International Law, 1993 which has been ratified by a number of countries deals with various safeguards to ensure that inter-country adoptions take place in the best interest of the child and also emphasizes respect for his or her fundamental rights as recognized in international law etc. Here it has been stated that before the child is surrendered, the persons, institutions and authorities whose consent is necessary for adoption, have to be counselled as may be necessary and duly informed about the effects of their consent, in particular whether or not an adoption will result in the termination of the legal relationship between the child and his or her family of origin. Such persons, institutions and authorities have to give their consent freely, in the required legal form.

The New Zealand survey carried by Sue Wells among 262 respondents constituting biological mothers demonstrates an overwhelming negative experience for the birth mothers both at the time of relinquishment and current anxieties about the child's welfare. Considering that the mothering instinct is universal, can the situation in India be different. Some of the major finding can be summed up as under:

1. Most birth mothers felt that they had no choice about relinquishing their child for adoption. Many recollect being coerced and only later realized that they did not know enough about adoption at the time, particularly how it would affect them later on and were given wrong, misleading or inadequate information about alternatives to adoption.
2. Birth mothers did not want to forget about their children.
3. Almost all wanted to know basic information about their children. Most of the respondents had no support or counselling services.
4. Far from being able to make "a fresh start", the loss of their babies and subsequent denial of that loss by professionals had meant unresolved grief. Almost all said that they were not actively involved in making the decision to have their babies adopted.
5. Many birthmothers had stable relationships with the birthfathers but had not planned marriage.
6. Almost all birthmothers said that they had been adversely affected emotionally and/or physically and that the effects of relinquishment were profound and long lasting. Difficulties with relationships and trust were cited as the most common symptoms, which may be associated with blocking or suppressing feelings, linked to have their child adopted. Almost half said that it had affected their physical health.
7. Almost all wanted to see their child.
8. The majority was dissatisfied with current adoption law and practice and thought that they should have the same legal rights to information about the child as the child had about them.
9. Given the same circumstances today, most said they would have decided against adoption because of the deep and long lasting emotional effects.
10. Over half felt a clean break was not the best choice because of long-term emotional effect. Two-thirds had searched or tried to find out about their child.

The Hague Convention on Inter-country Adoption

The Hague Conference on Private International Law is an inter-

Governmental Organisation set up on a permanent basis in 1953 and is based at the Hague, Netherlands. It has been associated with various treaties in the field of Private International Law including international judicial and administrative cooperation, and is an international forum, which gives positive directions in solving many complex socio-economic and legal problems. The Hague Convention on Protection of Children and Cooperation in Respect of Inter-country Adoption (the Hague Convention) was adopted on 29 May, 1993 and entered into force on 1 May, 1995. More than 60 countries and about 10 international NGOs took part in its drafting. It has as its principle objectives

(a) to establish safeguards to ensure that inter-country adoptions take place in the best interests of the child and with respect for his or her fundamental rights as recognized in international law.
(b) to establish a system of cooperation amongst Contracting States to ensure that those safeguards are respected and thereby prevent the abduction, the sale of, or traffic in children.
(c) to secure the recognition in Contracting States of adoptions made in accordance with the Convention.

The Hague Convention was therefore designed principally to set up a mechanism for international cooperation to give practical effect to the CRC provisions relating to inter-country adoption. It provides for responsibilities and tasks to be shared between the States of origin and the receiving States, while respecting organisational diversities and national legislation. One of it basic premises is that adoption is not an individual affair, which can be left exclusively to the child's birthparents or legal measure for the protection of children. Consequently procedures for inter-country adoption should ultimately be the responsibility of the States involved, which must guarantee that adoption corresponds to the child's best interests and respects his or her fundamental rights.

The Hague Inter-country Adoption Convention was developed over a three-year period in discussions and negotiations that involved more than 70 States, five inter-governmental organisations and 12 non-governmental international organisations. The Permanent Bureau, and in particular, Hans van Loon (now

Secretary General), who was primarily responsible for the preparatory work, had already begun work on the project in 1988. One of the most important elements of the preparation was to secure the participation of many States of origin from around the world, which would not normally be involved in the discussions at The Hague. Their participation was crucial to the success of the undertaking given the very different interests of States of origin and receiving States, and the very sensitive nature of the subject-matter, the degree of unanimity achieved when negotiations were completed was remarkable. The Convention was adopted unanimously by the 66 States represented in May 1993 at The Hague. The main reason for this harmony was perhaps the underlying philosophy of the convention, influenced by Article 21 of the *United Nations Convention of 20 November, 1989 on the Rights of the Child,* that the Convention should be designed to ensure that (a) the interests of the child should be foremost in the adoption process, (b) inter-country adoption should only be considered in the case of a child for whom a suitable family cannot be found in his or her State of origin, (c) abuses associated with inter-country adoption should be eliminated. Discussions benefited from many examples of good practice in inter-country adoption and there was awareness of the great benefit that had been brought to many children and families as a result of inter-country adoption in the past. However, there was also an understanding that the dramatic increase in inter-country adoption since the late 1960s, had unfortunately been accompanied by a wide range of complex social and legal problems, and by some malpractice. It was also recognized that unilateral action by individual States to control this situation was not sufficient. The objects of the *Hague Convention of 29 May, 1993 on Protection of Children and Co-operation in Respect of Inter-country Adoption,* as set out in Article I, are therefore to establish a system of cooperation between receiving States and States of origin for the purposes of minimizing abuse, ensuring that the interests of the child come uppermost in the adoption process and to guarantee the recognition of adoptions made under the Convention (http://www.hcch.net).

The Goal of the Convention is to protect the rights of children, birth families and adoptive parents involved in adoptions with other countries that are parties to the Convention. The Hague Convention/ Final Act consists of Seven Chapters spread over 48 Articles.

The Hague Convention essentially turns the 'principle' of subsidiary into a rule, recognizing that "inter-country adoption may offer the advantage of a permanent family to a child for whom a suitable family cannot be found in his or her State of Origin". This Convention reflects an internationally recommended policy concerning different child care measures, which-while recognizing that each child is special and that decisions affecting the child's life must be based on a full respect for his or her uniqueness—sets out the following hierarchy of options, generally held to safeguard the long-term "best interests" of the child:

- Family solutions (return to the birth family, foster care, and adoption) should generally be preferred to institutional placement;
- Permanent solutions (return to the birth family, adoption) should be preferred to provisional ones (institutional placement, foster care;
- National solutions (return to birth family, national adoption) should be preferred to international ones (inter-country adoption).

In addition, the Hague Convention sets out to establish a co-operation system based on the designation by each contracting state—be it a country of origin or a receiving country—of a "central authority", a type of single official service. The central authority in each country is responsible for all aspects of international adoption—whether children are leaving or arriving in the country—and deals, in each case, with the central authority of the other country concerned.

Since a home and the protective environment of a home is important for the healthy development of the child, the first option should be to locate the child's own family and if the child's family is not located, then the second option should be to find an alternative family for the child, either through adoption or foster care. The third option should be to create an atmosphere of family within the institution, through the involvement of community.

It rests on three major principles:

(i) Subsidiary, whereby international adoption may only be

considered in the absence of domestic solutions (i.e., only if the child cannot be brought up by his or her own parents, other members of the family or adoptive parents within the country of origin);

(ii) Prohibiting improper financial or other gain and requiring that only costs and expenses, including reasonable professional fees, be charged;

(iii) The primacy of the child's best interests (requiring a central point of contact or central authority in each country to coordinate inter-country adoption policy and practice; to establish legal safeguards to ensure that inter-country adoptions take place in the best interest of the child and with respect to his/her fundamental rights as recognized in International Law; to ensure and secure in the Contracting States International recognition of adoption, in other words, an adoption made in one country will be recognized in other countries; providing for a system of accreditation for inter-country adoption practitioners; requiring that consent to adopt be informed and freely given; and requiring preservation of medical and other records etc.).

Every Contracting State has to set up a Central Authority as per the Hague Convention.

The Central Authorities will discharge the following main functions:

(a) provide information as to the laws of their States concerning adoption and other general information, such as, statistics and standard forms;

(b) keep one another informed about the operation of the Convention and, as far as possible, eliminate any obstacles to its application;

(c) collect, preserve and exchange information about the situation of the child and the prospective adoptive parents, so far as it is necessary to complete the adoption;

(d) facilitate, follow and expedite proceedings with a view to obtaining the adoption;

(e) promote the development of adoption counselling and post-adoption services in their States;

(f) provide each other with general evaluation reports about experience with inter-country adoption.

The great majority of the states involved in international adoption—whether as receiving countries or countries of origin—had a hand in preparing the Hague Convention and it is, therefore, fair to conclude that the treaty as a whole reflects the collective vision of those concerned. The 60-70 countries in question include virtually no Islamic and only a few sub-Saharan states.

In order to safeguard the child's biological link with his or her parents, the Convention stipulates that the parents must freely consent to the adoption. It also prohibits any contact between the prospective adoptive parents and the natural parents before the latter have taken the initial steps in the adoption process.

In addition, the Hague Convention sets out to establish a co-operation system based on the designation by each contracting state—be it a country of origin or a receiving country—of a "central authority", a type of single official service. The central authority in each country is responsible for all aspects of international adoption—whether children are leaving or arriving in the country—and deals, in each case, with the central authority of the other country concerned.

Obviously, it takes time to put such a system in place—and it is a prerequisite to ratification of the convention. The convention does not cover the criminal aspects of abuses practiced on children, as these questions lie outside the remit of the Hague Conference.

The Hague Convention essentially turns the 'principle' of subsidiary into a rule, recognizing that "inter-country adoption may offer the advantage of a permanent family to a child for whom a suitable family cannot be found in his or her State of Origin". *For current status of the Convention about ratification and Guides to Good Practice, Hague Convention site can be accessed through www.hcch.net.*

The List of Ratifications and Accessions is remarkable for two reasons: First, the speed at which ratifications and accessions have proceeded, despite the complexity that may be involved in implementing the Convention into domestic law, is unusual. Some countries of origin take the position that they will only engage in making arrangements for inter-country adoption with States that have ratified the Hague Convention. Convention principles have influenced some of the bilateral arrangements, which are becoming more and more common as implementation of the Convention advances. And some of the key concepts within the Convention have been implemented in States, which have not ratified the Convention. The idea of the "Central Authority" in particular has taken a firm root. Adoption agencies in several countries have been reviewing their structures and organisation in the light of the Hague system. This has been so in Europe, where inter-country adoption agencies have established a European organisation called "Euro Adopt," which is helping to raise standards and develop practical procedures in the context of the Hague system. A similar process is occurring within the United State of America. Finally, the United Nations Committee on the Rights of the Child has strongly endorsed the Hague Convention by recommending ratification or accession to numerous States.

Role of the Permanent Bureau

The Permanent Bureau has a number of continuing functions in relation to the operation of the Convention. First, it receives and circulates basic contact details concerning the Central Authorities designated under the Convention, as well as the names and addresses of the bodies, which are accredited in accordance with Articles 10 and 11 of the Convention. The Permanent Bureau also keeps the latest information concerning ratifications and accessions. All this information is now contained on the website of the Hague Conference on Private International Law (http://www.hcch.net).

Article 42 of the Convention requires the Secretary General of the Hague Conference, at regular intervals, to convene a Special Commission to review the practical operation of the convention. The value of these Special Commission is that they provide and opportunity for States and their authorities to share good and bad experiences and to develop uniform procedures.

The Permanent Bureau performs a continuing role in helping to facilitate operation of the Convention. This involves a number of informal activities, including: promoting further ratification of the Convention, assisting with its implementation, spreading information concerning good practice under the Convention, and helping from time to time to promote, or to remove obstacles to, cooperation between Central Authorities.

Safeguards

Adoption offers an excellent alternative to institutional care for an abandoned, destitute or neglected child in an atmosphere of happiness, love and understanding which only a family can provide. It meets the needs of persons who are considering parenthood through adoption and also ensures the best interest of the child by providing the child the right to a family.

Inter-country adoption of homeless Indian children is governed by an extensive set of rules, which are basically drawn up, with the intent of safeguarding the interest of the child. While there is a whole infrastructure in place to assist in inter-country adoption, in-country adoption is encouraged most in India. The intension behind the whole program is that an orphan child should get parental care and simultaneously he or she should be adopted preferably in his or her own society or cultural milieu. There should not be abuse of any kind while the child is in institution or is placed in family care. There should not be any ulterior motive behind the placement. It should be entirely a safe journey at least till the child attains adulthood. Various country laws and international conventions protect orphan children. This begins with priority or promotion to in-country adoption by each sending country. There is wide agreement that before inter-country adoption is chosen as a suitable alternative for a child, sufficient consideration should be given to other alternatives within the country. This is because of the fact that a child can best adjust with his own cultural milieu and society.

India is a large country having more than 1 billion population and has 35 States and Union Territories. There are a number of gaps in child welfare system in India. There is no segregated database on all children in need of care and protection and children in conflict with law. The new Juvenile Justice Act (2000) now amended in 2006 is yet to be implemented in all the states. Inadequate infrastructure under JJ system like constitution of Juvenile Justice Boards, Child Welfare Committees and Special

Juvenile Police Units are noticeable. Lack of coordination and convergence of programs/services and inadequate budgetary allocation for child protection are other important observations so also inadequate training and capacity building of functionaries under juvenile justice system.

All over the world, there is emphasis now on preventive measures, early identification and early intervention. Prevention of abandonment of children should be followed by to frothly presanation efforts.

Social conditions of children before adoption are important issues. Children who are relinquished or abandoned live in institutions such as orphanages or remand homes and they come from different religious and ethnic backgrounds. Children have to live in the institutions for several reasons. Sources of such children include hospitals, nursing homes, unmarried biological mother, criminal parents, insane parents, street children, children from poor socio-economic strata, family breakdown, lost children, children with families in crisis, i.e. affected by HIV/AIDS, children of commercial sex workers, children of substance abusers, children of prisoners, children rescued from trafficking and exploitation, children who have been abused and neglected, children with special needs, etc.

An adoption agency has to ensure that it has employed professional social worker/s, trained nurse/s and other child care staff as per requirement to cater to the well-being of children in the institution and further to prevent any kind of abuse and neglect of children, i.e. sexual abuse, physical abuse and emotional abuse and ensure conducive environment essential for adequate physical and emotional development of a child. The agency has to provide immediate treatment to such children as most of them are low birth weight babies (2.5 kg or less).

Teri Bell, an expert on adoption matters is more concerned about the procedural lapses. "In my opinion, the systematic abuses taking place, jeopardize our abilities to find permanence for children all over the world. In most, but not all, sending countries, the information supplied regarding each child available for adoptive placement is scant if present. Children must be represented thoroughly before they are considered as a new family member by an adoptive parent(s). This information should include all background information, how they came into care and why they are considered to be available for placement. In some countries, this is thoroughly covered in the child reports, in many, little or no information is given. This is not acceptable. If information is not known, it must be investigated. There is no excuse for adoptive children having to return to their countries of birth to find the "truth" or information about their backgrounds. This is not the job of the children; this is the job of the professionals involved with the placement of the children. Birth parents must be interviewed, they must receive counselling, they must be offered alternatives to adoption for their children. As I personally do not consider institutional care or long-term foster care as an alternative to a permanent family, adoption should be the last resource for the children if joining their family of birth is not an option for them. This will entail much more work on the part of the social work community and the officials, however, the words 'unknown' or 'abandoned' should not be acceptable as the end of the story".

Each child care institution should take care to:

(a) promote high standards of health and nutrition,
(b) assure basic minimum needs and security, play and leisure,
(c) provide early childhood care for survival, growth and development,
(d) protection of the girl-child, and
(e) protection of children with special needs.

New CARA Inter-country Guidelines (2006)

Over the years, India has evolved a system of inter-country adoption procedure which takes care of all issues of safeguards. While Central Adoption Resource Authority (CARA) is the nodal body to implement all adoption related guidelines, the Placement Agencies have been given lot of freedom to deal with adoption matters. The 2006 Guidelines on Inter-country Adoption has replaced the 1995 Guidelines. Although matching and processing of applications of foreign parents still remain with the adoption agencies, there are some noticeable features in the new Guidelines:

- All Indian adoption agencies processing foreign adoptions

have to be licensed by respective State Governments and also to be recognized by CARA.

- Provision of regular inspections by state government as well as by CARA.
- Criteria of adoption agencies for foreign adoptions defined so also for children and perspective adoptive parents.
- Curtailing delays at all level and provision of time stipulation.
- Adoption fee has been fixed that will cover the cost involved in providing quality child care, medical and legal services, passport, visa, payment towards professional staff, monitoring, correspondence, preparation of child study reports, medical report, etc.
- Donation by foreign prospective adoptive parents and foreign agencies has been stopped.

Para 5.23 of the Guidelines deals with various safeguards for children placed in inter-country adoption.

(i) No contact between the FPAPs (Foreign Prospective Adoptive Parents) and the biological parents will be allowed. Counselling facilities should be made available to biological mother/parents by the adoption agency. Consent of the biological mother cannot be obtained before the birth of the child.

(ii) No child should be proposed for inter-country adoption before ACA (Adoption Coordination Agency) Clearance except in the case of NRIs (Non-Residence Indians).

(iii) RIPA will maintain the confidentiality of the child's origin, his or her parents.

(iv) No one shall derive improper financial gain or other gain from an activity related to adoption. A receipt shall be issued in case of receipt of any payment for any service rendered.

(v) There can't be any direct adoption by any FPAPs and all such adoptions shall be through recognized/enlisted agencies as defined under the Guidelines.

(vi) All RIPAs (Recognized Indian Placement Agencies) shall adhere to strict ethical practices and work in the best interest of children as defined in the Guidelines and described in Hague Convention on Inter-country Adoption, 1993 failing which action as deems fit will be taken against any defaulting agency/ies. The office-bearers of the agency/ies will be held responsible for any breach of procedural safeguards or non-compliance of ethical practices. (See details in http://www.adoptionindia.nic.in/carahome.html)

In case of sending countries like India, certain other ethical standards have been stipulated by Supreme Court of India (L. K. Pandey vs. *Union of India* case in 1171 of 1982 and subsequent judgements) *and circulars/guidelines issued from time to time by Government of India.*

Authorities

1. Strategies related to prevention of abandonment and relinquishment particularly by biological parents on the ground of poverty should be included in the programmes of the governments as well as NGOs so as to prevent separation of children from their parents. This would involve ensuring that the environment at home is one of love, support and care. Since a home and the protective environment of a home is important for the healthy development of the child, the first option should be to locate the child's own family and if the child's family is not located, then the second option should be to find an alternative family for the child, either through adoption or foster care. The third option should be to create an atmosphere of family within the institution, through the involvement of community.
2. It is the responsibility of the appropriate authority or agency to ensure that when the parents relinquish a child for adoption, all the legal requirements are met. If the parents state a preference for the religious upbringing of the child, these wishes shall be respected as far as possible, but the best interest of the child will be the paramount consideration. If the parents are not known, the appropriate authority or agency, in whose care the child has been placed, shall endeavour to trace the parents and ensure

that the above services are provided, before taking any action in relation to adoption of the child.

3. Government may promote ethics that may include respect for human dignity, respect for moral integrity, promotion of justice, fostering of transparency and renunciation of all forms of corruption.
4. Central authority of each country should fix adoption fee both in case of domestic adoption and inter-country adoption to prevent improper financial gain as per Article 8 of Hague Convention. Thus financial transparency has got to deal with ethical practices. Adoption should be part of other social and child welfare activities so that other programs can support adoption program and not the *vice versa*. When an agency is dependant on donations on a regular basis to run its adoption program, it is bound to compromise with ethics.

   When a child goes to another country to be adopted, the appropriate authority or agency of the receiving country shall accept responsibility for supervision of the placement, and for the provision of progress reports for the adoption authority or agency in the sending country for the period agreed upon.
5. Approval of inter-country adoption applicants is a responsibility of the appropriate authorities or agencies in both sending and receiving countries. An application to adopt a child shall not be considered by a sending country unless it is forwarded through the appropriate authority or agency in the receiving country.
6. Government may discourage large scale institutional care for the sole reason that in a large institution, personal care cannot be guaranteed to all. It may result in poor vaccination schedule, sever nutritional deficiency, signs of protein deficiency, developmental delay, poor stimulation and poor immune capacity etc. It should be part of other social and child welfare activities.
7. Use of MIS and ICT in child welfare system has brought forward effective results in developed countries, which may be replicated, in developing countries like India where there is no accurate database and central pool of information. Without accurate data and access to infor-

mation, the desired result is unlikely to come. Particularly in USA, the universities have been greatly involved in child welfare training activities and preparing large number of trained social workers which is a best practice to be followed by other countries.

8. The period of waiting and uncertainty of the child must be reduced as much as possible. Continuity of bond must be insured and transition between one situations of the life to another must be prepared and carefully supported in order to avoid disruption and distress. As per Article 35, the competent authorities of the Contracting States shall act expeditiously in the process of adoption. All efforts must be made to reduce the stay of orphan, abandoned and surrendered children in the institutions. Central Adoption Resource Authority (CARA) in India has come out with the following time schedule to limit institutionalisation of children, which is certainly a positive footstep.

Sl. No.	*Services to be Rendered by Concerned Agency/Authority*	*Proposed Time Frame*
1.	*RIPA* to place a child in domestic adoption.	Within 30 days from the date on which the child is legally free for adoption.
2.	*ACA* to issue a Clearance Certificate.	On 31st day in case of a normal child and within 10 days in case of a special needs child.
3.	*CARA* to issue NOC for inter-country adoption.	Within 15 days from the date of receipt of NOC application from RIPA, complete in all respect.
4.	*RIPA* to file the case in the competent Court for an appropriate order after CARA NOC.	Within 15 days from the date of receipt of NOC from CARA.

(*Contd.*)

(Contd.)

Sl. No.	*Services to be Rendered by Concerned Agency/Authority*	*Proposed Time Frame*
5.	The competent *Court* to dispose the case.	Within 2 months from the date of filing of application by RIPA, complete in all respect.
6.	The concerned *Passport Office* to issue passport for the child.	Within 10 days from the date of submission.

(*Source*: www.adoptionindia.nic.in)

RIPA: Recognized Indian Placement Agency to process cases of foreign adoptions.

ACA: Adoption Coordinating Agency—promotes domestic adoption in the country.

CARA: Central Adoption Resource Agency—functions as central authority in the matter of adoptions in the country.

9. Guidelines on special needs children should be developed by each country to deal with such children so that such children are fast-tracked.
10. As per Article 7, 8, 9 and 20 of Hague Convention, there should be regular interaction among central authorities to protect children and achieve other objects of the Convention. Central Authorities should provide the administrative framework for the Convention. It should promote cooperation amongst competent authorities in their states to:
    (a) protect children; and
    (b) achieve the other objects of the Convention.
11. Research and documentation on children issues have to be encouraged in order to understand trends, impact and outcomes of child welfare measures. More resource centers and advocacy based organisations may be encouraged to work in the area as we have neglected and abused children on the one hand, so also vast majority of children who are homeless and are leading joyless life.

Agencies

1. Each adoption agency should prepare a Child Study Report (CSR) which should contain all information about the child, about a brief social history of the child, his or her medical treatment, immunisations undergone and such other information as considered important for the child. Only after matching a child study report with a home study report by a professional social worker, a child should be proposed for adoption and while handing over the child, the adoptive parents should be provided as much information about the child such as:
   - Brief social history of the child,
   - Child Study Report,
   - Record of medical treatment/immunisations undergone etc.
2. It is pertinent that child's behaviour and development, i.e. motor development, perceptual development, cognitive development, development of language and communication, emotional and social development etc. should be observed minutely and observations should be made in the Child Study Report.

   In most of the cases the foreign adoptive parents do not have opportunity to see the child physically before signing the Child Study Report (CSR) which contains very limited information about the child. It is important that the CSR should contain as much information as possible so that the parents are in a position to take an information decision without any hesitation.

   Professionally qualified workers should offer biological parents social work services. No commitment to an adoption plan should be permitted before the birth of the child. If the parents decide to relinquish the child for adoption, they shall be helped to understand all the implications, including the possibility of adoption by foreigners and of no further contact with the child. Parents should be encouraged, where possible, to provide information about the child's background and develop-ment, and their own health.

The adoption agency is responsible for procuring available information about the child's background.

3. All admissions and deaths should be reported to the appropriate authority and all agencies have to provide quality childcare to such children.
4. Each adoption home or Placement Agency has to maintain a number of files/registers including the Master Admission Register. Admission Register should contain information about the child from the day it arrives in the institution till the child has progress reports and adoption decree. Further, the Adoption agencies have to work in the best interest of children as defined under UNCRC, Hague Convention on Inter-country Adoption and various Guidelines issued by CARA/Government of India from time to time, build confidence and bring together parents and children for legal adoption to ensure smooth transition, dispel all confusion and misinformation related to child adoption, educate and enrich the staff working in the Agency in early childhood care, guard itself against the violations of established norms and rule of law, ensure quality child care and promote non-institutional care.
5. No commitment to an adoption plan should be permitted before the birth of the child. If the parents decide to relinquish the child for adoption, they shall be helped to understand all the implications, including the possibility of adoption by foreigners and of no further contact with the child. Parents should be encouraged, where possible, to provide information about the child's background and development, and their own health. It is the responsibility of the appropriate authority or agency to ensure that when the parents relinquish a child for adoption all of the legal requirements are met. If the parents state a preference for the religious upbringing of the child, these wishes shall be respected as far as possible, but the best interest of the child will be the paramount consideration. If the parents are not known, the appropriate authority or agency, in whose care the child has been placed, shall endeavour to trace the parents and ensure that the above services are provided, before taking any action in relation to adoption of the child.

There must not be any promise of or any direct financial support to biological parents, which could influence their decision to give up their child for adoption.

6. No child should be disadvantaged in securing a permanent family placement because of the lack of the ability of an agency to make such a placement. The child should then be transferred to an agency who can effectively handle special needs placements. Children with special needs have the same right as any other child to a secure and permanent family relationship. When an older child joins a new family, there are both joys and challenges for the child, parent and other family members. It is indeed wonderful to see a child settle into a new family and to make enduring links with other family members, friends and neighbours. Children who join permanent care of adoptive families at an older age may bring many of the stressful experiences of their earlier lives into their new families. Their behaviour may become very disruptive and sometimes aggressive and they can be indiscriminate and inappropriate in their relationships with family members and other people.
7. Brothers and sisters and other children who have been cared for as siblings should not be separated by adoption placement except for special reasons. Before any adoption placement is finalized, the child concerned shall be consulted in a manner appropriate to his or her age or level of development. There should not be separation of siblings/twins either at the time of proposal and even after placement as a result of disruption of any case unless it is unavoidable and in the interest of the children.
8. The adoptive parents should be continuously updated about the status of their applications. The adoptive parents should receive information about the medical and social history of the child and some information about the biological parent/s if possible.

   Research shows that the bulk of disrupted children are such children who have been placed in adoption at an older age. All such children have faint memories of their biological mothers or part of their life, who have been severely traumatized, before placement.

Although disruptions cannot be predicted, but can be avoided by more careful matching. All disruptions must be dealt as per Section 21 of Hague Convention.

The careful matching between a given child and a given prospective adoptive family must take place taking into account the characteristics and specific needs of the child and the characteristics and apparent ability of the family so that this relationship may be durable and smooth. The matching should be based on both the detailed Reports (CSR and HSR). Those who treat children as commodities deserve to be cursed. Careful matching can avoid chances of disruption.

Conclusion

An unfaltering commitment of adoption should be that it is intended as a means to provide families for children, rather than children for families. This is especially critical in international adoption where it is the children of one country being taken to another. The simplistic assumption that a poor child in a developing country will have a preferred life with a family in a 'rich' country is misguided. Ethics in adoption...an issue not often publicly explored, yet an issue that should be on the highest list of priorities. It can be concluded that...for thousands of children throughout the world, international adoption may provide the only possibility of finding a permanent family. We must all make a commitment to ensure ethical adoption practices as a means of securing the futures of orphaned children worldwide.

A very clear conviction and commitment to transparency and ethical practices is very important for all stakeholders involved in the adoption process from micro to the macro level. Centralized database and multi-media campaign are other requirements. All efforts have to be made to expedite the adoption process, reduce the time period and prevent delays in the adoption process so that a child gets a family without any delay. India is a vast country with large number of homeless children. For effective implementation of child welfare policies, all districts can be connected to the State Department of Women and Child Development and the state to the Central Government. Access to information has to be promoted at all level to enable mass to take informed decision. Now the attitude towards adoption of unrelated children particularly in urban India seems changing. The adoption of an unrelated child is now receiving acceptance in the Indian society. The sensitisation and awareness of society to this issue has also helped to create a more positive climate for adoption.

Reorganizing the adoption procedure in India has almost become inevitable now when we see large number of children are languishing in the institutions and such children have a right to be placed with loving and caring families.

Since the mandate of all UNCRC ratified countries is to cover all children in need of care and protection, it important for countries to come out with broad Guideline on "*Guidelines for Strengthening Family and Providing Alternative Care*" that may be based on "Draft UN Guidelines on the Protection and Alternative Care of Children without Parental Care". The purpose is not to limit the benefit to orphan and abandoned children alone but cover all such children who are deprived of family care for some reason or other. No child should be without the support and protection of a legal guardian or other recognised responsible adult at any time. Most children without parental care are looked after informally by relatives or others. States should devise appropriate means to ensure their welfare and protection while in such informal care arrangements. Thus reorganizing adoption system in India, becomes inevitable.

References

A Child Rights Agenda for the Coming Decade, Statement of the Child Rights Caucus for 2001, UN General Assembly Special Session on Children, October, 2000.

Eufemio Flora (29th to Ist April, 1984), Special Address in Child's Basic Right to family: A Search of Alternative Strategies within the Country in An International Seminar held at Delhi, Organized by TDH (Germany) and IAPA.

Hague Convention on Inter-country Adoption http://www.hcch.net

http://www.adoptionindia.nic.in/carahome.html.

http://www.adoptioninstitute.org/policy/hagueregs.html

http://www.jcics.org/2005Programs.htm.

Innocent Digest (1998), UNICEF, International Child Development Center, Florence, Italy.

ISS/IRC News Bulletin No. 72-73, Dec. 2004, http://www.iss-ssi.org

Menon, N.R. (22-23 Dec., 1994), Situational Analysis of Children in India in the Context of Constitutional and legal provisions and UN Convention on the Rights of the Child, Two Day Meet on Rights of the Child, NIPCCD, New Delhi.

Nilima Mehta (2003), 'Dilemma in Adoption Counselling', paper presented in International Meet on Adoption India, 2004, New Delhi.

Sue Wells (1994), *Within Me, without Me*; Scarlet P. Press.

Website of International Adoption Consortium.

www.unicef.org

Annexures

Annexure-I

Declaration on Social and Legal Principles relating to the Protection and Welfare of Children, with special reference to Foster Placement and Adoption Nationally and Internationally

Adopted by General Assembly Resolution 41/85 of 3 December, 1986

The General Assembly,

Recalling the Universal Declaration of Human Rights, the International Covenant on Economic, Social and Cultural Rights, the International Covenant on Civil and Political Rights, the International Convention on the Elimination of All Forms of Racial Discrimination and the Convention on the Elimination of All Forms of Discrimination against Women,

Recalling also the Declaration of the Rights of the Child, which it proclaimed by its Resolution 1386 (XIV) of 20 November, 1959,

Reaffirming principle 6 of that Declaration, which states that the child shall, wherever possible, grow up in the care and under the responsibility of his parents and, in any case, in an atmosphere of affection and of moral and material security,

Concerned at the large number of children who are abandoned or become orphans owing to violence, internal disturbance, armed conflicts, natural disasters, economic crises or social problems,

Bearing in mind that in all foster placement and adoption procedures the best interests of the child should be the paramount consideration,

Recognizing that under the principal legal systems of the world, various valuable alternative institutions exist, such as the kafalah of Islamic Law, which provide substitute care to children who cannot be cared for by their own parents,

Recognizing further that only where a particular institution is recognized and regulated by the domestic law of a State would the provisions of this Declaration relating to that institution be relevant and that such provisions would in no way affect the existing alternative institutions in other legal systems,

Conscious of the need to proclaim universal principles to be taken into account in cases where procedures are instituted relating to foster placement or adoption of a child, either nationally or internationally,

Bearing in mind, however, that the principles set forth hereunder do not impose on States such legal institutions as foster placement or adoption,

Proclaims the following principles:

A. *General Family and Child Welfare*

Article 1

Every State should give a high priority to family and child welfare.

Article 2

Child welfare depends upon good family welfare.

Article 3

The first priority for a child is to be cared for by his or her own parents.

Article 4

When care by the child's own parents is unavailable or inappropriate, care by relatives of the child's parents, by another substitute—foster or adoptive—family or, if necessary, by an appropriate institution should be considered.

Article 5

In all matters relating to the placement of a child outside the care of the child's own parents, the best interests of the child, particularly his or her need for affection and right to security and continuing care, should be the paramount consideration.

Article 6

Persons responsible for foster placement or adoption procedures should have professional or other appropriate training.

Article 7

Governments should determine the adequacy of their national child welfare services and consider appropriate actions.

Article 8

The child should at all times have a name, a nationality and a legal representative. The child should not, as a result of foster placement, adoption or any alternative rgime, be deprived or his or her name, nationality or legal representative unless the child thereby acquires a new name, nationality or legal representative.

Article 9

The need of a foster or an adopted child to know about his or her background should be recognized by persons responsible for the child's care unless this is contrary to the child's best interests.

B. Foster Placement

Article 10

Foster placement of children should be regulated by law.

Article 11

Foster family care, though temporary in nature, may continue, if necessary, until adulthood but should not preclude either prior return to the child's own parents or adoption.

Article 12

In all matters of foster family care, the prospective foster parents and, as appropriate, the child and his or her own parents should be properly involved. A competent authority or agency should be responsible for supervision to ensure the welfare of the child.

C. Adoption

Article 13

The primary aim of adoption is to provide the child who cannot be cared for by his or her own parents with a permanent family.

Article 14

In considering possible adoption placements, persons responsible for them should select the most appropriate environment for the child.

Article 15

Sufficient time and adequate counselling should be given to the child's own parents, the prospective adoptive parents and, as appropriate, the child in order to reach a decision on the child's future as early as possible.

Article 16

The relationship between the child to be adopted and the prospective adoptive parents should be observed by child welfare agencies or services prior to the adoption. Legislation should ensure that the child is recognized in law as a member of the adoptive family and enjoys all the rights pertinent thereto.

Article 17

If a child cannot be placed in a foster or an adoptive family or cannot in any suitable manner be cared for in the country of origin, inter-country adoption may be considered as an alternative means of providing the child with a family.

Article 18

Governments should establish policy, legislation and effective supervision for the protection of children involved in inter-country adoption. Inter-country adoption should, wherever possible, only be undertaken when such measures have been established in the States concerned.

Article 19

Policies should be established and laws enacted, where necessary, for the prohibition of abduction and of any other act for illicit placement of children.

Article 20

In inter-country adoption, placements should, as a rule, be made through competent authorities or agencies with application of safeguards and standards equivalent to those existing in respect of national adoption. In no case should the placement result in improper financial gain for those involved in it.

Article 21

In inter-country adoption through persons acting as agents for prospective adoptive parents, special precautions should be taken in order to protect the child's legal and social interests.

Article 22

No inter-country adoption should be considered before it has been established that the child is legally free for adoption and that any pertinent documents necessary to complete the adoption, such as the consent of competent authorities, will become available. It must also be established that the child will be able to migrate and to join the prospective adoptive parents and may obtain their nationality.

Article 23

In inter-country adoption, as a rule, the legal validity of the adoption should be assured in each of the countries involved.

Article 24

Where the nationality of the child differs from that of the prospective adoptive parents, all due weight shall be given to both the law of the State of which the child is a national and the law of the State of which the prospective adoptive parents are nationals. In this connection due regard shall be given to the child's cultural and religious background and interests.

Annexure-II

Convention on the Rights of the Child, G.A. Res. 44/25, Annex, 44 U.N. GAOR Supp. (No. 49) at 167, U.N. Doc. A/44/49 (1989), entered into force September 2, 1990

Ratification Information

Preamble

The States Parties to the present Convention,

Considering that, in accordance with the principles proclaimed in the Charter of the United Nations, recognition of the inherent dignity and of the equal and inalienable rights of all members of the human family is the foundation of freedom, justice and peace in the world,

Bearing in mind that the peoples of the United Nations have, in the Charter, reaffirmed their faith in fundamental human rights and in the dignity and worth of the human person, and have determined to promote social progress and better standards of life in larger freedom,

Recognizing that the United Nations has, in the Universal Declaration of Human Rights and in the International Covenants on Human Rights, proclaimed and agreed that everyone is entitled to all the rights and freedoms set forth therein, without distinction of any kind, such as race, colour, sex, language, religion, political or other opinion, national or social origin, property, birth or other status,

Recalling that, in the Universal Declaration of Human Rights, the United Nations has proclaimed that childhood is entitled to special care and assistance,

Convinced that the family, as the fundamental group of society and the natural environment for the growth and well-being of all its members and particularly children, should be afforded the necessary protection and assistance so that it can fully assume its responsibilities within the community,

Recognizing that the child, for the full and harmonious development of his or her personality, should grow up in a family environment, in an atmosphere of happiness, love and understanding,

Considering that the child should be fully prepared to live an individual life in society, and brought up in the spirit of the ideals proclaimed in the Charter of the United Nations, and in particular in the spirit of peace, dignity, tolerance, freedom, equality and solidarity,

Bearing in mind that the need to extend particular care to the child has been stated in the Geneva Declaration of the Rights of the Child of 1924 and in the Declaration of the Rights of the Child adopted by the General Assembly on 20 November, 1959 and recognized in the Universal Declaration of Human Rights, in the International Covenant on Civil and Political Rights (in particular in articles 23 and 24), in the International Covenant on Economic, Social and Cultural Rights (in particular in article 10) and in the statutes and relevant instruments of specialized agencies and international organisations concerned with the welfare of children,

Bearing in mind that, as indicated in the Declaration of the Rights of the Child, "the child, by reason of his physical and mental immaturity, needs special safeguards and care, including appropriate legal protection, before as well as after birth",

Recalling the provisions of the Declaration on Social and Legal Principles relating to the Protection and Welfare of Children, with Special Reference to Foster Placement and Adoption Nationally and Internationally; the United Nations Standard Minimum Rules for the Administration of Juvenile Justice (The Beijing Rules); and the Declaration on the Protection of Women and Children in Emergency and Armed Conflict,

Recognizing that, in all countries in the world, there are children living in exceptionally difficult conditions, and that such children need special consideration,

Taking due account of the importance of the traditions and cultural values of each people for the protection and harmonious development of the child,

Recognizing the importance of international co-operation for improving the living conditions of children in every country, in particular in the developing countries,

Have agreed as follows:

PART I

Article 1

For the purposes of the present Convention, a child means every human being below the age of eighteen years unless under the law applicable to the child, majority is attained earlier.

Article 2

1. States Parties shall respect and ensure the rights set forth in the present Convention to each child within their jurisdiction without discrimination of any kind, irrespective of the child's or his or her parent's or legal guardian's race, colour, sex, language, religion, political or other opinion, national, ethnic or social origin, property, disability, birth or other status.
2. States Parties shall take all appropriate measures to ensure that the child is protected against all forms of discrimination or punishment on the basis of the status, activities, expressed opinions, or beliefs of the child's parents, legal guardians, or family members.

Article 3

1. In all actions concerning children, whether undertaken by public or private social welfare institutions, courts of law, administrative authorities or legislative bodies, the best interests of the child shall be a primary consideration.
2. States Parties undertake to ensure the child such protection and care as is necessary for his or her well-being, taking into account the rights and duties of his or her parents, legal guardians, or other individuals legally responsible for him or her, and, to this end, shall take all appropriate legislative and administrative measures.
3. States Parties shall ensure that the institutions, services and facilities responsible for the care or protection of children shall conform with the standards established by competent authorities, particularly in the areas of safety, health, in the number and suitability of their staff, as well as competent supervision.

Article 4

States Parties shall undertake all appropriate legislative, administrative, and other measures for the implementation of the rights recognized in the present Convention. With regard to economic, social and cultural rights, States Parties shall undertake such measures to the maximum extent of their available resources and, where needed, within the framework of international co-operation.

Article 5

States Parties shall respect the responsibilities, rights and duties of parents or, where applicable, the members of the extended family or community as provided for by local custom, legal guardians or other persons legally responsible for the child, to provide, in a manner consistent with the evolving capacities of the child, appropriate direction and guidance in the exercise by the child of the rights recognized in the present Convention.

Article 6

1. States Parties recognize that every child has the inherent right to life.
2. States Parties shall ensure to the maximum extent possible the survival and development of the child.

Article 7

1. The child shall be registered immediately after birth and shall have the right from birth to a name, the right to acquire a nationality and as far as possible, the right to know and be cared for by his or her parents.
2. States Parties shall ensure the implementation of these rights in accordance with their national law and their obligations under the relevant international instruments in this field, in particular where the child would otherwise be stateless.

Article 8

1. States Parties undertake to respect the right of the child to preserve his or her identity, including nationality, name and family relations as recognized by law without unlawful interference.
2. Where a child is illegally deprived of some or all of the

elements of his or her identity, States Parties shall provide appropriate assistance and protection, with a view to re-establishing speedily his or her identity.

Article 9

1. States Parties shall ensure that a child shall not be separated from his or her parents against their will, except when competent authorities subject to judicial review determine, in accordance with applicable law and procedures, that such separation is necessary for the best interests of the child. Such determination may be necessary in a particular case such as one involving abuse or neglect of the child by the parents, or one where the parents are living separately and a decision must be made as to the child's place of residence.
2. In any proceedings pursuant to paragraph 1 of the present article, all interested parties shall be given an opportunity to participate in the proceedings and make their views known.
3. States Parties shall respect the right of the child who is separated from one or both parents to maintain personal relations and direct contact with both parents on a regular basis, except if it is contrary to the child's best interests.
4. Where such separation results from any action initiated by a State Party, such as the detention, imprisonment, exile, deportation or death (including death arising from any cause while the person is in the custody of the State) of one or both parents or of the child, that State Party shall, upon request, provide the parents, the child or, if appropriate, another member of the family with the essential information concerning the whereabouts of the absent member(s) of the family unless the provision of the information would be detrimental to the well-being of the child. States Parties shall further ensure that the submission of such a request shall of itself entail no adverse consequences for the person(s) concerned.

Article 10

1. In accordance with the obligation of States Parties under article 9, paragraph 1, applications by a child or his or her

parents to enter or leave a State Party for the purpose of family reunification shall be dealt with by States Parties in a positive, humane and expeditious manner. States Parties shall further ensure that the submission of such a request shall entail no adverse consequences for the applicants and for the members of their family.

2. A child whose parents reside in different States shall have the right to maintain on a regular basis, save in exceptional circumstances personal relations and direct contacts with both parents. Towards that end and in accordance with the obligation of States Parties under article 9, paragraph 1, States Parties shall respect the right of the child and his or her parents to leave any country, including their own, and to enter their own country. The right to leave any country shall be subject only to such restrictions as are prescribed by law and which are necessary to protect the national security, public order (ordre public), public health or morals or the rights and freedoms of others and are consistent with the other rights recognized in the present Con-vention.

Article 11

1 States Parties shall take measures to combat the illicit transfer and non-return of children abroad.

2. To this end, States Parties shall promote the conclusion of bilateral or multilateral agreements or accession to existing agreements.

Article 12

1. States Parties shall assure to the child who is capable of forming his or her own views the right to express those views freely in all matters affecting the child, the views of the child being given due weight in accordance with the age and maturity of the child.

2. For this purpose, the child shall in particular be provided the opportunity to be heard in any judicial and administrative proceedings affecting the child, either directly, or through a representative or an appropriate body, in a manner consistent with the procedural rules of national law.

Article 13

1. The child shall have the right to freedom of expression; this right shall include freedom to seek, receive and impart information and ideas of all kinds, regardless of frontiers, either orally, in writing or in print, in the form of art, or through any other media of the child's choice.
2. The exercise of this right may be subject to certain restrictions, but these shall only be such as are provided by law and are necessary:
   (a) For respect of the rights or reputations of others; or
   (b) For the protection of national security or of public order (ordre public), or of public health or morals.

Article 14

1. States Parties shall respect the right of the child to freedom of thought, conscience and religion.
2. States Parties shall respect the rights and duties of the parents and, when applicable, legal guardians, to provide direction to the child in the exercise of his or her right in a manner consistent with the evolving capacities of the child.
3. Freedom to manifest one's religion or beliefs may be subject only to such limitations as are prescribed by law and are necessary to protect public safety, order, health or morals, or the fundamental rights and freedoms of others.

Article 15

1. States Parties recognize the rights of the child to freedom of association and to freedom of peaceful assembly.
2. No restrictions may be placed on the exercise of these rights other than those imposed in conformity with the law and which are necessary in a democratic society in the interests of national security or public safety, public order (ordre public), the protection of public health or morals or the protection of the rights and freedoms of others.

Article 16

1. No child shall be subjected to arbitrary or unlawful

interference with his or her privacy, family, home or correspondence, nor to unlawful attacks on his or her honour and reputation.

2. The child has the right to the protection of the law against such interference or attacks.

Article 17

States Parties recognize the important function performed by the mass media and shall ensure that the child has access to information and material from a diversity of national and international sources, especially those aimed at the promotion of his or her social, spiritual and moral well-being and physical and mental health. To this end, States Parties shall:

(a) Encourage the mass media to disseminate information and material of social and cultural benefit to the child and in accordance with the spirit of article 29;
(b) Encourage international co-operation in the production, exchange and dissemination of such information and material from a diversity of cultural, national and international sources;
(c) Encourage the production and dissemination of children's books;
(d) Encourage the mass media to have particular regard to the linguistic needs of the child who belongs to a minority group or who is indigenous;
(e) Encourage the development of appropriate guidelines for the protection of the child from information and material injurious to his or her well-being, bearing in mind the provisions of articles 13 and 18.

Article 18

1. States Parties shall use their best efforts to ensure recognition of the principle that both parents have common responsibilities for the upbringing and development of the child. Parents or, as the case may be, legal guardians, have the primary responsibility for the upbringing and development of the child. The best interests of the child will be their basic concern.
2. For the purpose of guaranteeing and promoting the rights set forth in the present Convention, States Parties shall

render appropriate assistance to parents and legal guardians in the performance of their child-rearing responsibilities and shall ensure the development of institutions, facilities and services for the care of children.

3. States Parties shall take all appropriate measures to ensure that children of working parents have the right to benefit from child-care services and facilities for which they are eligible.

Article 19

1. States Parties shall take all appropriate legislative, administrative, social and educational measures to protect the child from all forms of physical or mental violence, injury or abuse, neglect or negligent treatment, maltreatment or exploitation, including sexual abuse, while in the care of parent(s), legal guardian(s) or any other person who has the care of the child.
2. Such protective measures should, as appropriate, include effective procedures for the establishment of social programmes to provide necessary support for the child and for those who have the care of the child, as well as for other forms of prevention and for identification, reporting, referral, investigation, treatment and follow-up of instances of child maltreatment described heretofore, and, as appropriate, for judicial involvement.

Article 20

1. A child temporarily or permanently deprived of his or her family environment, or in whose own best interests cannot be allowed to remain in that environment, shall be entitled to special protection and assistance provided by the State.
2. States Parties shall in accordance with their national laws ensure alternative care for such a child.
3. Such care could include, *inter alia*, foster placement, kafalah of Islamic law, adoption or if necessary placement in suitable institutions for the care of children. When considering solutions, due regard shall be paid to the desirability of continuity in a child's upbringing and to the child's ethnic, religious, cultural and linguistic background.

Article 21

States Parties that recognize and/or permit the system of adoption shall ensure that the best interests of the child shall be the paramount consideration and they shall:

(a) Ensure that the adoption of a child is authorized only by competent authorities who determine, in accordance with applicable law and procedures and on the basis of all pertinent and reliable information, that the adoption is permissible in view of the child's status concerning parents, relatives and legal guardians and that, if required, the persons concerned have given their informed consent to the adoption on the basis of such counselling as may be necessary;

(b) Recognize that inter-country adoption may be considered as an alternative means of child's care, if the child cannot be placed in a foster or an adoptive family or cannot in any suitable manner be cared for in the child's country of origin;

(c) Ensure that the child concerned by inter-country adoption enjoys safeguards and standards equivalent to those existing in the case of national adoption;

(d) Take all appropriate measures to ensure that, in inter-country adoption, the placement does not result in improper financial gain for those involved in it;

(e) Promote, where appropriate, the objectives of the present article by concluding bilateral or multilateral arrangements or agreements, and endeavour, within this framework, to ensure that the placement of the child in another country is carried out by competent authorities or organs.

Article 22

1. States Parties shall take appropriate measures to ensure that a child who is seeking refugee status or who is considered a refugee in accordance with applicable international or domestic law and procedures shall, whether unaccompanied or accompanied by his or her parents or by any other person, receive appropriate protection and humanitarian assistance in the enjoyment of applicable rights set forth in the present Convention

and in other international human rights or humanitarian instruments to which the said States are Parties.

2. For this purpose, States Parties shall provide, as they consider appropriate, co-operation in any efforts by the United Nations and other competent inter-governmental organisations or non-governmental organisations co-operating with the United Nations to protect and assist such a child and to trace the parents or other members of the family of any refugee child in order to obtain information necessary for reunification with his or her family. In cases where no parents or other members of the family can be found, the child shall be accorded the same protection as any other child permanently or temporarily deprived of his or her family environment for any reason, as set forth in the present Convention.

Article 23

1. States Parties recognize that a mentally or physically disabled child should enjoy a full and decent life, in conditions which ensure dignity, promote self-reliance and facilitate the child's active participation in the community.
2. States Parties recognize the right of the disabled child to special care and shall encourage and ensure the extension, subject to available resources, to the eligible child and those responsible for his or her care, of assistance for which application is made and which is appropriate to the child's condition and to the circumstances of the parents or others caring for the child.
3. Recognizing the special needs of a disabled child, assistance extended in accordance with paragraph 2 of the present article shall be provided free of charge, whenever possible, taking into account the financial resources of the parents or others caring for the child, and shall be designed to ensure that the disabled child has effective access to and receives education, training, health care services, rehabilitation services, preparation for employment and recreation opportunities in a manner conducive to the child's achieving the fullest possible social integration and individual development, including his or her cultural and spiritual development.

4. States Parties shall promote, in the spirit of international cooperation, the exchange of appropriate information in the field of preventive health care and of medical, psychological and functional treatment of disabled children, including dissemination of and access to information concerning methods of rehabilitation, education and vocational services, with the aim of enabling States Parties to improve their capabilities and skills and to widen their experience in these areas. In this regard, particular account shall be taken of the needs of developing countries.

Article 24

1. States Parties recognize the right of the child to the enjoyment of the highest attainable standard of health and to facilities for the treatment of illness and rehabilitation of health. States Parties shall strive to ensure that no child is deprived of his or her right of access to such health care services.
2. States Parties shall pursue full implementation of this right and, in particular, shall take appropriate measures:
   (a) To diminish infant and child mortality;
   (b) To ensure the provision of necessary medical assistance and health care to all children with emphasis on the development of primary health care;
   (c) To combat disease and malnutrition, including within the framework of primary health care, through, *inter alia*, the application of readily available technology and through the provision of adequate nutritious foods and clean drinking-water, taking into consideration the dangers and risks of environmental pollution;
   (d) To ensure appropriate pre-natal and post-natal health care for mothers;
   (e) To ensure that all segments of society, in particular parents and children, are informed, have access to education and are supported in the use of basic knowledge of child health and nutrition, the advantages of breastfeeding, hygiene and environmental sanitation and the prevention of accidents;
   (f) To develop preventive health care, guidance for parents and family planning education and services.

3. States Parties shall take all effective and appropriate measures with a view to abolishing traditional practices prejudicial to the health of children.
4. States Parties undertake to promote and encourage international co-operation with a view to achieving progressively the full realisation of the right recognized in the present article. In this regard, particular account shall be taken of the needs of developing countries.

Article 25

States Parties recognize the right of a child who has been placed by the competent authorities for the purposes of care, protection or treatment of his or her physical or mental health, to a periodic review of the treatment provided to the child and all other circumstances relevant to his or her placement.

Article 26

1. States Parties shall recognize for every child the right to benefit from social security, including social insurance, and shall take the necessary measures to achieve the full realisation of this right in accordance with their national law.
2. The benefits should, where appropriate, be granted, taking into account the resources and the circumstances of the child and persons having responsibility for the maintenance of the child, as well as any other consideration relevant to an application for benefits made by or on behalf of the child.

Article 27

1. States Parties recognize the right of every child to a standard of living adequate for the child's physical, mental, spiritual, moral and social development.
2. The parent(s) or others responsible for the child have the primary responsibility to secure, within their abilities and financial capacities, the conditions of living necessary for the child's development.
3. States Parties, in accordance with national conditions and within their means, shall take appropriate measures to assist parents and others responsible for the child to implement this right and shall in case of need provide

material assistance and support programmes, particularly with regard to nutrition, clothing and housing.

4. States Parties shall take all appropriate measures to secure the recovery of maintenance for the child from the parents or other persons having financial responsibility for the child, both within the State Party and from abroad. In particular, where the person having financial responsibility for the child lives in a State different from that of the child, States Parties shall promote the accession to international agreements or the conclusion of such agreements, as well as the making of other appropriate arrangements.

Article 28

1. States Parties recognize the right of the child to education, and with a view to achieving this right progressively and on the basis of equal opportunity, they shall, in particular:
   (a) Make primary education compulsory and available free to all;
   (b) Encourage the development of different forms of secondary education, including general and vocational education, make them available and accessible to every child, and take appropriate measures such as the introduction of free education and offering financial assistance in case of need;
   (c) Make higher education accessible to all on the basis of capacity by every appropriate means;
   (d) Make educational and vocational information and guidance available and accessible to all children;
   (e) Take measures to encourage regular attendance at schools and the reduction of drop-out rates.
2. States Parties shall take all appropriate measures to ensure that school discipline is administered in a manner consistent with the child's human dignity and in conformity with the present Convention.
3. States Parties shall promote and encourage international cooperation in matters relating to education, in particular with a view to contributing to the elimination of ignorance and illiteracy throughout the world and facilitating access to scientific and technical knowledge and modern teaching

methods. In this regard, particular account shall be taken of the needs of developing countries.

Article 29

1. States Parties agree that the education of the child shall be directed to:
   (a) The development of the child's personality, talents and mental and physical abilities to their fullest potential;
   (b) The development of respect for human rights and fundamental freedoms, and for the principles enshrined in the Charter of the United Nations;
   (c) The development of respect for the child's parents, his or her own cultural identity, language and values, for the national values of the country in which the child is living, the country from which he or she may originate, and for civilisations different from his or her own;
   (d) The preparation of the child for responsible life in a free society, in the spirit of understanding, peace, tolerance, equality of sexes, and friendship among all peoples, ethnic, national and religious groups and persons of indigenous origin;
   (e) The development of respect for the natural environment.
2. No part of the present article or article 28 shall be construed so as to interfere with the liberty of individuals and bodies to establish and direct educational institutions, subject always to the observance of the principle set forth in paragraph 1 of the present article and to the requirements that the education given in such institutions shall conform to such minimum standards as may be laid down by the State.

Article 30

In those States in which ethnic, religious or linguistic minorities or persons of indigenous origin exist, a child belonging to such a minority or who is indigenous shall not be denied the right, in community with other members of his or her group, to enjoy his or her own culture, to profess and practise his or her own religion, or to use his or her own language.

Article 31

1. States Parties recognize the right of the child to rest and leisure, to engage in play and recreational activities appropriate to the age of the child and to participate freely in cultural life and the arts.
2. States Parties shall respect and promote the right of the child to participate fully in cultural and artistic life and shall encourage the provision of appropriate and equal opportunities for cultural, artistic, recreational and leisure activity.

Article 32

1. States Parties recognize the right of the child to be protected from economic exploitation and from performing any work that is likely to be hazardous or to interfere with the child's education, or to be harmful to the child's health or physical, mental, spiritual, moral or social development.
2. States Parties shall take legislative, administrative, social and educational measures to ensure the implementation of the present article. To this end, and having regard to the relevant provisions of other international instruments, States Parties shall in particular:
   (a) Provide for a minimum age or minimum ages for admission to employment;
   (b) Provide for appropriate regulation of the hours and conditions of employment;
   (c) Provide for appropriate penalties or other sanctions to ensure the effective enforcement of the present article.

Article 33

States Parties shall take all appropriate measures, including legislative, administrative, social and educational measures, to protect children from the illicit use of narcotic drugs and psychotropic substances as defined in the relevant international treaties, and to prevent the use of children in the illicit production and trafficking of such substances.

Article 34

States Parties undertake to protect the child from all forms of sexual exploitation and sexual abuse. For these purposes, States Parties shall in particular take all appropriate national, bilateral and multilateral measures to prevent:

(a) The inducement or coercion of a child to engage in any unlawful sexual activity;
(b) The exploitative use of children in prostitution or other unlawful sexual practices;
(c) The exploitative use of children in pornographic performances and materials.

Article 35

States Parties shall take all appropriate national, bilateral and multilateral measures to prevent the abduction of, the sale of or traffic in children for any purpose or in any form.

Article 36

States Parties shall protect the child against all other forms of exploitation prejudicial to any aspects of the child's welfare.

Article 37

States Parties shall ensure that:

(a) No child shall be subjected to torture or other cruel, inhuman or degrading treatment or punishment. Neither capital punishment nor life imprisonment without possibility of release shall be imposed for offences committed by persons below eighteen years of age;
(b) No child shall be deprived of his or her liberty unlawfully or arbitrarily. The arrest, detention or imprisonment of a child shall be in conformity with the law and shall be used only as a measure of last resort and for the shortest appropriate period of time;
(c) Every child deprived of liberty shall be treated with humanity and respect for the inherent dignity of the human person, and in a manner which takes into account the needs of persons of his or her age. In particular, every child deprived of liberty shall be separated from adults unless it is considered in the child's best interest not to do so and shall have the right to maintain contact with his or her family through correspondence and visits, save in exceptional circumstances;

(d) Every child deprived of his or her liberty shall have the right to prompt access to legal and other appropriate assistance, as well as the right to challenge the legality of the deprivation of his or her liberty before a court or other competent, independent and impartial authority, and to a prompt decision on any such action.

Article 38

1. States Parties undertake to respect and to ensure respect for rules of international humanitarian law applicable to them in armed conflicts which are relevant to the child.
2. States Parties shall take all feasible measures to ensure that persons who have not attained the age of fifteen years do not take a direct part in hostilities.
3. States Parties shall refrain from recruiting any person who has not attained the age of fifteen years into their armed forces. In recruiting among those persons who have attained the age of fifteen years but who have not attained the age of eighteen years, States Parties shall endeavour to give priority to those who are oldest.
4. In accordance with their obligations under international humanitarian law to protect the civilian population in armed conflicts, States Parties shall take all feasible measures to ensure protection and care of children who are affected by an armed conflict.

Article 39

States Parties shall take all appropriate measures to promote physical and psychological recovery and social reintegration of a child victim of: any form of neglect, exploitation, or abuse; torture or any other form of cruel, inhuman or degrading treatment or punishment; or armed conflicts. Such recovery and reintegration shall take place in an environment which fosters the health, self-respect and dignity of the child.

Article 40

1. States Parties recognize the right of every child alleged as, accused of, or recognized as having infringed the penal law to be treated in a manner consistent with the promotion of the child's sense of dignity and worth, which

reinforces the child's respect for the human rights and fundamental freedoms of others and which takes into account the child's age and the desirability of promoting the child's reintegration and the child's assuming a constructive role in society.

2. To this end, and having regard to the relevant provisions of international instruments, States Parties shall, in particular, ensure that:
   (a) No child shall be alleged as, be accused of, or recognized as having infringed the penal law by reason of acts or omissions that were not prohibited by national or international law at the time they were committed;
   (b) Every child alleged as or accused of having infringed the penal law has at least the following guarantees:
      (i) To be presumed innocent until proven guilty according to law;
      (ii) To be informed promptly and directly of the charges against him or her, and, if appropriate, through his or her parents or legal guardians, and to have legal or other appropriate assistance in the preparation and presentation of his or her defence;
      (iii) To have the matter determined without delay by a competent, independent and impartial authority or judicial body in a fair hearing according to law, in the presence of legal or other appropriate assistance and, unless it is considered not to be in the best interest of the child, in particular, taking into account his or her age or situation, his or her parents or legal guardians;
      (iv) Not to be compelled to give testimony or to confess guilt; to examine or have examined adverse witnesses and to obtain the participation and examination of witnesses on his or her behalf under conditions of equality;
      (v) If considered to have infringed the penal law, to have this decision and any measures imposed in consequence thereof reviewed by a higher competent, independent and impartial authority or judicial body according to law;

(vi) To have the free assistance of an interpreter if the child cannot understand or speak the language used;

(vii) To have his or her privacy fully respected at all stages of the proceedings.

3. States Parties shall seek to promote the establishment of laws, procedures, authorities and institutions specifically applicable to children alleged as, accused of, or recognized as having infringed the penal law, and, in particular:
   (a) The establishment of a minimum age below which children shall be presumed not to have the capacity to infringe the penal law;
   (b) Whenever appropriate and desirable, measures for dealing with such children without resorting to judicial proceedings, providing that human rights and legal safeguards are fully respected.
4. A variety of dispositions, such as care, guidance and supervision orders; counselling; probation; foster care; education and vocational training programmes and other alternatives to institutional care shall be available to ensure that children are dealt with in a manner appropriate to their well-being and proportionate both to their circumstances and the offence.

Article 41

Nothing in the present Convention shall affect any provisions which are more conducive to the realisation of the rights of the child and which may be contained in:
(a) The law of a State party; or
(b) International law in force for that State.

PART II

Article 42

States Parties undertake to make the principles and provisions of the Convention widely known, by appropriate and active means, to adults and children alike.

Article 43

1. For the purpose of examining the progress made by States

Parties in achieving the realisation of the obligations undertaken in the present Convention, there shall be established a Committee on the Rights of the Child, which shall carry out the functions hereinafter provided.

2. The Committee shall consist of ten experts of high moral standing and recognized competence in the field covered by this Convention. The members of the Committee shall be elected by States Parties from among their nationals and shall serve in their personal capacity, consideration being given to equitable geographical distribution, as well as to the principal legal systems.
3. The members of the Committee shall be elected by secret ballot from a list of persons nominated by States Parties. Each State Party may nominate one person from among its own nationals.
4. The initial election to the Committee shall be held no later than six months after the date of the entry into force of the present Convention and thereafter every second year. At least four months before the date of each election, the Secretary-General of the United Nations shall address a letter to States Parties inviting them to submit their nominations within two months. The Secretary-General shall subsequently prepare a list in alphabetical order of all persons thus nominated, indicating States Parties which have nominated them, and shall submit it to the States Parties to the present Convention.
5. The elections shall be held at meetings of States Parties convened by the Secretary-General at United Nations Headquarters. At those meetings, for which two-thirds of States Parties shall constitute a quorum, the persons elected to the Committee shall be those who obtain the largest number of votes and an absolute majority of the votes of the representatives of States Parties present and voting.
6. The members of the Committee shall be elected for a term of four years. They shall be eligible for re-election if renominated. The term of five of the members elected at the first election shall expire at the end of two years; immediately after the first election, the names of these five members shall be chosen by lot by the Chairman of the meeting.

7. If a member of the Committee dies or resigns or declares that for any other cause he or she can no longer perform the duties of the Committee, the State Party which nominated the member shall appoint another expert from among its nationals to serve for the remainder of the term, subject to the approval of the Committee.
8. The Committee shall establish its own rules of procedure.
9. The Committee shall elect its officers for a period of two years.
10. The meetings of the Committee shall normally be held at United Nations Headquarters or at any other convenient place as determined by the Committee. The Committee shall normally meet annually. The duration of the meetings of the Committee shall be determined, and reviewed, if necessary, by a meeting of the States Parties to the present Convention, subject to the approval of the General Assembly.
11. The Secretary-General of the United Nations shall provide the necessary staff and facilities for the effective performance of the functions of the Committee under the present Convention.
12. With the approval of the General Assembly, the members of the Committee established under the present Convention shall receive emoluments from United Nations resources on such terms and conditions as the Assembly may decide.

Article 44

1. States Parties undertake to submit to the Committee, through the Secretary-General of the United Nations, reports on the measures they have adopted which give effect to the rights recognized herein and on the progress made on the enjoyment of those rights:
   (a) Within two years of the entry into force of the Convention for the State Party concerned;
   (b) Thereafter every five years.
2. Reports made under the present article shall indicate factors and difficulties, if any, affecting the degree of fulfilment of the obligations under the present Convention. Reports shall also contain sufficient information to provide the Committee with a comprehensive understanding of

the implementation of the Convention in the country concerned.

3. A State Party which has submitted a comprehensive initial report to the Committee need not, in its subsequent reports submitted in accordance with paragraph 1 (b) of the present article, repeat basic information previously provided.
4. The Committee may request from States Parties further information relevant to the implementation of the Convention.
5. The Committee shall submit to the General Assembly, through the Economic and Social Council, every two years, reports on its activities.
6. States Parties shall make their reports widely available to the public in their own countries.

Article 45

In order to foster the effective implementation of the Convention and to encourage international co-operation in the field covered by the Convention:

(a) The specialized agencies, the United Nations Children's Fund, and other United Nations organs shall be entitled to be represented at the consideration of the implementation of such provisions of the present Convention as fall within the scope of their mandate. The Committee may invite the specialized agencies, the United Nations Children's Fund and other competent bodies as it may consider appropriate to provide expert advice on the implementation of the Convention in areas falling within the scope of their respective mandates. The Committee may invite the specialized agencies, the United Nations Children's Fund, and other United Nations organs to submit reports on the implementation of the Convention in areas falling within the scope of their activities;

(b) The Committee shall transmit, as it may consider appropriate, to the specialized agencies, the United Nations Children's Fund and other competent bodies, any reports from States Parties that contain a request, or indicate a need, for technical advice or assistance, along with the Committee's observations and suggestions, if any, on these requests or indications;

(c) The Committee may recommend to the General Assembly to request the Secretary-General to undertake on its behalf studies on specific issues relating to the rights of the child;

(d) The Committee may make suggestions and general recommendations based on information received pursuant to articles 44 and 45 of the present Convention. Such suggestions and general recommendations shall be transmitted to any State Party concerned and reported to the General Assembly, together with comments, if any, from States Parties.

PART III

Article 46

The present Convention shall be open for signature by all States.

Article 47

The present Convention is subject to ratification. Instruments of ratification shall be deposited with the Secretary-General of the United Nations.

Article 48

The present Convention shall remain open for accession by any State. The instruments of accession shall be deposited with the Secretary-General of the United Nations.

Article 49

1. The present Convention shall enter into force on the thirtieth day following the date of deposit with the Secretary-General of the United Nations of the twentieth instrument of ratification or accession.
2. For each State ratifying or acceding to the Convention after the deposit of the twentieth instrument of ratification or accession, the Convention shall enter into force on the thirtieth day after the deposit by such State of its instrument of ratification or accession.

Article 50

1. Any State Party may propose an amendment and file it

with the Secretary-General of the United Nations. The Secretary-General shall thereupon communicate the proposed amendment to States Parties, with a request that they indicate whether they favour a conference of States Parties for the purpose of considering and voting upon the proposals. In the event that, within four months from the date of such communication, at least one-third of the States Parties favour such a conference, the Secretary-General shall convene the conference under the auspices of the United Nations. Any amendment adopted by a majority of States Parties present and voting at the conference shall be submitted to the General Assembly for approval.

2. An amendment adopted in accordance with paragraph 1 of the present article shall enter into force when it has been approved by the General Assembly of the United Nations and accepted by a two-thirds majority of States Parties.
3. When an amendment enters into force, it shall be binding on those States Parties which have accepted it, other States Parties still being bound by the provisions of the present Convention and any earlier amendments which they have accepted.

Article 51

1. The Secretary-General of the United Nations shall receive and circulate to all States the text of reservations made by States at the time of ratification or accession.
2. A reservation incompatible with the object and purpose of the present Convention shall not be permitted.
3. Reservations may be withdrawn at any time by notification to that effect addressed to the Secretary-General of the United Nations, who shall then inform all States. Such notification shall take effect on the date on which it is received by the Secretary-General.

Article 52

A State Party may denounce the present Convention by written notification to the Secretary-General of the United Nations. Denunciation becomes effective one year after the date of receipt of the notification by the Secretary-General.

Article 53

The Secretary-General of the United Nations is designated as the depositary of the present Convention.

Article 54

The original of the present Convention, of which the Arabic, Chinese, English, French, Russian and Spanish texts are equally authentic, shall be deposited with the Secretary-General of the United Nations.

In Witness thereof the undersigned plenipotentiaries, being duly authorized thereto by their respective governments, have signed the present Convention.

Annexure-III

Convention on Protection of Children and Co-operation in Respect of Inter-country Adoption

(Concluded 29 May, 1993)

The States signatory to the present Convention,

Recognizing that the child, for the full and harmonious development of his or her personality, should grow up in a family environment, in an atmosphere of happiness, love and understanding,

Recalling that each State should take, as a matter of priority, appropriate measures to enable the child to remain in the care of his or her family of origin,

Recognizing that inter-country adoption may offer the advantage of a permanent family to a child for whom a suitable family cannot be found in his or her State of origin,

Convinced of the necessity to take measures to ensure that inter-country adoptions are made in the best interests of the child and with respect for his or her fundamental rights, and to prevent the abduction, the sale of, or traffic in children,

Desiring to establish common provisions to this effect, taking into account the principles set forth in international instruments, in particular the United Nations Convention on the Rights of the Child, of 20 November, 1989, and the United Nations Declaration on Social and Legal Principles relating to the Protection and Welfare of Children, with Special Reference to Foster Placement and Adoption Nationally and Internationally (General Assembly Resolution 41/85, of 3 December, 1986),

Have agreed upon the following provisions—

Chapter I—Scope of the Convention

Article 1

The objects of the present Convention are:

(a) to establish safeguards to ensure that inter-country adoptions take place in the best interests of the child and with respect for his or her fundamental rights as recognized in international law;

(b) to establish a system of co-operation amongst Contracting States to ensure that those safeguards are respected and thereby prevent the abduction, the sale of, or traffic in children;

(c) to secure the recognition in Contracting States of adoptions made in accordance with the Convention.

Article 2

1. The Convention shall apply where a child habitually resident in one Contracting State ("the State of origin") has been, is being, or is to be moved to another Contracting State ("the receiving State") either after his or her adoption in the State of origin by spouses or a person habitually resident in the receiving State, or for the purposes of such an adoption in the receiving State or in the State of origin.
2. The Convention covers only adoptions which create a permanent parent-child relationship.

Article 3

The Convention ceases to apply if the agreements mentioned in Article 17, sub-paragraph (c), have not been given before the child attains the age of eighteen years.

Chapter II—Requirements for Inter-country Adoptions

Article 4

An adoption within the scope of the Convention shall take place only if the competent authorities of the State of origin:

(a) have established that the child is adoptable;

(b) have determined, after possibilities for placement of the child within the State of origin have been given due consideration, that an inter-country adoption is in the child's best interests;

(c) have ensured that

    (i) the persons, institutions and authorities whose consent is necessary for adoption, have been counselled as may be necessary and duly informed of the effects of their consent, in particular whether or not an adoption will result in the termination of the legal relationship between the child and his or her family of origin,

    (ii) such persons, institutions and authorities have given their consent freely, in the required legal form, and expressed or evidenced in writing,

    (iii) the consents have not been induced by payment or compensation of any kind and have not been withdrawn, and

    (iv) the consent of the mother, where required, has been given only after the birth of the child; and

(d) have ensured, having regard to the age and degree of maturity of the child, that

    (i) he or she has been counselled and duly informed of the effects of the adoption and of his or her consent to the adoption, where such consent is required,

    (ii) consideration has been given to the child's wishes and opinions,

    (iii) the child's consent to the adoption, where such consent is required, has been given freely, in the required legal form, and expressed or evidenced in writing, and

    (iv) such consent has not been induced by payment or compensation of any kind.

Article 5

An adoption within the scope of the Convention shall take place only if the competent authorities of the receiving State:

(a) have determined that the prospective adoptive parents are eligible and suited to adopt;

(b) have ensured that the prospective adoptive parents have been counselled as may be necessary; and

(c) have determined that the child is or will be authorized to enter and reside permanently in that State.

Chapter III—Central Authorities and Accredited Bodies

Article 6

1. A Contracting State shall designate a Central Authority to discharge the duties which are imposed by the Convention upon such authorities.
2. Federal States, States with more than one system of law or States having autonomous territorial units shall be free to appoint more than one Central Authority and to specify the territorial or personal extent of their functions. Where a State has appointed more than one Central Authority, it shall designate the Central Authority to which any communication may be addressed for transmission to the appropriate Central Authority within that State.

Article 7

1. Central Authorities shall co-operate with each other and promote co-operation amongst the competent authorities in their States to protect children and to achieve the other objects of the Convention.
2. They shall take directly all appropriate measures to:
   (a) provide information as to the laws of their States concerning adoption and other general information, such as statistics and standard forms;
   (b) keep one another informed about the operation of the Convention and, as far as possible, eliminate any obstacles to its application.

Article 8

Central Authorities shall take, directly or through public authorities, all appropriate measures to prevent improper financial or other gain in connection with an adoption and to deter all practices contrary to the objects of the Convention.

Article 9

Central Authorities shall take, directly or through public authorities or other bodies duly accredited in their State, all appropriate measures, in particular to:

(a) collect, preserve and exchange information about the

situation of the child and the prospective adoptive parents, so far as is necessary to complete the adoption;

(b) facilitate, follow and expedite proceedings with a view to obtaining the adoption;

(c) promote the development of adoption counselling and post-adoption services in their States;

(d) provide each other with general evaluation reports about experience with inter-country adoption;

(e) reply, in so far as is permitted by the law of their State, to justified requests from other Central Authorities or public authorities for information about a particular adoption situation.

Article 10

Accreditation shall only be granted to and maintained by bodies demonstrating their competence to carry out properly the tasks with which they may be entrusted.

Article 11

An accredited body shall:

(a) pursue only non-profit objectives according to such conditions and within such limits as may be established by the competent authorities of the State of accreditation;

(b) be directed and staffed by persons qualified by their ethical standards and by training or experience to work in the field of inter-country adoption; and

(c) be subject to supervision by competent authorities of that State as to its composition, operation and financial situation.

Article 12

A body accredited in one Contracting State may act in another Contracting State only if the competent authorities of both States have authorized it to do so.

Article 13

The designation of the Central Authorities and, where appropriate, the extent of their functions, as well as the names and addresses of the accredited bodies shall be communicated by each Contracting

State to the Permanent Bureau of the Hague Conference on Private International Law.

Chapter IV—Procedural Requirements in Inter-country Adoption

Article 14

Persons habitually resident in a Contracting State, who wish to adopt a child habitually resident in another Contracting State, shall apply to the Central Authority in the State of their habitual residence.

Article 15

1. If the Central Authority of the receiving State is satisfied that the applicants are eligible and suited to adopt, it shall prepare a report including information about their identity, eligibility and suitability to adopt, background, family and medical history, social environment, reasons for adoption, ability to undertake an inter-country adoption, as well as the characteristics of the children for whom they would be qualified to care.
2. It shall transmit the report to the Central Authority of the State of origin.

Article 16

1. If the Central Authority of the State of origin is satisfied that the child is adoptable, it shall –
   (a) prepare a report including information about his or her identity, adoptability, background, social environment, family history, medical history including that of the child's family, and any special needs of the child;
   (b) give due consideration to the child's upbringing and to his or her ethnic, religious and cultural background;
   (c) ensure that consents have been obtained in accordance with Article 4; and
   (d) determine, on the basis in particular of the reports relating to the child and the prospective adoptive parents, whether the envisaged placement is in the best interests of the child.

2. It shall transmit to the Central Authority of the receiving State its report on the child, proof that the necessary consents have been obtained and the reasons for its determination on the placement, taking care not to reveal the identity of the mother and the father if, in the State of origin, these identities may not be disclosed.

Article 17

Any decision in the State of origin that a child should be entrusted to prospective adoptive parents may only be made if:

(a) the Central Authority of that State has ensured that the prospective adoptive parents agree;
(b) the Central Authority of the receiving State has approved such decision, where such approval is required by the law of that State or by the Central Authority of the State of origin;
(c) the Central Authorities of both States have agreed that the adoption may proceed; and
(d) it has been determined, in accordance with Article 5, that the prospective adoptive parents are eligible and suited to adopt and that the child is or will be authorized to enter and reside permanently in the receiving State.

Article 18

The Central Authorities of both States shall take all necessary steps to obtain permission for the child to leave the State of origin and to enter and reside permanently in the receiving State.

Article 19

1. The transfer of the child to the receiving State may only be carried out if the requirements of Article 17 have been satisfied.
2. The Central Authorities of both States shall ensure that this transfer takes place in secure and appropriate circumstances and, if possible, in the company of the adoptive or prospective adoptive parents.
3. If the transfer of the child does not take place, the reports referred to in Articles 15 and 16 are to be sent back to the authorities who forwarded them.

Article 20

The Central Authorities shall keep each other informed about the adoption process and the measures taken to complete it, as well as about the progress of the placement if a probationary period is required.

Article 21

1. Where the adoption is to take place after the transfer of the child to the receiving State and it appears to the Central Authority of that State that the continued placement of the child with the prospective adoptive parents is not in the child's best interests, such Central Authority shall take the measures necessary to protect the child, in particular:
   (a) to cause the child to be withdrawn from the prospective adoptive parents and to arrange temporary care;
   (b) in consultation with the Central Authority of the State of origin, to arrange without delay a new placement of the child with a view to adoption or, if this is not appropriate, to arrange alternative long-term care; an adoption shall not take place until the Central Authority of the State of origin has been duly informed concerning the new prospective adoptive parents;
   (c) as a last resort, to arrange the return of the child, if his or her interests so require.
2. Having regard in particular to the age and degree of maturity of the child, he or she shall be consulted and, where appropriate, his or her consent obtained in relation to measures to be taken under this Article.

Article 22

1. The functions of a Central Authority under this Chapter may be performed by public authorities or by bodies accredited under Chapter III, to the extent permitted by the law of its State.
2. Any Contracting State may declare to the depositary of the Convention that the functions of the Central Authority under Articles 15 to 21 may be performed in that State, to the extent permitted by the law and subject to the supervision of the competent authorities of that State, also by bodies or persons who—

(a) meet the requirements of integrity, professional competence, experience and accountability of that State; and

(b) are qualified by their ethical standards and by training or experience to work in the field of inter-country adoption.

3. A Contracting State which makes the declaration provided for in paragraph 2 shall keep the Permanent Bureau of the Hague Conference on Private International Law informed of the names and addresses of these bodies and persons.

4. Any Contracting State may declare to the depositary of the Convention that adoptions of children habitually resident in its territory may only take place if the functions of the Central Authorities are performed in accordance with paragraph 1.

5. Notwithstanding any declaration made under paragraph 2, the reports provided for in Articles 15 and 16 shall, in every case, be prepared under the responsibility of the Central Authority or other authorities or bodies in accordance with paragraph 1.

Chapter V—Recognition and Effects of the Adoption

Article 23

1. An adoption certified by the competent authority of the State of the adoption as having been made in accordance with the Convention shall be recognized by operation of law in the other Contracting States. The certificate shall specify when and by whom the agreements under Article 17, sub-paragraph (c), were given.

2. Each Contracting State shall, at the time of signature, ratification, acceptance, approval or accession, notify the depositary of the Convention of the identity and the functions of the authority or the authorities which, in that State, are competent to make the certification. It shall also notify the depositary of any modification in the designation of these authorities.

Article 24

The recognition of an adoption may be refused in a Contracting State only if the adoption is manifestly contrary to its public policy, taking into account the best interests of the child.

Article 25

Any Contracting State may declare to the depositary of the Convention that it will not be bound under this Convention to recognize adoptions made in accordance with an agreement concluded by application of Article 39, paragraph 2.

Article 26

1. The recognition of an adoption includes recognition of:
   (a) the legal parent-child relationship between the child and his or her adoptive parents;
   (b) parental responsibility of the adoptive parents for the child;
   (c) the termination of a pre-existing legal relationship between the child and his or her mother and father, if the adoption has this effect in the Contracting State where it was made.
2. In the case of an adoption having the effect of terminating a pre-existing legal parent-child relationship, the child shall enjoy in the receiving State, and in any other Contracting State where the adoption is recognized, rights equivalent to those resulting from adoptions having this effect in each such State.
3. The preceding paragraphs shall not prejudice the application of any provision more favourable for the child, in force in the Contracting State which recognizes the adoption.

Article 27

1. Where an adoption granted in the State of origin does not have the effect of terminating a pre-existing legal parent-child relationship, it may, in the receiving State which recognizes the adoption under the Convention, be converted into an adoption having such an effect—
   (a) if the law of the receiving State so permits; and
   (b) if the consents referred to in Article 4, sub-paragraphs (c) and (d), have been or are given for the purpose of such an adoption.
2. Article 23 applies to the decision converting the adoption.

Chapter VI—General Provisions

Article 28

The Convention does not affect any law of a State of origin which requires that the adoption of a child habitually resident within that State take place in that State or which prohibits the child's placement in, or transfer to, the receiving State prior to adoption.

Article 29

There shall be no contact between the prospective adoptive parents and the child's parents or any other person who has care of the child until the requirements of Article 4, sub-paragraphs (a) to (c), and Article 5, sub-paragraph (a), have been met, unless the adoption takes place within a family or unless the contact is in compliance with the conditions established by the competent authority of the State of origin.

Article 30

1. The competent authorities of a Contracting State shall ensure that information held by them concerning the child's origin, in particular information concerning the identity of his or her parents, as well as the medical history, is preserved.
2. They shall ensure that the child or his or her representative has access to such information, under appropriate guidance, in so far as is permitted by the law of that State.

Article 31

Without prejudice to Article 30, personal data gathered or transmitted under the Convention, especially data referred to in Articles 15 and 16, shall be used only for the purposes for which they were gathered or transmitted.

Article 32

1. No one shall derive improper financial or other gain from an activity related to an inter-country adoption.
2. Only costs and expenses, including reasonable professional fees of persons involved in the adoption, may be charged or paid.

3. The directors, administrators and employees of bodies involved in an adoption shall not receive remuneration which is unreasonably high in relation to services rendered.

Article 33

A competent authority which finds that any provision of the Convention has not been respected or that there is a serious risk that it may not be respected, shall immediately inform the Central Authority of its State. This Central Authority shall be responsible for ensuring that appropriate measures are taken.

Article 34

If the competent authority of the State of destination of a document so requests, a translation certified as being in conformity with the original must be furnished. Unless otherwise provided, the costs of such translation are to be borne by the prospective adoptive parents.

Article 35

The competent authorities of the Contracting States shall act expeditiously in the process of adoption.

Article 36

In relation to a State which has two or more systems of law with regard to adoption applicable in different territorial units:

(a) any reference to habitual residence in that State shall be construed as referring to habitual residence in a territorial unit of that State;
(b) any reference to the law of that State shall be construed as referring to the law in force in the relevant territorial unit;
(c) any reference to the competent authorities or to the public authorities of that State shall be construed as referring to those authorized to act in the relevant territorial unit;
(d) any reference to the accredited bodies of that State shall be construed as referring to bodies accredited in the relevant territorial unit.

Article 37

In relation to a State which with regard to adoption has two or more systems of law applicable to different categories of persons, any reference to the law of that State shall be construed as referring to the legal system specified by the law of that State.

Article 38

A State within which different territorial units have their own rules of law in respect of adoption shall not be bound to apply the Convention where a State with a unified system of law would not be bound to do so.

Article 39

1. The Convention does not affect any international instrument to which Contracting States are Parties and which contains provisions on matters governed by the Convention, unless a contrary declaration is made by the States Parties to such instrument.
2. Any Contracting State may enter into agreements with one or more other Contracting States, with a view to improving the application of the Convention in their mutual relations. These agreements may derogate only from the provisions of Articles 14 to 16 and 18 to 21. The States which have concluded such an agreement shall transmit a copy to the depositary of the Convention.

Article 40

No reservation to the Convention shall be permitted.

Article 41

The Convention shall apply in every case where an application pursuant to Article 14 has been received after the Convention has entered into force in the receiving State and the State of origin.

Article 42

The Secretary-General of the Hague Conference on Private International Law shall at regular intervals convene a Special Commission in order to review the practical operation of the Convention.

Chapter VII—Final Clauses

Article 43

1. The Convention shall be open for signature by the States which were Members of the Hague Conference on Private International Law at the time of its Seventeenth Session and by the other States which participated in that Session.
2. It shall be ratified, accepted or approved and the instruments of ratification, acceptance or approval shall be deposited with the Ministry of Foreign Affairs of the Kingdom of the Netherlands, depositary of the Convention.

Article 44

1. Any other State may accede to the Convention after it has entered into force in accordance with Article 46, paragraph 1.
2. The instrument of accession shall be deposited with the depositary.
3. Such accession shall have effect only as regards the relations between the acceding State and those Contracting States which have not raised an objection to its accession in the six months after the receipt of the notification referred to in sub-paragraph (b) of Article 48. Such an objection may also be raised by States at the time when they ratify, accept or approve the Convention after an accession. Any such objection shall be notified to the depositary.

Article 45

1. If a State has two or more territorial units in which different systems of law are applicable in relation to matters dealt with in the Convention, it may at the time of signature, ratification, acceptance, approval or accession declare that this Convention shall extend to all its territorial units or only to one or more of them and may modify this declaration by submitting another declaration at any time.

2. Any such declaration shall be notified to the depositary and shall state expressly the territorial units to which the Convention applies.
3. If a State makes no declaration under this Article, the Convention is to extend to all territorial units of that State.

Article 46

1. The Convention shall enter into force on the first day of the month following the expiration of three months after the deposit of the third instrument of ratification, acceptance or approval referred to in Article 43.
2. Thereafter the Convention shall enter into force:
   (a) for each State ratifying, accepting or approving it subsequently, or acceding to it, on the first day of the month following the expiration of three months after the deposit of its instrument of ratification, acceptance, approval or accession;
   (b) for a territorial unit to which the Convention has been extended in conformity with Article 45, on the first day of the month following the expiration of three months after the notification referred to in that Article.

Article 47

1. A State Party to the Convention may denounce it by a notification in writing addressed to the depositary.
2. The denunciation takes effect on the first day of the month following the expiration of twelve months after the notification is received by the depositary. Where a longer period for the denunciation to take effect is specified in the notification, the denunciation takes effect upon the expiration of such longer period after the notification is received by the depositary.

Article 48

The depositary shall notify the States Members of the Hague Conference on Private International Law, the other States which participated in the Seventeenth Session and the States which have acceded in accordance with Article 44, of the following:

(a) the signatures, ratifications, acceptances and approvals referred to in Article 43;

(b) the accessions and objections raised to accessions referred to in Article 44;
(c) the date on which the Convention enters into force in accordance with Article 46;
(d) the declarations and designations referred to in Articles 22, 23, 25 and 45;
(e) the agreements referred to in Article 39;
(f) the denunciations referred to in Article 47.

In witness whereof the undersigned, being duly authorized thereto, have signed this Convention.

Done at The Hague, on the 29th day of May, 1993, in the English and French languages, both texts being equally authentic, in a single copy which shall be deposited in the archives of the Government of the Kingdom of the Netherlands, and of which a certified copy shall be sent, through diplomatic channels, to each of the States Members of the Hague Conference on Private International Law at the date of its Seventeenth Session and to each of the other States which participated in that Session.

Annexure–IV

The Rights of the Child in Internal and Inter-country Adoption Ethics and Principles—Guidelines for Practice

Introduction

To mark the tenth anniversary of the United Nations Convention on the Rights of the Child the International Social Service has prepared this document for its interlocutors in the network of the International Resource Centre for the Protection of Children in Adoption (IRC/ISS), and all those active in upholding the rights of the child. It deals with both internal and inter-country adoption. While certain principles and practices referred to relate more to inter-country adoption, it is the protection of the child that must continue to be the primary concern in both areas.

- ISS/IRC deems it essential to define the *ethics and principles* that should govern adoption, a fundamental decision in the life of several human beings, among them a child in a vulnerable position.
- Although the ethical principles are conceived essentially as a frame of reference, ISS/IRC considers it important to supplement them with *a number of guidelines to ensure that the ethics and principles are respected in practice.* They are the product of exchanges of views with professionals from all over the world. They reflect and complement the principles enshrined in the 1989 Convention on the Rights of the Child (CRC) and the 1993 Hague Convention on the Protection of Children and Cooperation in respect of Inter-country Adoption (THC). ISS/IRC hopes to be able to enhance them with future publications.

Source: International Social Services: International Resource Center for the Protection of Children in Adoption, Geneva.

We hope this paper will be of use to you in your practice and that your contributions will help us to supplement and improve upon it. Please write and share with us your experience, indicating your points of agreement or disagreement. We would be grateful to have brought to our attention other documents published for the same purpose.

I. Adoption: A Social and Legal Protective Measure for Children

(a) *Adoption is not an arrangement between individuals.* It is a social and legal protective measure for children. It should be considered and authorized with this sole aim in view. The State bears the responsibility to ensure it is so.

(b) *It should be made available to all children whose personal and family situation warrants it, without prejudice* against their social situation, physical features, ethnicity, culture, physical or mental health disorders. (CRC* art. 2/THC* preamb., art. 1-a and b)

II. Best Interests and Fundamental Rights of the Child

Any protective measure taken for a child shall be governed by the child's best interests and by respect for his/her fundamental rights. (CRC art. 3/THC preamb. para. 4, art. 1-a)

This signifies that:

(a) *It is the child who must be the starting point in the process leading up to adoption*. This process is initiated because the child's situation warrants it, not because others have expressed the wish to adopt the child or are in quest of a child.

---

* *CRC* : The 1989 United Nations Convention on the Rights of the Child.

* *THC* : The 1993 Hague Convention on the Protection of Children and Cooperation in respect of Inter-country Adoption. The texts of those Conventions are available on the International Social Service's web site,http://www.iss-ssi.org/Resource Centre/Resource Center EN/Int Conventions/int conventions.html

(b) The handling of any child's case cannot be left to the birth parents, to unqualified protagonists or those of doubtful ethics, or to prospective adoptive parents. It must be carried out by *services competent* in the protection of children*, which as far as possible, should be pluridisciplinary and subject to accreditation and periodic inspection by the competent national authorities. Direct adoption from one family to another must be banned, except under extraordinary circumstances supervised by child protection services.

(c) Professionals engaged in adoption proceedings should be guided as *a priority*, in the perception of their work and in their practice, by *the needs of the child*. While they must be careful to listen to and respect the wishes of prospective adoptive parents and the demands of birth parents, whatever their particularities may be, they are not required to accord them priority, but rather to consider the extent to which they correspond to the best interests of the child. Professionals must be aware that adoption in the best interests of the child is one that fosters the creation of an environment or family relationships that satisfy all parties.

(d) Since time is essential in a child's development, professionals should *act as quickly as possible* without jeopardizing overall respect for procedures. They should cut as much as possible the periods of waiting, uncertainty or transition that children live through.

(e) The child, in a manner appropriate to his/her age and degree of maturity, must be kept informed and consulted about any life plan for him/her.

The above applies equally to internal and inter-country adoption. (CRC art. 21-a, art. 12/THC art. 29, art. 4-d, art. 21.2)

III. Adoption must be Embodied in a Global Policy on the Child and the Family, Composed of an Array of Measures

One can envisage a desirable hierarchy of life environments that can be offered a child:

---

* *Competent* : in this paper, it means governmental or private bodies whose official responsibility is to carry out the tasks implied by the child protection.

- family solutions (prevention of abandonment and keeping the child in his/her family, returning the child to his/her family of origin, foster care, internal or inter-country adoption) must take precedence over long-term institutionalisation.
- Permanent solutions (keeping or reintegrating the child in his/her family of origin, adoption) must take precedence over temporary solutions that perpetuate themselves.
- Temporary solutions (foster care, placement in an institution) must give priority to the reintegration of the child in his/her family of origin, or else to the search for a permanent solution.
- National solutions (family reintegration, internal adoption) must take precedence over international solutions (inter-country adoption).

Nonetheless, the important thing is not to apply this range of measures mechanically or rigidly. Every child is different; his/her history and his/her personal and family situation are special. His/her protection must be understood:

- in conjunction with the child's and the family's own particular characteristics;
- in choosing the one measure or those that best meet the interest of the child in question (for example, in certain cases, normally temporary measures could prove to be appropriate in the long run);
- as a dynamic process where the available protective environments must be seen to complement each other in the way they are used, in striving to ensure coordination and continuity between them in the best interest of the child and the family. (CRC arts. 18, 19, 20, 21/THC preamble)

IV. Subsidiarity of Internal Adoption to Keeping or Returning the Child to his/her family of origin/Priority to preventing abandonment

Priority must go to allowing children to be raised in their own family, i.e., staying with the birth parents or the extended family (avoiding relinquishment); being reunited with the immediate or extended family (children at the pre-abandonment stage). Governments and civil society must do their utmost to ensure that families of origin have the possibility and are encouraged, to care for their children.

This requires the formulation of policies and programmes that take human development and equity into account, resulting among other things, in:

- psychosocial support services and/or financial support for mothers or families in difficulty;
- social dialogue with the extended family, especially the grandparents, so that they help in preventing abandonment;
- sensitisation to the importance of the father's role, training for parenthood;
- awareness of the needs and rights of the child;
- conscious and responsible sex education and family planning;
- promotion and upholding of women's rights;
- fair incomes, access to employment;
- a reduction of world economic imbalances. (CRC art. 18/ THC preamb. para. 2)

V. Search for Alternatives

When the birth family does not meet the conditions that ensure the psycho-social development as well as the physical and emotional integrity of the child, competent child protection bodies must seek for adequate alternatives. *Poverty alone should not be a criterion for severing a child's bonds with his/her birth family.* But attention should be given not to use poverty as a criterion to refuse a child the alternative of a substitute family which respects his/her rights and integrity. (CRC art. 20 para. 2)

VI. Priority for an Alternative Family

The family is the best environment for a child's development: *offering a child a substitute family should, other than exceptional and justified cases, prevail over his/her placement or long-term residence in an institution.* It is the responsibility of the competent* authorities to ensure that whenever a child enters an institution, his/her personal and family situation is investigated rapidly and suitable family protective measures are sought. (CRC art. 20-3/THC preamb. para. 1)

VII. Priority for a Permanent Solution

To flourish, a child needs stability in his/her contacts with the adults around him/her: *permanent solutions must prevail* over provisional arrangements for an undetermined period of time. (THC preamb. para. 3)

VIII. Subsidiarity of Inter-country Adoption

Inter-country adoption is subsidiary to internal adoption. As a priority, a child must be placed for adoption in his/her own country or in a cultural, linguistic and religious environment akin to his/her community of origin. A decision in favour of inter-country adoption should be taken only after an unsuccessful search has been conducted for a satisfactory solution in the child's country of origin. In the interest of the child, the competent* authorities shall see to it that *such a search is carried out without undue delay.* (CCRC art. 21-b/THC preamb. para. 3, art. 4-b)

IX. Adoptability of the Child

Adoption is a personalized life plan for a child. Such a plan can be decided upon only after a preliminary psycho-medico-social study of the child and his/her birth family. The conclusion that it is impossible for the birth family to care for the child, and the assessment of the child's capacity to benefit from a family environment, *determine his/her psycho-social adoptability.* This is supplemented by his/her *legal adoptability,* which forms the basis for severance of the filiation links with birth parents, in the ways specified by the law of the State. *The adoptability of the child must be determined before starting adoption proceedings.* (THC art. 4, art. 16-1)

X. Prospective Parents' Eligibility to Adopt

Adoption aims at offering a child who has lived through traumatic experiences (the incapacity or impossibility of the birth family to care for him/her being one of them) and who may have little in common with the society about to receive him/her, the family best suited to meet his/her needs. *The adoptive family must therefore be recognized ahead of time as being apt* and able to ensure, in a lasting and satisfactory manner, the protection and respect of a child with such a background and characteristics. A psycho-medico-social and legal family study should therefore be undertaken *before adoption proceedings are started.* It will help to confirm or disqualify the *family's adoptive capacity which must be officially certified.*

In the case of internal adoption, adoption by nationals of the child's country of origin resident in a receiving country, or intra-family adoption, the adoptive capacity of the adopters must equally well be examined and certified. The child's best interest is at stake. For nationals of the country of origin permanently resident in a receiving country, the extent of their integration in that country must be considered a factor to facilitate the child's future integration. (THC art. 5, art. 15)

XI. Pre-placement Preparation

The child, the adoptive family, and the birth parents should be prepared for adoption. Adoption will satisfy the interests of all parties, only if adequate preparation permits each person to understand the short- and long-term implications of adoption on his/her life and on the child's life. Moreover, counselling must help the child and the adoptive family to approach their first meeting and the start of life together with more serenity. (THC art. 4-c-1, art. 4-d-1, art. 5-b, art. 9-c)

XII. Post-adoption Support

Access to qualified post-adoption support services should be made *available* to the child, the adoptive parents and siblings, as well as the birth parents, in order to answer questions and unravel or resolve any problem which might arise. (THC art. 9-c)

XIII. Right to Confidentiality

The child, the birth parents and the adoptive family have the right to confidentiality and to respect for their private lives. *Access to their file will be strictly controlled.* When deemed necessary to the best interests of the child, the publication of personal data will be issued by appropriate means, *to recipients chosen* for their ability or interest in problem solving but will not be made available to a wide and unspecified public through channels such as internet. (CRC art. 16)

XIV. Search for Origins

Children have the right, if they feel the need and when age and maturity permit, to know their history, especially information relating to their birth mother and father, and siblings, wherever possible. *It is essential to have this information gathered and preserved. A qualified psycho-social assistance is necessary for processing the search for origins.* Specialized professional services should be set up or reinforced to encompass this process.

This right may be difficult to respect in the present social context of certain States. However, given the growing number of searches for origins by young and adult adoptees, each State must do its utmost to improve the exercise of this right. (CRC art. 8/ THC art. 30)

XV. Profit–Abuse–Trafficking–Sale

The protection of children in a vulnerable position must not be a source of material or other profit. Any abuse, trading or trafficking in this field flouts the rights of the individual human and, as such, must be combated and severely prosecuted. (CRC art. 21-d, art. 35/THC preamb. para. 4, art. 1-b, art. 11-a, art. 32)

XVI. Armed Conflict—Natural Disasters

Inter-country adoption is not a step to consider in countries were armed conflict prevails or among victims of natural disasters. It may only be contemplated after a sufficient period (two years are generally recommended) to allow the competent bodies to ensure that no member of the child's family or community is still living and wishing to care for the child. Meanwhile, priority must be given to put the child in a safe location, to "in situ" assistance measures to enable the child to remain in his/her community, and in his/her country or region if possible. (CRC art. 22, art. 38/THC recommendation 24 October, 1994)

Guidelines to Ensure that Ethics and Principles are Respected in Practice

These guidelines provide a frame of reference. But ISS/IRC is aware that their application will run into numerous obstacles. Nonetheless, it is hoped that they will facilitate progress towards practices which accord greater respect to children. Moreover, we recommend that their application be adapted to circumstances and in the best interests of each particular child.

Certain States of origin* may find it difficult to make available the necessary human and material resources. Receiving States* must assist them in order to develop capacities for assuming these responsibilities.

Both receiving States and States of origin are responsible for the exercise of the rights of the child in adoption. Only genuine cooperation between the two can make it possible to provide greater protection of children.

I. Adoptability of the Child

Adoptability

1. Determination of a child's *adoptability is a matter for both the child and his/her birth family*: mother, father, and extended family, sometimes the community.
2. A child's adoptability must be established *before* a particular matching is considered.
3. Adoptability is more than a mere legal concept. *Psychological, social, medical and legal factors must be taken into account.* Adoptability establishes that:
   3.1 A child is in need of an adoptive family, since he/she cannot be kept in or reunited with his/her birth family.

---

* **The State of origin :** the term used in the THC (art. 2-1). The State where the child is habitually resident before being considered for adoption.
* **The receiving State :** the term used in the THC (art. 2-1). The State where the child has been, is being or is to be moved either after his or her adoption in the State of origin, or for the purposes of such an adoption in the receiving State or in the State of origin.

3.2 A child is psychologically and medically fit to benefit from adoption. Due to earlier experiences, some children may lose the ability/desire to develop a new bond of emotional dependency, or they may show clear limitations in adjusting to a family environment. However, *the great majority of children are capable of reaping the benefits from a permanent family environment.* Some children, because they may present more serious challenges (physical and/or mental handicaps, serious psychological traumas, illnesses, etc.) will need an adoptive family setting with special characteristics to make physical, emotional or psychic recovery possible. But *families willing and able to provide them a suitable human environment do exist.* It is essential to ensure that there is no discrimination and that the utmost is done to provide these children with access to the benefits of adoption.

3.3 A child is legally adoptable.

Study of the Child and His/Her Birth Family

4. Adoptability must be established through *psycho-medico-social studies of the child and the birth family.*

4.1 No time should be lost before undertaking and carrying out the study of a child's adoptability. *The child's situation should be investigated as soon as he/she enters an institution* (hospital, maternity clinic, temporary or long-term child care institution). This to avoid the harmful effects of keeping children in an institution without proper consideration. It will help, also, to clarify transitory or dubious situations that can harm a child's development.

4.2 *A life book should be created as soon as a child enters an institution,* to record his/her experience, to collect the history and details of the child's lifespan in the interests of the child and his/her future adoptive family. This book will form part of the file to be handed over later to the family with whom the child is placed.

4.3 *Child protection and family professionals* will be responsible for carrying out the psychosocial studies.

5. The child study must be as thorough as possible, since the child's future, that of his/her birth family, and of the prospective substitute family will depend upon it.

   As far as possible, *the study, which is confidential, should cover:*

   5.1 The identity of the child, his/her parents and extended family; if the child's parents are unknown, a search should be made to trace them and discuss the child's future with them.

   5.2 The situation of the child's birth family—immediate family (parents and siblings), and extended family (grandparents, etc.)—socio-economic situation, nature of relationships between relatives, relationships with the social environment, main difficulties, positive factors, etc.

   5.3 The child's past, in as much detail as possible, about the stages of his/her *personal and family history,* ethnic and religious upbringing.

   5.4 The reasons for the child's ties with the birth family to be weakened or severed, for the abandonment decree, or the adoption consent.

   5.5 The stages of the child's physical, motor, intellectual, and socio-emotional development.

   5.6 His/her state of health; medical history (including available information about the mother's pregnancy and delivery, vaccinations, etc.) and that of the birth family.

   5.7 His/her physical and general appearance, personality and behaviour.

   5.8 The child's present situation, with all available information about his/her present environment, way of life, habits, ability to be self-reliant according to his/her age, relations with other children and adults around him/her, his/her pace, etc.

6. It must be made certain that a child's relinquished status is not the result of abuse, trafficking, sale or kidnapping.

   6.1 *The child's origin must be carefully established.*

   6.2 When the child seems legally adoptable by virtue of *parental consent,* it must be checked that consent is/

was freely given, without pressure, without material compensation, or otherwise. The social services must:

- counsel and assist the parents of the child to consider other alternatives than adoption;
- inform the parents and ensure they have a proper understanding of the consequences of adoption, which might become inter-country adoption;
- make sure the parents have grasped clearly the implications for the child, themselves and the future of their legal bond, and their social and personal attachment to the child;
- ensure the parents are informed of the possibility of a future contact in the event of a search for origins by the then full-grown child;
- collect the parents' possible wishes in regard to the profile of the substitute family, that such wishes may be respected as far as possible if in the interests of the child.

6.3 *Parental consent* (and especially that of the mother) *must not be given before birth or during the first weeks of the child's life.* The mother and the father must be given the opportunity to form an attachment with the child and to avail themselves of a period of reflection after the birth of the child. Throughout pregnancy and during the reflection period, it is very important to provide psychosocial and economic support services to the parents to reduce the risk of abandonment or,—in that eventuality—to help them part with the child with dignity and respect.

Life Plan for the Child

7. *The studies should result in a life plan for the child,* drawn up by *a team* of child protection professionals, pluridisciplinary as far as possible. A life plan is: the most appropriate protective social measure (or series of measures) for the child—one of which may be adoption.
8. The life plan for the future must be *built around the interests of the child.*

   8.1 *Every child is unique,* and duly considered as such in the plan.

8.2 The child's birth mother and father should participate in the definition of the plan, as far as possible.

8.3 The child, too, should participate, in the drawing up, carrying out and eventual reassessment of the plan, in a manner appropriate to his/her age and degree of maturity.

8.4 The plan will take care that blood (or possibly love) brothers and sisters are not separated, especially when they know one another; if, under extraordinary circumstances, separation should occur, provision must be made for them to remain in contact.

8.5 Adoption will only be selected as the life plan when keeping or reuniting the child *in the immediate birth family, or extended family,* prove impossible or contrary to the interests of the child, despite all efforts.

8.6 Adoption should be selected as the appropriate step only if it appears to *fit the child's personal characteristics* (see 3.2).

8.7 *Inter-country adoption* of a child should be considered only (i) if the child could not benefit from adoption by a family in his/her country of origin despite efforts to that effect, and (ii) when it appears appropriate to the child's personal characteristics (i.e., ability to adapt to: a different family, social, ethnic, cultural, linguistic, educational environment; different physical features; etc.).

8.8 Except in very special cases, *adoption must prevail over indefinite institutionalisation* of children for whom it proves impossible to reunite with their birth family, *without prejudice* for ethnic aspects, physical characteristics, age, physical or mental health disorders.

8.9 If adoption is chosen as the life plan for the child, *his/her legal adoptability must be clearly established and certified.*

Child Report for Adoption Purposes

9. *A report on the child is prepared on the basis of the above-mentioned studies.* This report is passed to the entities responsible for matching and for the adoption decision. *It*

must present as complete a picture of the child and his/her birth family as possible so as to help the competent bodies achieve matching in the interests of the child and the family that will adopt him/her.

Moreover, thanks to the information contained in the file they receive, the adoptive parents will better know and understand the child and his/her past, as well as be better equipped to answer questions the child might ask about his/her life story and to receive and accompany him/her throughout life.

As far as possible, the report will contain:

9.1 The reasons why adoption is the proposed measure. In the case of inter-country adoption, a particular justification will be added;

9.2 A synthesis of the psycho-social information gathered during the child and birth family study;

9.3 The medical file on the child's history, state of health, and his/her birth family's antecedents;

9.4 The legal file dealing with his/her adoptability;

9.5 A description of his/her present environment, habits, relationships, behaviour;

9.6 An assessment of the positive factors and risks in the child's personality, experience and characteristics which have a bearing on the development of a satisfactory adoptive relationship;

9.7 Guidelines for the type of family (family composition, character, age, etc.) likely to meet the child's needs and to facilitate his/her bonding with it and the surrounding society;

9.8 Any further information that can help matching in the interests of the child and the adoptive family;

9.9 Photographs, or possibly a video of the child.

10. *Information about the child's origins must be preserved by one of the bodies responsible for adoption.* If the adopted child feels the need later and when his/her age and degree of maturity permit, he/she could receive this information with appropriate psychosocial support services, taking into consideration the rights of the birth family and the law of the State concerned.

The possible renewal of contact with the birth family must take place within a specialized psychosocial framework, as much for the birth family as for the adopted child. It should only be continued if both parties accept to do so and appear able to assume the consequences. ISS/IRC recommends that contact be considered only when the adoptee is no longer an adolescent. Any steps taken must preserve the confidentiality due to each person involved.

II. Adoptive Eligibility and Suitability of Parents

11. *Opinion of ISS*: Adoption must be a meeting of the child's needs and the wishes of the adoptive parents. This does not mean that adoption has to meet the various wishes of the prospective adoptive parents (hereafter referred to as PAPs) but that PAPs must desire a child and wish for the specific child placed in their care. However, *adoption is a right of the child* in need of permanent substitute parental care. *Adults do not have a right to be entrusted with the care of a child simply because they want one.* The right to equality between people is too often used to justify recognition of anyone's right to adopt.

    The child in need of adoption is a child who has suffered serious deprivation. His/her history, situation as an adopted child, and sometimes even his/her physical features, make the child initially a different person in the environment of the State or the community envisaged for his/her placement. The receiving family should not add to the child's differences or deficiencies. They should:

    - provide or revalorize the maternal or paternal representation that he/she has lacked or suffered from;
    - ensure an environment that will ease his/her social inclusion;
    - enable him/her to face up to the particular difficulties of the adoptive family relationship.

    For these reasons ISS/IRC considers that, except for justified special cases, a couple, comprising a man and a woman, of an age in keeping with that of the child, offers a more appropriate environment for the development of the child than a single person, a couple of the same sex or a couple with certain characteristics (an advanced age of one or both partners, a serious health problem, etc.) that constitute an obstacle in adapting to the needs of the child or a risk as to how long parental protection would be forthcoming.

12. It is essential to ascertain whether those with whom a child will be placed for adoption are equipped to assume this responsibility in the best interests of the child. *The adoptive family must be capable, on a lasting and satisfactory basis, of caring for a child who:*
    - is a stranger to them;
    - comes to them with a past prior to them knowing him/her that must be taken into account and respected;
    - has, in most cases, lived through traumatic experiences, i.e., death or incapacity of birth parents to take care of him/her, an insecurity in his/her attachment to adults, prolonged periods of institutionalisation, hardships, etc.; all of which give rise to special needs and are a potential source of particular problems;
    - bears, especially for inter-country adoption, a culture, a language, physical features, behaviour, etc., that are different.
13. *The adoptive eligibility* and suitability of parents *must be determined before* a specific matching is considered.
14. Adoptive eligibility and suitability of parents cannot be reduced to a mere legal, economic or religious concept. *Consideration must be given to ethical, psychological, social and medical factors* and established on the basis of a thorough psycho-medico-social and legal study of applicants. The study must be carried out by professionals in child and family protection.
15. *The study,* which is *confidential,* must gather information, as far as possible, concerning:

    15.1 The composition of the family;

    15.2 The civil, legal and judicial status of the PAPs;

    15.3 The PAPs' level of education, professional status, economic situation, place of residence, and social, ethno-cultural and linguistic identity.

An advanced education, economic comfort or high social standing of PAPs are not, in themselves, sufficient guarantees for the interests of the child. A family of modest means can be very satisfactory for the child.

It is essential to assess the adoptive family's psycho-emotional capacity to raise the child who may be placed in their care, as well as their ethics about the rights of that child. Information should be collected concerning;

15.4 The physical, mental and emotional health of both PAPs;

15.5 The general appearance and personality of both PAPs, their personal history, the aspects of their family history with their own parents and siblings that would help understanding how such relationships could strengthen or inhibit them as parents;

15.6 Their history and relationship as a couple;

15.7 The extent of their integration in their community; their fields of interest;

15.8 The future possibility and probability of having children of their own;

15.9 Their experience of children, their educative capacity, their ability to cope with difficulties which might create differences between the child and the social or family environment;

15.10 If appropriate, the personality of their own children and their relationship with their parents and their environment, as well as their attitude towards the contemplated adoption;

15.11 The social environment in which the adopted child will be placed (extended family, social circle in which the family moves, community) and the attitude to be expected towards the child, especially if he/she is different from these surroundings; mention of emotional or other kinds of support that PAPs and the child can expect; foreseeable difficulties;

15.12 The PAPs' wish for children and the reasons why each of them wants to adopt a child;

15.13 Their concept and ethics concerning adoption,

awareness of difficulties they may encounter at different stages of their life with the adopted child, attitude towards the child's past, his/her history and secrets, his/her differences, the adoption disclosure and the child's search for birth parents;

15.14 The profile of the child they would like to adopt and reasons behind it; and

15.15 The PAPs' plans for their future and that of the child they wish to adopt.

16. As a follow-up to the study, *a team* (as far as possible pluridisciplinary: social worker, psychologist, etc.) will decide upon the adoptive eligibility of the PAPs. This team will draft a report for the bodies responsible for matching and the adoption decision. *This report will provide as complete a picture as possible to assist the competent bodies to achieve a matching in the interest of the child, and family that will adopt him/her.*

The report will contain, to the extent possible:

16.1 The reasons why the PAPs were considered apt to be entrusted with a child for adoption. In the case of inter-country adoption, justification will take into account particular requirements (e.g., need to cope with the problems arising from physical, ethnic and cultural diversity, the traumatic circumstances related to a possible long period of institutionalisation, health problems);

16.2 A synthesis of the psycho-medico-social information gathered during the study of the PAPs and their surroundings;

16.3 The administrative or judicial file on their identification and civil status, as well as the certification of adoptive eligibility;

16.4 Photos of the family;

16.5 A description of the PAPs' expectations of adoption, with appropriate comments;

16.6 Assessments of (i) the positive factors, within the adoptive family and its environment that will ensure an emotionally, morally, educationally and materially satisfactory framework for the child, and ease his/her integration; (ii) the limits that risk jeopardizing them in the case of a internal and/or inter-country adoption. The latter calls for a wider range of abilities, given its more complex nature;

16.7 Assessment of the family's capacity to care on a long-term basis for a child who does not necessarily correspond to the family's image of him/her;

16.8 Guidance on the type of child the family seems best equipped to cope with (behaviour, character, age, particularities, etc.); the family's capacity to care for a sibling group;

16.9 Any further information that might help to achieve matching in the interests of the child and the adoptive family.

17. It is very important that *PAPs have access to systematic and thorough preparation for adoption,* preferably *before* the assessment of their adoptive capacity, including:

17.1 Ethics about adoption and the rights of the child in a vulnerable position;

17.2 Information about the nature of adoption and the profile of children in need of adoption in different countries of the world;

17.3 Stages, personal rewards and possible pitfalls in the adoptive relationship, and points that help to cope with them;

17.4 Issues to consider in order to ensure a better respect for the child, his/her experience, origins, needs and particularities, rights;

17.5 Special demands of intercountry adoption.

Good counselling helps PAPs to strengthen their resolve in their approach to adoption. It *is also an action in the interest of the child,* since it fosters in PAPs a greater capacity to receive the child and accompany him/her throughout his/her development. Therefore, it is an action *in the interests of the adoptive family as a whole.*

III. Matching

Matching is not the adoption decision. It is a proposal to establish an adoptive relationship between a particular child and a particular family. The decision of adoption comes later.

18. An adoption in the best interest of the child is one that creates both a situation which respects the biological family

and family relationships that satisfy the child and the adoptive family. Matching is therefore a key point in time. It is the convergence of two life plans: that of the child, and that of the family in whose care he/she is to be placed.

19. Matching should be *the proposal of an adoptive family for a child* that fits the life experience, characteristics and needs of that child.
20. Matching should take place *after child protection professionals have established the psycho-medico-social and legal adoptability of the child.*
21. Matching should take place *after child and family protection professionals have established the psycho-medico-social and legal adoptive eligibility of the possible PAPs.*
22. *Matching should be assigned to a team* and not be left to the responsibility of an individual; the team should be composed of *child protection professionals* trained in adoption policies and practices. They should preferably be specialists in psychosocial fields. In the case of inter-country adoption, it is desirable to invite a lawyer to join the team to check that the legal requirements are met and are compatible between the States concerned.
23. Matching should not be left to the initiative of the birth family, other than in duly justified exceptional cases. Whatever the circumstances, it must be supervised by a competent child protection service and take place *after* reception of consent.
24. Matching must not be left to the sole initiative of the staff of child care institutions, or the child's guardian or tutor. Although, as they know the child, these people should be included in, or consulted by the team that makes the proposal, as far as possible.
25. Matching must never be left to the initiative of PAPs choosing a child among others when visiting institutions for children, during visits to families in the State of origin, or from catalogues.
26. Matching must not be left to the initiative of PAPs choosing a child from a catalogue of public advertisements on internet.
27. *Professionals from the State of origin and from the receiving State must be jointly responsible for matching* in the case of inter-country adoption. As far as possible, the proposal should be put forward following consultations between:

- **In the State of origin:** a professional who knows the child, and a representative of the central authority (or of the competent authority, or the accredited body).
- **In the receiving State:** a professional who knows the chosen family, and a representative of the central authority (or of the competent authority, or the accredited body).

28. Before the decision order of adoption is confirmed, it should be submitted for approval to the chosen adoptive family through the good offices of one of the competent bodies involved in adoption procedures in the family's State of residence.
29. Before matching is officially confirmed, *it is desirable, both in the interests of the child and of the adoptive family, that the proposal be followed by a face-to-face meeting between the child and the future adoptive family,* and wherever possible, by a brief period of getting to know each other.
30. When bringing the child and the adoptive family together, it is very important that:
    30.1 *The child and the future adoptive family first be prepared* for the proposed meeting (photos, exchange of information, information about attitudes or points to be careful about, etc.).
    30.2 The meeting be held in privacy and assisted by persons who have been caring for the child.

Protagonists Directly Involved in Adoption Procedures

Bodies or persons who play a role in adoption procedures, whatever the importance or level of their participation, are defined here as protagonists.

The 1993 Hague Convention on the Protection of Children and Co-operation in respect of Inter-country Adoption refers to the protagonists described below under items 1 to 3. Those considered under items 4 and 5 are not accepted by the Convention.

The ISS clearly prefers the bodies mentioned under items 1 and 2, particularly those whose staff is composed of pluridisciplinary professionals in child protection (social workers, psychologists, jurists), who have benefited from special training in adoption and the rights of the child, and are guided by ethical standards in the best interests of the child.

ISS believes that experience as an adoptive parent is not a sufficient qualification to play a role in adoption procedures. Moreover, while acknowledging the indisputable value of volunteer work, ISS considers that it cannot be recognized as a skill in itself, and does not justify overlooking professional qualifications in child protection.

1. *Central authority* in internal and/or inter-country adoption (THC art. 6).
   Other competent public or judicial authorities (THC art. 7, 8, 9).
2. *National accredited bodies* in the receiving State – in the State of origin (THC art. 10, 11, 12). The THC considers their existence as being possible but not compulsory.
3. *Bodies or persons,* not accredited but who are officially recognized (under the terms of the Hague Convention) to act in adoption procedures (THC art. 22-2). They are not subject to all the demands made upon the accredited bodies (i.e., being not-for-profit).
   A State party to the THC may refuse the participation of such protagonists in adoption procedures (at stages that take place on its territory or in other countries concerned) when the procedures concern persons who reside in its State. To do so, it must make a declaration in accordance with the terms of THC art. 22-4.
4. Bodies and persons acting in adoption procedures without being accredited or officially recognized to do so (under the terms of the Hague Convention), without it being against the law or the administrative regulations of the State (their own State or the other concerned), but who are beyond the scope of the THC.
5. Bodies and persons acting in adoption procedures without being accredited or officially recognized to do so (under the terms of the Hague Convention), it being against the law or the administrative regulations of the State (their State or the other involved).

For inter-country adoption, ISS favours the participation of accredited bodies (listed under item 2 above), *especially in the receiving*

State, since they provide a firm link case by case between the State of origin and the receiving State, between the child and the adoptive family, between the field and the governmental levels.

However in the interest of the child, ISS insists on the need to:

- reinforce the criteria for accreditation,
- systematise the accreditation methodology,
- deepen the training of these bodies on the rights of the child and adoption,
- improve their periodic supervision.

Without underestimating volunteer work, ISS recommends that sufficient material resources be made available to accredited bodies for the hiring of professionally qualified staff, for training in adoption and the rights of the child and for organizing their work in an appropriate manner to ensure the genuine protection of children. A part of the tasks performed by accredited bodies is delegated to them by the State, which should ensure or assist with the provision of adequate resources and qualifications.

IRC/ISS strongly opposes any undue or obviously exaggerated material gain in the context of adoption. Protection of the child in a vulnerable position must not become a source of inappropriate revenue or profit. *ISS considers it essential that the following be proposed rapidly and periodically updated at the national and international level, in both receiving States and States of origin:*

- a list of the steps involved in adoption procedures, or related to adoption, that could justify a payment;
- ranges of emoluments, fees and the cost of services in adoption that could be considered reasonable.

Annexure-V

Conclusions and Recommendations of the Second Meeting of the Special Commission on the Practical Operation of the Hague Convention of 29 May, 1993 on Protection of Children and Co-operation in Respect of Inter-country Adoption (17-23 September, 2005)

Guide to Good Practice

1. The Special Commission gives its general endorsement to the draft Guide to Good Practice dealing with Implementation of the 1993 Convention prepared by the Permanent Bureau. It requests the Permanent Bureau, with the assistance of a group of experts appointed by the Special Commission, to review the draft in the light of comments made in the Special Commission on which there was consensus, and in particular by the addition of appropriate references to the situation of children with special needs. The revised text should then be circulated for their comments/approval to Contracting States, Member States of the Hague Conference and organisations represented at the Special Commission. Once there is a consensus, the Permanent Bureau will prepare the text for publication. The Permanent Bureau is authorised, in preparing the Guide to Good Practice for publication, to make changes of an editorial nature, to update where necessary any factual information contained in the Guide, to determine the presentation of the material in the Guide, provided that this does not involve any changes in substance or emphasis.
2. The Special Commission recommends that the Permanent Bureau, in consultation with Contracting States and non-

---

Source: http:/www.hcch.net

governmental organisations, collect information on issues including, *inter alia,* the financial aspects of inter-country adoption, reports on prospective adoptive parents, preparation of prospective adoptive parents, and post-adoption reports, with the view to the possible development of future Parts of the Guide to Good Practice.

Designation of Central Authorities, Other Authorities and Bodies under the Convention

3. The Special Commission reaffirms Recommendation No. 2 of the Special Commission of November/December 2000, and underlines, in particular, the importance of designating Central Authorities without delay:

"2. The following recommendations are designed to improve communication under the Convention, as well as understanding of how the Convention operates in the different Contracting States:

(a) The designation of the Central Authorities, required by Article 13, as well as their contact details, should be communicated to the Permanent Bureau not later than the date of the entry into force of the Convention in that State.

(b) Such communication should, in accordance with Article 13 and paragraph 274 of the Explanatory Report on the Convention by G. Parra- Aranguren (Proceedings of the Seventeenth Session (1993), Tome II, Adoption – Co-operation, page 591), give notice of any other public authorities (including their contact details) which, under Article 8 or 9 discharge functions assigned to the Central Authorities.

(c) The extent of the functions of the Central Authorities and any such public authorities should be explained.

(d) The designation of accredited bodies, required by Article 13, as well as their contact details, should be communicated to the Permanent Bureau at the time of their accreditation.

(e) Where a body accredited in one Contracting State is, in accordance with Article 12, authorised to act in another Contracting State, such authorisation should be communicated to the Permanent Bureau by the competent authorities of both States without delay.

(f) The extent of the functions of accredited bodies should also be explained.

(g) All the information referred to above should be kept up-to-date and the Permanent Bureau informed promptly of any changes, including in particular any withdrawals of accreditation or authorisation to act.

(h) Designations, in accordance with Article 23, of authorities competent to certify an adoption as having been made in accordance with the Convention should also be kept up-to-date."

Accreditation

4. The Special Commission recommends that the Permanent Bureau should continue to gather information from different Contracting States regarding accreditation with the view to the development of a future Part of the Guide to Good Practice dealing with accreditation. The experience of non-governmental organisations in this field should be taken into account. Such information should include financial matters and should also be considered in the development of a set of model accreditation criteria.
5. The Special Commission reaffirms Recommendation Nos. 6-9 of the Special Commission of November/December 2000:

"6. Accreditation requirements for agencies providing inter-country adoption services should include evidence of a sound financial basis and an effective internal system of financial control, as well as external auditing. Accredited bodies should be required to maintain accounts, to be submitted to the supervising authority, including an itemised statement of the average costs and charges associated with different categories of adoptions.

7. Prospective adopters should be provided in advance with an itemised list of the costs and expenses likely to

arise from the adoption process itself. Authorities and agencies in the receiving State and the State of origin should co-operate in ensuring that this information is made available.

8. Information concerning the costs and expenses and fees charged for the provision of inter-country adoption services by different agencies should be made available to the public.
9. Donations by prospective adopters to bodies concerned in the adoption process must not be sought, offered or made."

Collection and Dissemination of Information

6. The Special Commission reaffirms the usefulness of the Model Form—Medical Report on the Child and notes the usefulness, in particular in the case of very young children, of the supplement to this form as proposed in Working Document No. 6, pp. 8-9.
7. The Special Commission recommends that the Permanent Bureau, in consultation with Contracting States and non-governmental organisations, develop a model form for the consent of the child [Article 4(d)(3)] as well as model forms or protocols regarding the operation of Articles 15 and 16 of the Convention.
8. To further the work commenced by the development of the organigram (Appendix 6 of Prel. Doc. No. 2), the Special Commission invites the Permanent Bureau, to collect specific information from Contracting States, including, *inter alia*, procedures, website addresses and how the various responsibilities and tasks under the Convention are divided between Central Authorities, public authorities, accredited bodies and any bodies and persons under Article 22(2). This information should be made available on the website of the Hague Conference.

Statistics

9. The Special Commission welcomes the development of the draft forms for the gathering of general statistical

information (Appendix 5 of Prel. Doc. No. 2) and underlines the importance for States Parties to submit general statistics to the Permanent Bureau using these forms on an annual basis.

Co-operation and Communication

10. The Special Commission stresses the importance of enhancing co-operation and exchange of information between Central Authorities, public authorities, accredited bodies and any bodies and persons under Article 22(2), notably with a view to promoting good practice and to ensuring that illegal and unethical procedures prior to the adoption of a child be effectively and systematically combatted.
11. Contracting States are encouraged to undertake and participate in regional and/or bilateral meetings to exchange information and good practices.
12. The Special Commission recognises the importance of States of origin sending information to receiving States on the needs of children to better identify prospective adoptive parents.
13. The Special Commission recognises that as a matter of good practice, authorities in receiving States should co-operate with authorities in States of origin in order to better understand the needs of children in States of origin.
14. The Special Commission reminds States Parties to the Convention of their obligations under Article 35 to act expeditiously in the process of adoption, and notes in particular the need to avoid unnecessary delay in finding a permanent family for the child.
15. The Special Commission recommends that States actively discourage direct contacts between prospective adoptive parents and authorities in the State of origin until authorised to do so. Exceptionally, such contact at the appropriate time may be desirable, for example in the case of a child with special needs.
16. The Special Commission recommends the use of flexible and efficient systems of communication taking into account, where available, advances in technology.

Nationality

17. The Special Commission recommends that the child be accorded automatically the nationality of one of the adoptive parents or of the receiving State, without the need to rely on any action of the adoptive parents. Where this is not possible, the receiving States are encouraged to provide the necessary assistance to ensure the child obtains such citizenship. The policy of Contracting States regarding the nationality of the child should be guided by the overriding importance of avoiding a situation in which an adopted child is stateless.

Post-adoption Reporting

18. The Special Commission recommends to receiving States to encourage compliance with post-adoption reporting requirements of States of origin; a model form might be developed for this purpose. Similarly, the Special Commission recommends to States of origin to limit the period in which they require post-adoption reporting in recognition of the mutual confidence which provides the framework for co-operation under the Convention.

Application of Convention Principles to Non-Convention Countries

19. The Special Commission reaffirms Recommendation No. 11 of the Special Commission of November/December 2000:

"11. Recognising that the Convention of 1993 is founded on universally accepted principles and that States Parties are "convinced of the necessity to take measures to ensure that inter-country adoptions are made in the best interests of the child and with respect for his or her fundamental rights, and to prevent the abduction, the sale of, or traffic in children", the Special Commission recommends that States Parties, as far as practicable, apply the standards and safeguards of the Convention to the arrangements for inter-country adoption which they make in respect of non-Contracting States. States Parties should also encourage such States without delay to take all necessary steps, possibly including the enactment of legislation and the creation of a Central Authority, so as to enable them to accede to or ratify the Convention."

Other Conventions

20. The Special Commission stresses the usefulness of linking the application of the Hague Adoption Convention of 1993 to the *Hague Convention of 5 October, 1961 Abolishing the Requirement of Legalisation for Foreign Public Documents* (the Apostille Convention). In the light of the high number of public documents included in a typical adoption procedure, the Special Commission recommends that States Parties to the Adoption Convention but not to the Apostille Convention, consider the possibility of becoming a party to the latter.
21. The Special Commission recognises the need to consider how best to regulate the different types of international placement falling outside the scope of the Convention. The value in this context of the *Hague Convention of 19 October, 1996 on Jurisdiction, Applicable Law, Recognition, Enforcement and Co-operation in respect of Parental Responsibility and Measures for the Protection of Children*, in particular Article 33, was recognised. The Special Commission also recognised the reference to this Convention in the important Decision of the United Nations Committee on the Rights of the Child, 37th Session, "Children without parental care", October 2004.

Implementation of the Convention in Guatemala

22. The Special Commission:
    (a) *Recognises* the initiative of the Government of

Guatemala, which led to the visit of the Secretary General to Guatemala from 31 May—3 June, 2005;

(b) *Takes note* of the Report of the Secretary General of 15 June, 2005, in particular the "action points"[1] (Work. Doc. No. 8) on which a consensus emerged during this visit;

(c) *Appreciates* the presence at the Special Commission of a high-level delegation from Guatemala, including the Vice-Minister of Foreign Affairs; the *Procurador General de la Nación* (the Central Authority under the Convention); Chairmen of three Parliamentary Committees, and others;

(d) *Recognises* the efforts being made by the Government of Guatemala towards the full implementation of the Convention;

(e) *Urges* Guatemala to confirm, as soon as possible, the legal effect of the Convention within its legal order consistent with Guatemala's international obligations under the Convention;

(f) Having regard to the request for support made during the Special Commission by the delegation of Guatemala, *calls upon* the States and international organisations represented at the Special Commission to co-operate with the Government in its endeavours to fully implement the Convention.

---

1. The "action points" refer to commitments by the Government of Guatemala (1) to send a high-level delegation to the Special Commission, (2) to respond positively to an offer made in 2003 on behalf of 13 States to provide assistance to Guatemala in respect of implementation of the 1993 Convention, (3) to propose to Congress the formal withdrawal of the reservations made to Articles 11 and 12 of the Vienna Convention on the Law of Treaties, which were identified by the Constitutional Court of Guatemala in its ruling of 13 August, 2003 as reasons for considering that *Decreto 50-2002*, by which Guatemala had approved the accession to the 1993 Convention, was unconstitutional, and (4) to take urgent steps to resubmit the 1993 Convention to Congress for it to confirm its legal effect within Guatemala.

Index